Education Law & Policy Review

Volume 1

A Publication of the Education Law Consortium in Cooperation with the Education Law Association

Education Law & Policy Review™
Education Law Consortium © 2014

Permission is granted to make and distribute free copies of this publication for educational purposes. Commercial use is prohibited.

The *Education Law & Policy Review*™ (ELPR) is a trademark wholly owned by the *Education Law Consortium* (ELC) as Publisher of the ELPR. As Publisher of the ELPR the ELC holds the copyright to the published journal as a whole in all formats. Authors retain separate and individual copyright over those materials that were produced by the Authors, conditioned on granting full permission and legal rights to publish included works in the *Education Law & Policy Review* and in any derivative works by the Publisher, in print, electronic, and all other formats, and to allow unlimited reproduction and distribution for free educational purposes. Publication of the ELPR is supported in part through a charitable gift from *Wisdom Builders Press*, making the very best academic and educational works available to everyone:

Wisdom Builders Press ™

www.wisdombuilderspress.com

Education Law Consortium
850 College Station Road
University of Georgia
Athens, Georgia, USA
John Dayton, J.D., Ed. D., Editor-in-Chief 2013-2014 Term

Nota bene: These materials and any derivative works contain academic information and opinions and are intended for educational purposes only. The ELPR provides a pro bono forum for scholarly commentary. Authors are solely responsible for their comments and opinions. These materials are not intended as legal advice and should in no way be interpreted as legal advice. Legal advice can only be obtained from an attorney licensed to practice law in your jurisdiction and with specific knowledge concerning the facts in your case. Authors and the Publisher have made good faith efforts in the preparation of these materials, but neither the Authors nor the Publisher make any warranties of comprehensiveness, accurateness, or fitness for a particular purpose. Further, any opinions or strategies suggested in these materials may not be appropriate for your circumstances. Consult with an appropriate professional concerning your specific circumstances. This notice serves as an express disclaimer of all liability and warranties by the Authors and the Publisher.

ISBN-13: 978-0615989983
ISBN-10: 0615989985

Education Law & Policy Review Personnel
Volume 1
2013-2014 Term

Faculty Editorial Board
Volume 1
2013-2014 Term

Student Editorial Board
Volume 1
2013-2014 Term

Acknowledgments

As founding *Editor-in-Chief* of the *Education Law & Policy Review* (ELPR), I want to acknowledge and thank everyone who has made this exciting new venture in scholarship possible, including the members of our Executive Advisory Board, Editors, Faculty Editorial Board, Student Editorial Board, and *Education Law Association* (ELA) partners. I also want to thank our deans, faculty, students, and staff in the University of Georgia College of Education, Institute of Higher Education, and School of Law for their continued encouragement and support for the advancement of scholarship and practice.

I want to dedicate this inaugural issue of the *Education Law & Policy Review* to the memory of Anne Proffitt Dupre, as this project was in part Anne's dream also. All projects begin as an idea, and ideas are born from the minds of people. Anne had a most fertile mind for great ideas. Anne Proffitt Dupre came to the University of Georgia after serving as a judicial law clerk for Justice Harry A. Blackmun at the United States Supreme Court. As a former teacher Anne had always been interested in education, and especially education law and policy.

In order to promote the public good and support educational improvement, Anne and I created the *Education Law Consortium* (ELC) in 2003, providing non-partisan information and scholarly analyses of significant state, regional, national, and international education law and policy issues. The ELC brings together a multi-disciplinary assemblage of leading scholars, policy analysts, and practitioners to cooperate in the production and dissemination of research and analyses of significant education law and policy issues.

In 2010, Anne and I were having one of our regular ELC Directors meetings at our unofficial office, the Thai Spoon, in downtown Athens, GA. We both decided that what was needed to advance scholarship and practice in education law was a journal focused on the intersection of law and policy: The *Education Law & Policy Review* was born. Sadly, Anne passed away in 2011, before this work could be completed. She is greatly missed by all, and constantly remembered for her concern for students, education, and her kindness to all.

Anne was kind to her very core, but she was also fiery and full of passion for issues she cared about. Anne was a zealous advocate for justice and civility in schools and in the workplace. For all of these reasons, this inaugural issue of the *Education Law & Policy Review*, and the first article on *Law and Policy Remedies for Workplace Bullying in Higher Education*, are dedicated to the memory of my good friend and colleague Anne Proffitt Dupre.

John Dayton, March 14, 2014

Forward to the Inaugural Issue of the *Education Law & Policy Review*

Consistent with our initial vision in 2010 for the *Education Law and Policy Review* (ELPR), the ELPR is a peer-reviewed law and policy journal providing scholarly reviews and commentary on national and international issues in education law and policy in K-12 and Higher Education. The *Education Law & Policy Review* publishes leading law and policy research and analysis for use by scholars, policymakers, judges, lawyers, and educators. This is an open access journal published in both electronic and printed formats to serve the broadest audience of readers, and permission is granted to make and distribute free copies of this publication for educational purposes.

The *Education Law & Policy Review* fills a much needed role in scholarly research by focusing on the vital intersection between education law and policy. The ELPR provides scholarly reviews of the law, and encourages improvements in law and policy, supporting advances in both scholarship and practice. The ELPR Editors view scholarship and practice as two sides of the same essential coin, with scholarship informing practice, and practice driving scholarship, creating a vital synergy to support law and policy improvement.

The *Education Law & Policy Review* team wants to thank all of our authors, as exemplars of effectively connecting scholarship to practice and promoting improvements in law and policy. The ELPR wants to enthusiastically encourage further scholarship and improvements in practice in this vital area through future issues. Please consider becoming a member the ELPR team as a regular reader, reviewer, or author. See further information on forthcoming issues at the end of this volume, including a *Special Issue on Free Speech*, with a forward by Mary Beth Tinker, famed plaintiff in *Tinker v. Des Moines*, and featuring invited commentary from leading First Amendment scholars. Please also see an open call for papers for the next regular issue of the *Education Law & Policy Review*.

We hope that you will find this issue of the *Education Law & Policy Review* informative and inspiring, that you will cite it in your work, share it with students and colleagues, and that you will be encouraged to take an active role in improving education in your community. Further, we hope that you will consider supporting education law and policy improvement nationally and internationally. Please see further information on the forthcoming *Special Issue on Free Speech* for how you can help support the ongoing *pro bono* work of Mary Beth Tinker, and the invitation to join the *Education Law Association* (ELA) to become a part of the Nation's leading professional association in education law. ELA members have exclusive first access to the ELPR for 30 days. Thereafter the ELPR is available in a free open access electronic format through the *Education Law Consortium* (ELC) website, www.educationlawconsortium.org or in printed format at cost through AMAZON www.amazon.com. We hope you will enjoy this first issue of the ELPR and join us for future issues.

Education Law & Policy Review
Volume 1 Spring 2014

Contents

Contents (cont'd)

Law and Policy Remedies for Workplace Bullying in Higher Education

John Dayton, J.D., Ed. D.*

A dark and not so well kept secret lurks the halls of higher education institutions. Even among people who should certainly know better than to tolerate such abuse, personnel misconduct in the form of workplace bullying remains a serious but largely neglected problem.[1] A problem so serious it can devastate academic programs and the people in them. If allowed to maraud unchecked, workplace bullies can poison the office culture; shut down progress and productivity; drive off the most promising and productive people; and make the workplace increasingly toxic for everyone who remains in the bully dominated environment.[2] A toxic workplace can even turn deadly when stress begins to take its all too predictable toll on victims' mental and physical health, or interpersonal stress leads to acts of violence.[3]

---

* This article is dedicated to the memory of Anne Proffitt Dupre, Co-Director of the Education Law Consortium, Professor of Law, Law Clerk for the U.S. Supreme Court and the U.S. Court of Appeals for the Eleventh Circuit, trusted friend and colleague, and zealous advocate for justice and civility in the workplace. John Dayton is a Professor of Education Law and Adjunct Professor of Higher Education at the University of Georgia.

[1] *See* David C. Yamada, *Workplace Bullying and American Employment Law: A Ten-Year Progress Report and Assessment*, 32 COMP. LAB. L. & POL'Y J. 251, 253 (2010) ("Overall, workplace bullying remains the most neglected form of serious worker mistreatment in American employment law"). *See also* Irvin Lawrence et al., *Bullying and Harassment in the Workplace: An International Perspective*, 23 EMP. & INDUS. REL. L. 24, 24 (2013) ("In spite of its increasing prevalence, workplace harassment and specifically bullying continues to be under-reported and is often ignored by employers"); Susan H. Duncan, *College Bullies—Precursors to Campus Violence: What Should Universities and College Administrators Know About the Law?*, 55 VILL. L. REV. 269, 269 (2010). ("attention has not been devoted to post-adolescent bullying, despite the continuing propensities of grade school and high school bullies to torment others in college and later in the workplace").

[2] Yamada, *supra* note 1, at 274 (2010) (citing a 2008 Joint Commission medical accrediting standard recognizing that acts such as workplace bullying and harassment "can foster medical errors, contribute to poor patient satisfaction and to preventable adverse outcomes, increase the cost of care, and cause qualified clinicians, administrators and managers to seek new positions in more professional environments").

[3] *See* Florence Z. Mao, *Is Litigation Your Final Answer? Why the Healthy Workplace Bill Should Include an ADR Provision*, 21 J.L. & POL'Y 679, 686 (2013) ("Targets

Higher education institutions are especially vulnerable to some of the most toxic forms of workplace bullying. When workplace bullies are tenured professors they can become like bullying zombies seemingly invulnerable to efforts to stop them while faculty, staff, students, and even university administrators run for cover apparently unable or unwilling to do anything about the loose-cannons that threaten to sink them all. This article examines the problem of workplace bullying in higher education; reviews possible remedies; and makes suggestions for law and policy reforms to more effectively address this very serious but too often tolerated problem in higher education.

Defining Workplace Bullying

Workplace bullying may take as many forms as there are perpetrators and circumstances. It may be overt or covert; simple-minded or elaborately Machiavellian. The most candid definition for workplace bullying may be the definition given to obscenity by Justice Douglas: "I know it when I see it."[4] But while those exposed to workplace bullying may recognize it when they see it,[5] articulating a precise legal definition can be challenging. Nonetheless, an adequate working definition is essential to assure due process and the fair, efficient, and effective administration of employment laws and institutional policies.[6]

In understanding and defining workplace bullying it may also be useful to define what it is not. Workplace bullying is not an expression of free speech.[7] It is not the exercise of academic freedom.[8] Nor is it mere

---

experience psychological effects such as stress, depression, loss of sleep, and low self-esteem, as well as feelings of shame, guilt, and embarrassment. In more severe instances, they may develop posttraumatic stress disorder, which, if left untreated, may cause an individual to react violently against either the bully or another coworker"). *See also* Duncan, *supra* note 1, at 276 (describing campus violence resulting from bullying).

[4] Jacobellis v. Ohio, 378 U.S. 184, 197 (1964) (Stewart, J., concurring).

[5] A key challenge in rallying support for the adoption of protective policies is that people often don't get the problem until it gets them. *Compare* Pastor Martin Niemöller (1892-1984) ("They came for the Jews, and I didn't speak up because I wasn't a Jew. Then they came for me and by that time no one was left to speak up").

[6] JOHN DAYTON, EDUCATION LAW: PRINCIPLES, POLICIES, AND PRACTICE 240 (2012) (summarizing essential principles of due process in educational institutions).

[7] Connick v. Myers, 461 U.S. 138 (1983) (matters of personal concern and not public concern are not protected speech in the workplace).

[8] AMERICAN ASSOCIATION OF UNIVERSITY PROFESSORS (AAUP), STATEMENT OF PRINCIPLES ON ACADEMIC FREEDOM AND TENURE (1940) (recognizing that concerning the exercise of academic freedom faculty "should at all times be accurate, should exercise appropriate restraint, should show respect for the opinions of others").

incivility or interpersonal rudeness.[9] Workplace bullying is an egocentric, intentional, and systematic effort to harm others in the workplace, a serious act of employment misconduct. Perpetrators do not commonly cross the line to criminality. But like a criminal act there is both an *actus reas* and a *mens rea* in workplace bullying. Workplace bullying involves acts that breach the bounds of acceptable workplace conduct and do so with the intent to harm others. Workplace bullying is not a mere accident or interpersonal misunderstanding. It involves intentional acts knowingly aimed at targeted victims with the purpose of inflicting psychological suffering and other harms.[10]

There are varied definitions of workplace bullying, but many share common elements including language concerning prohibited acts; intent to harm; patterns of interpersonal misconduct; negative impacts on victims; and interference with workplace performance.[11] Yamada defined workplace bullying as "the intentional infliction of a hostile work environment upon an employee by a coworker or coworkers, typically through a combination of verbal and nonverbal behaviors."[12] Tepper & White defined workplace bullying in academic settings as follows:

> [W]orkplace bullying . . . is commonly defined as behavior by a
> perpetrator that may involve repeated verbal abuse, offensive
> conduct that may threaten, humiliate, or intimidate a target, or
> efforts to sabotage a target's performance. As commonly defined,
> the subject behavior is intentional, results in physical or

---

[9] *See* Mao, supra note 3, at 684-685 (2013) ("Unlike general aggression or incivility, which involve isolated instances of rudeness or crass behavior, workplace bullying involves *repetition, duration,* and *escalation*, creating an ongoing pattern of abusive behavior"). *See also* GARY NAMIE & RUTH F. NAMIE, THE BULLY-FREE WORKPLACE 6 (2011) ("Compared with incivility, bullying is a laser-focused, systematic campaign of interpersonal destruction").

[10] *See* Jordan F. Kaplan, *Help is on the Way: A Recent Case Sheds Light on Workplace Bullying*, 47 HOUS. L. REV. 141, 142 (2010) ("Workplace bullying consists of repeated hostile behavior designed to empower the bully at the expense of the victim"; "Many victims of bullying suffer psychological damage similar to post-traumatic stress disorder").

[11] *See also* Mao, *supra* note 3, at 684 (2013) ("definitions have three unifying themes: (1) the bullying activity is persistent and intentional; (2) the Target suffers a combination of psychological, physical, and economic harm as a result; and (3) the bullying activity creates an overall hostile work environment").

[12] David C. Yamada, *The Phenomenon of "Workplace Bullying" and the Need for Status-Blind Hostile Work Environment Protection*, 88 GEO. L.J. 475, 481 (2000).

psychological harm to the target, and makes the target's job performance more difficult.[13]

Workplace bullying in academia is often not just the employment misconduct of a lone perpetrator. Tepper & White recognized an especially dangerous form of workplace bullying in academia, "academic mobbing" perpetrated by groups: "At times, perpetrators, who may include administrators and faculty members, combine their efforts to abuse and harass the target, a phenomenon known as 'mobbing.'"[14]

Concerning the prevalence of workplace bullying evidence suggests that workplace bully is "an epidemic, with fifty-four million people-- amounting to 37% of American workers--who have reported being the victims of bullying."[15] Further, the impact of workplace bullying is likely to extend far beyond its direct targets, damaging morale and productivity throughout the organization.[16] Although workplace bullying may sometimes include status-based harassment related to race, color, religion, sex, national origin, age, disability, etc., non-status based workplace bullying is 400% more common than status based workplace discrimination addressed by current U.S. employment laws.[17]

Despite the harms and prevalence of workplace bullying in the U.S.[18] "the United States is the last among all Western industrialized nations to acknowledge workplace bullying. We're finally joining the rest of the world when we identify the acts of perpetrators of anti-corporate, anti-organizational, and anti-worker aggressive actions as bullying."[19]

---

[13] Robert J. Tepper & Craig G. White, *Workplace Harassment in the Academic Environment*, 56 ST. LOUIS U. L.J. 81, 81 (2011).

[14] *Id.*

[15] Duncan, *supra* note 1, at 273, *citing* WORKPLACE BULLYING INST. & ZOGBY INT'L, U.S. WORKPLACE BULLYING SURVEY (2007), available at http://www.workplacebullying.org/res/N-N-Zogby2007.pdf.

[16] David C. Yamada, *Human Dignity and American Employment Law*, 43 U. RICH. L. REV. 523, 562 (2009) ("bullying hurts employees and organizations alike, causing psychological and physical harm to workers and sapping productivity from the workplace").

[17] Tepper & White, *supra* note 13, at 83.

[18] Mao, *supra* note 3, at 686 ("WBI-Zogby survey results reveal that workplace bullying is a pervasive phenomenon with harmful effects that are widely felt by a large portion of the American workforce").

[19] NAMIE & NAMIE, *supra* note 9, at 3-4.

Assessing the Impacts of Workplace Bullying

The impacts of workplace bullying range from the wasteful and annoying to the destructive and even deadly.[20] Workplace bullies directly waste time and resources by using institutional time and resources to pursue their own selfish agendas and interfering with the work of others. Internally, workplace bullies create a toxic culture that lowers morale and productivity. And externally, workplace bullies damage the reputation of the institution making it far more difficult to recruit and retain the most talented employees.[21] A culture under the influence of workplace bullies is characterized by decreased job satisfaction, productivity, and success; increased absenteeism, turnover, health-care costs, human resources and legal costs; and elevated risks of suicide and violence.[22]

Recruiting and retaining the best people becomes impossible with such a toxic workplace culture. As Sutton recognized in his bestseller, *The No Asshole Rule*, no sane, talented person with other options wants to work with "assholes."[23] Competitors will thrive at your expense until your institution adopts a strict "no asshole rule."[24] No bully is talented enough to justify the costs of keeping the bully and allowing the workplace misconduct to continue. The bully must either stop the misconduct, leave

---

[20] Lawrence, *supra* note 1 ("It is estimated that it costs a business between US $30,000 and US $100,000 per year for each individual that is bullied in the workplace", *id.*, at 25; and *citing* a study finding that workplace bullying was "associated with at least three suicides a week in Belgium alone", *id.*, at 27).

[21] NAMIE & NAMIE, *supra* note 9, at 34.

[22] *See* Mao, *supra* note 3, at 687 (cataloguing direct and indirect costs of workplace bullying and noting that "a 2002 survey of 9,000 federal employees revealed that workplace harassment over a two-year period cost the U.S. government more than $180 million in lost time and productivity").

[23] *See* Sutton's *Total Cost of Assholes* (TCA), *in* ROBERT I. SUTTON, THE NO ASSHOLE RULE: BUILDING A CIVILIZED WORKPLACE AND SURVIVING ONE THAT ISN'T 43-44 (2010). Sutton argues there are few worse business decisions than hiring and retaining a workplace bully. As workplace research confirms, bullies destroy morale; disrupt work; diminish productivity; misdirect resources to non-productive and unnecessary conflicts; cause higher absenteeism; diminish everyone's health, happiness, and job satisfaction; increase health care costs; damage the reputation of the institution and everyone in it; increase human resources and legal costs; increase the risk of suicide and violence; and increase worker turnover, especially of your most talented and supportive personnel who have the most options in employment. As the best personnel leave, the concentration of workplace bullies and people not talented enough to leave increases, making the workplace increasingly undesirable and unproductive.

[24] *Id.*

the workplace, or be terminated. As Kohut recognized: "The mission of entire organizations can be scuttled by just a few demeaning creeps."[25]

Workplace Bullying in Higher Education

Higher education institutions are in many ways an ideal venue for workplace bullies. Persons working in higher education generally have high degrees of personal autonomy; limited oversight; substantial differentials in power among persons; and there is an abundance of talented, hardworking, and well-intentioned altruists who are the preferred prey of workplace bullies. Further, the highly individualistic and careerist culture in higher education tends to reinforce self-interested behavior and provides limited or negative incentives for those with institutional power to step-up and protect vulnerable persons and the common culture.[26]

But bullies do not just go away when they are ignored by institutional officials. An administrator that ignores the misconduct of a workplace bully today is likely to have far more serious problems in the future. Further, in higher education the granting of tenure creates special problems for dealing with workplace bullies. There should be no pretense concerning the serious threat workplace bullies pose to the health and survival of institutions and the people in them:

> Bullies have declared war. They don't care about your mission, your responsibility to ensure fiduciary soundness, or your commitment to the health and well-being of the majority of employees. Bullying prevents work from getting done. It undermines your mission. It satisfies only the perpetrator's

---

[25] MARGARET R. KOHUT, UNDERSTANDING, CONTROLLING, AND STOPPING BULLIES & BULLYING AT WORK 223 (2008).

[26] Many administrators are hesitant to address workplace bullying, even though it is their job to protect the institution and its people, because once they confront the bully, they fear the bully will become a problem for them personally, and not just other people's problems. They may hope the problem will go away or at least stay off the radar of their superiors long enough for them to be promoted to a higher position (and the situation to become someone else's problem). For these reasons it is necessary to make addressing incidents of workplace bullying an affirmative job duty for all administrators with their performance of this duty assessed in their annual reviews. Allowing administrators to neglect their duties in this area, in favor of protecting their own self-interests, can have devastating impacts on the institution and the people in it. Clear mandates to protect the institution and its people must be woven into personnel policies. *See* SUTTON, *supra* note 23, at 62.

personal agenda, and it does so at the expense of people, their productivity, and their passion. It is the antithesis of work.[27]

Despite the obvious damage done by workplace bullies, however, in many higher education institutions there is a long history of denial, appeasement, and even rewards for workplace bullies. It may seem easier in the short-term to deny, appease, or reward bad behavior to avoid confrontation. In the longer-run, however, denial empowers workplace bullies and appeasement and reward further encourage this workplace misconduct. But what can be done? As Namie and Namie noted:

> It's your choice: Stay in denial and coddle the few or protect the vast majority . . . Bullying is a malignancy that invades your workplace. The problem metastasizes and threatens the functional integrity of your company, agency, or ministry. Like any undesirable cancer, it must be neutralized and eventually excised. Your organization's health cannot be restored if it is ignored.[28]

In terms of total damage to people and programs, there is no single more destructive force in higher education than the workplace bully.[29] Workplace bullies, however, do not take responsibility for the harm they do, and they are highly unlikely to change their behaviors unless changed is forced on them.[30] Part of the psychological profile of workplace bullies is a pathological focus on their own needs and desires, seeing others simply as a means of achieving their selfish goals, and commonly blaming their victims for any resulting harms.[31]

In higher education workplace bullies will often assert that their attacks on victims are motivated only by their "high standards"; that they are the true keepers of these high standards; and that the real problem is that the targeted victims are frauds, inferior, weak, hypersensitive, etc., and it is their professional duty to hold these persons fully accountable. But Namie & Namie provided a simple test to distinguish between these asserted

---

[27] *Id.* at 77.

[28] *Id.* at 78-79.

[29] *See* Yamada, *supra* note 12 ("The emerging literature on workplace bullying confirms that this behavior inflicts harmful, even devastating, effects on its targets and can sabotage employee morale in ways that severely undercut productivity and loyalty. *Id.* at 478; "A 1995 study of university faculty and staff reported that over half of the respondents had been subjected to verbal abuse, and twenty-three percent had been mistreated." *Id.* at 485).

[30] *See* NAMIE & NAMIE, *supra* note 9, at 78 ("What stops an aggressor is aggression").

[31] *See* KOHUT, *supra* note 25, at 35.

legitimate motivations and workplace bullying: What do their actions genuinely have to do with work and advancing the institutional mission?[32]

In higher education workplace bullies commonly attempt to mask their personal misconduct as part of the institutional mission. Skilled workplace bullies often succeed in convincing their superiors that an attack on an employee is somehow protecting the institution, allowing bullies to opportunistically morph their attacks on a targeted victim into a battle between the victim and the institution. One of the workplace bully's most potent weapons is bringing the full weight of institutional processes down on the victim by manipulating institutional administrators.

Before getting drawn into this deal with the devil, however, institutional leaders should objectively assess facts and circumstances for themselves, and not just listen to one-sided claims from potentially self-interested parties who may be engaged in workplace bullying. In fact, workplace bullies commonly target persons they see as personal threats to their ego or status, persons who are more talented, hardworking, or respected than the bullies.[33] The people most needed for the long-term success of the institution may be perceived as personal threats by workplace bullies who fear being exposed as less competent.

Unmasking Workplace Bullies in Higher Education Institutions

As a lamentable manifestation of the dark-side of human nature, there may always be a number of potential bullies among us. Generally, however, only the most talented and experienced abusers find their way into positions of power in successful institutions of higher education. Those that are too brazen in committing their misdeeds, or that cross the line of criminality, are likely to be found out and branded as unfit employees early in their careers. But based on a life-time of practice, the most able bullies have mastered the dark arts of not only using well-targeted persecution and harassment to destroy their victims, but also at using interpersonal deception and manipulation to cover their tracks.

Many have crafted a mask of civility to perfection for use when it benefits them and serves to protect them from the consequences of their own destructive behaviors. Those who look closer, however, will find that it is generally a very thin disguise. Bullies' masks commonly involve excessive ingratiating behavior to those in power and those they want something from, contrasted with disrespectful and demeaning behavior to those they seek to control and harm. Experienced observers may

---

[32] NAMIE & NAMIE, *supra* note 9, at 77.
[33] *Id.* at 32

commonly see a "kiss-up/kick-down" behavior pattern, often accompanied by a false bravado masking the bully's true insecurity and lack of competence.

To unmask workplace bullies, you must learn to recognize their telltale behaviors. Bullies are best identified by their conduct and its impact on others. Bullies are as bullies do. In higher education workplace bully red-flags include the following behaviors:[34]

> *Destructive Predatory Agenda*: An institutional objective may be offered as a pretext, but patterns of conduct reveal that the real objective is not related to any genuine institutional mission, but is in fact motivated by a destructive and predatory personal agenda.

> *Projected Arrogance/Hidden Fear*: Projected confidence may far exceed actual competence. Bullies commonly harbor morbid fears of being exposed as less competent than others, but they are unlikely to acknowledge these fears even though these fears are at the core of their motivations for the harassment of co-workers. Instead a bully is obsessed with solidifying a false facade of superiority over others and attacking anyone who might threaten this faux image and status (*n.b.*, genuine high achievers are too busy with productive work to waste time attacking others).

> *Authoritarian Personality*: Exhibits an overly simplistic black and white world view; rejects suggestions of situational complexity or shades of grey. There is only absolute right and wrong, and the bully is always "right" of course. Imposes arbitrary rules based on authority rather than reason or necessity; expects his or her orders to be followed without question or explanation; assigns demeaning tasks and meaningless busy work both to display power and to diminish the morale and productivity of targeted victims. Does not seem to understand cooperative relationships among equals; views

---

[34] Consistent with Justice Brandeis' declaration that "sunlight is said to be the best disinfectant", Buckley v. Valeo, 424 U.S. 1, 67 n. 80 (*quoting* L. BRANDEIS, OTHER PEOPLE'S MONEY 62 (1933)), this section attempts to illuminate common workplace bullying behaviors through a basic taxonomy of workplace bullying archetypes as an aid in recognizing and preventing these destructive behaviors. These are only illustrative archetypes, but they will no doubt ring true to those familiar with workplace bullies, and help the unfamiliar to more quickly recognize these behaviors in order to better mitigate damages to people and programs in their institutions through early preventive actions. These illustrative archetypes are not based on any real person and any resemblance to any real person is purely coincidental and unintended.

relationships as only dominate-submissive/exploiter-exploited, and will often become highly submissive when confronted with a clear and certain threat from a superior power.

Progress Roadblock: Intentionally impedes the progress and productivity of the institution and co-workers. May obstruct institutional decision-making processes (in effect holding everyone "hostage") in an attempt to extract personal benefits and concessions, or to stop the potential successes of others. Unless changes benefit the bully, changes are road-blocked, especially if targeted victims may be professionally elevated by the changes.

Powerphile: Obsessed with power and control over others; admires and seeks power; derives great pleasure from the exercise of power over others; believes those with power have a right to use it as they see fit; uses institutional power as personal power; does not recognize ethical and moral limits on the use of power. The only respected limits on the abuse of power result from the bully's fears of personal consequences if caught. Only power can stop the powerphile.

Control Freak: Covets opportunities to force his or her will on others. Seeks out positions of authority to acquire power to control others; but rejects institutional limits or controls on his or her own conduct. Aspects of the bully's life may be out of control even while the bully is desperately trying to micromanage and control others' lives.

Double-Standards: Manipulates rules and regulations to condemn and control victims. Rules are strictly applied to targeted victims, but not to the bully, allies, or minions. Commonly engages in bitter dissent to advance a personal agenda, but is intolerant of any dissent from others. Builds minor errors by victims into major incidents, but refuses to accept responsibility for personal errors and conduct.

Dual Personality: Dr. Jekyll & Mr. Hyde personality. Dr. Jekyll is the mask. Mr. Hyde is the true personality. But for the most talented and practiced bullies Dr. Jekyll may be so ostensibly charismatic that many do not see Mr. Hyde until it is too late.

Psychic Vampire: Feeds on negative emotions and is disturbingly energized by interpersonal conflicts or the suffering and misfortunes of others. May covertly orchestrate "chicken fights" between others in the workplace and take great pleasure in watching the resulting conflict and suffering.

Reputation Skunk: Damages the image of the institution and co-workers, both intentionally, *i.e.*, actively, by slandering the institution and co-workers, and unintentionally, *i.e.*, passively, by his/her personal bad reputation and known association with the institution and co-workers.

Social Illiterate: May display inappropriate social behaviors. The bully may seem to be trying to "read" others in order to know how to behave acceptably in a peer social situation. The bully may be masterful at interpersonal manipulation and attacking others, but may not be able to understand honest relationships among equals that do not involve coercion or exploitation. Bullies may believe, that like them, everyone is duplicitous, and like them, others are only pretending to be "nice" to gain advantage. Kindness and honest friendship are not real in their minds, and are not recognized as real in others.

Social Saboteur: Engages in covert efforts to sabotage victims' potential successes and destabilize their social support systems to make victims feel alone and paranoid. Bullies often do not recognize professional/personal boundaries and attacks may extend beyond the office into victims' personal lives (*e.g.*, attempts to harm relationships with spouses, friends, etc.). Tactics commonly include office-to-office closed door whispering campaigns, "warnings" to others about the victim, etc., all to sow the seeds of suspicion and poison the well for victims. Targeted victims may never know they have been slandered and lost relationships and opportunities because of the covert smear campaigns.

Manipulative: A skilled manipulator and fabricator often able to convince superiors and co-workers the targeted victim is the real problem; may attempt to inflame anger against the victim in order to escalate a minor or manufactured dispute into a full-blown academic mobbing.

Machiavellian: Obsessed with office politics and believes everyone else is; views others as little more than pawns in advancing the bully's selfish personal agenda and recognizes no ethical or moral limits. The only rule is to win, and the ends justify the means.

Obsessive Self-Promotion: May have received recognitions and awards that far exceed actual achievements, *i.e.*, awards were often self-promoted; bartered; received as appeasement; and/or coerced; may be obsessed with building a false image of personal greatness and historical importance even though an objective review would find the bully's works relatively insignificant and any belief of real historical significance delusional. Nonetheless, many in the workplace may continue to trade unearned recognitions for false peace, and pretend to admire "the Emperor's new clothes" just to avoid confrontations or becoming the next target of the bully's abuses.

Passive-Aggressive Attacks: Pokes at targeted victims until they react and then plays the victim. A master of back-handed "compliments" that are in fact provocations and insults. Rapidly shifts from attack mode to victim mode when challenged or exposed.

Histrionic Behavior: Uses excessive acts of ingratiation and overdramatic emotional outbursts to manipulate others; may include a full range of dramatic performances ranging from embarrassing displays of public sycophancy, to anger, shouting, slamming objects, tears, and pleadings, all calculated to manipulate observers into compliance.

Sadistic Behavior: Delights in the misfortunes of others. May set up targeted victims in lose-lose scenarios just to see them squirm and suffer.[35] Imposing suffering on targets is a tactic for all

---

[35] A common lose-lose scenario involves a series of false complaints by the bully aimed at the target, forcing the target to either passively submit to the unending allegations and abuses or have any reactions twisted as further "evidence" against the targeted person. If the target doesn't respond to the bully's baseless accusations and provocations they are deemed "true" by the bully (*i.e.* failure to reply/disprove equals "true") and widely broadcast to further harm and humiliate the target. If the target responds, any response is carefully dissected, twisted, and used against the target in the next round of accusations.

bullies, but for the sadist bully it is also a hobby. Offers of kindness or compromise by the target will be seen by the bully as weakness and a sign the bully is "winning" further energizing the bully's attacks on the victim like a shark smelling blood.

Narcissistic Behavior: Obsessed with his/her own greatness; everyone else is just an expendable supporting character or background extra in the great play that is his/her life; may have come to believe his/her own propaganda of greatness; exhibits a deep sense of entitlement, believing that he/she is owed special treatment and tribute from others.

Sociopathic Behavior: Consistently disregards the interests and feelings of others; may be unable to experience authentic human empathy or to believe it is real in others; feels no genuine remorse for harming others.

Inciter: Attempts to inflame fear and anger against the targeted person in order to drag co-workers and institutional support systems into the bully's personal attack on the targeted individual.

Workplace Spy: Snoops, stalks, and spies on targets, fishing to find any thread of "evidence" that could be used against the target. It doesn't matter that the "evidence" is false or amounts to nothing. To a bully determined to harm a targeted victim, "truth" is whatever the bully wants to be true, and lots of nothing equals something.

Workplace Destroyer: The workplace serial bully has a career-long path of workplace destruction. A careful look at the individual's past will show a person consistently surrounded by interpersonal conflict, high employee turnover, and institutional failure and decline. There may be a trail of "bodies" of damaged co-workers whose careers, health, and lives were damaged by the bully's endless barrage of attacks, and other evidence of a recurrent pattern of interpersonal aggression and workplace misconduct.[36]

---

[36] Important pre-employment caution: Current employers and co-workers may give a workplace bully positive recommendations just to be rid of the troublesome employee. Prior employers and co-workers may be more candid.

No workplace bully displays all of these disturbing traits. Nor is everyone who may display one or more of these traits necessarily a workplace bully. The way to distinguish the true workplace bully from those with less virulent human flaws is to carefully examine true motives, patterns of conduct, and reactions to harmful impacts on others. Although they may be masterful in hiding their misconduct, the true workplace bully clearly intends to harm targeted people; has a long history of doing so; and there is no genuine remorse for harms inflicted on people and institutions.

Examining Possible Pathologies of Workplace Bullies

Not all workplace bullies have diagnosable personality disorders, but many do.[37] Among the more recurrent personality disorders in workplace bullies observed by mental health professionals and researchers are those of the narcissist and the sociopath.[38] While all humans are to some degree self-interested, unhealthy and pathological narcissism occurs when individuals fail to acknowledge the legitimate feelings and rights of others because of obsessions with satisfying their own inflated egos. Narcissistic bullies display an arrogant, unhealthy sense of entitlement, overstated self-importance, and attitudes of superiority to others.[39] To sustain these false beliefs their own achievements are exaggerated and the achievements of others are diminished. Nonetheless, narcissistic bullies in fact envy others and want to prevent them from further successes that may threaten their fragile egos and status.[40]

Sociopathic bullies show a similar pattern of disregard for the feelings and rights of others, but these flaws are dangerously aggravated by their lack of capacity for normal human empathy and remorse. In the most successful workplace bullies, however, these character flaws may be well masked by a polished ability to fabricate, manipulate, and charm. Their warm facades are nonetheless masking icy souls that would feel nothing in inflicting great pain and suffering on others. Their inability to feel empathy for others, however, does not mean that sociopathic bullies do not understand consequences. In fact, the certainty of severe personal consequences may be the only means of stopping sociopathic bullies.[41]

Workplace bullies may show evidence of other psychological disorders, such as paranoia or neurosis, or there may be no diagnosable

---

[37] NAMIE & NAMIE, *supra* note 9, at 55.
[38] *Id.*
[39] *Id.*
[40] *See* KOHUT, *supra* note 25, at 44.
[41] *See* NAMIE & NAMIE, *supra* note 9, at 78.

disorder at all. Sometimes an opportunistic bully may simply choose to harm others as a misguided means of achieving desired personal goals. The bully "wanna-be" may be modeling behaviors observed as successful for other workplace bullies in the past. These copycat bullies are yet another cost of allowing bullies to prosper from their workplace misconduct. And the more bullies were allowed to prosper in the past, the more likely others with marginal ethics and morality will attempt similar workplace misconduct in the future.

Kohut argues that the most damaging yet disturbingly common type of workplace bully is the "serial bully."[42] Serial bullies are "extremely dangerous individuals that relentlessly and systematically destroy their targets in the workplace."[43] Serial bullies generally stop their misconduct short of criminality, but otherwise share many characteristics of common criminals from the lack of genuine remorse to life-long patterns of interpersonal misconduct and intentional harms to others.[44]

The serial bully is devastating to both individuals and the institution. The serial bully desperately needs a target, and will find a target, leaving a wake of pain and mounting ruin as each target and the institutional social fabric around them is destroyed. With years of practice, serial bullies are generally highly skilled at their craft. Attacks are well planned and expertly executed.[45] Further, serial bullies in higher education are often skilled at getting others to join them in their attack on a vulnerable individual, orchestrating an academic mobbing.[46] Few persons are able to

---

[42] KOHUT, *supra* note 25, at 157.

[43] *Id.* at 162.

[44] Some bullies do cross the line of criminality. *See* NAMIE & NAMIE, supra note 9, at 56 (*citing* the work of Dr. Robert Hare on psychopaths who estimates "1 in 100 executives is psychopathic, and . . . society is growing more psychopathic all the time").

[45] Victims often experience a sense of ambush as the trap is sprung when the victim is most vulnerable. Shock and denial may impair the victim's ability to respond, and others may find the vicious reality difficult to believe, as this type of behavior is outside of the realm of normal human conduct and experience. *See also* David C. Yamada, supra note 1, at *quoting* ANDREA ADAMS & NEIL CRAWFORD, BULLYING AT WORK: HOW TO CONFRONT AND OVERCOME IT 9 (1992) ("Bullying at work is like a malignant cancer. It creeps up on you long before you--or anyone else--are able to appreciate what it is that is making you feel the ill effects").

[46] *See* Yamada, *supra* note 12, at 481, *citing* NOA DAVENPORT, THE MOBBING SYNDROME: EMOTIONAL ABUSE IN THE AMERICAN WORKPLACE 10 (1999) ("Mobbing is an emotional assault. It begins when an individual becomes the target of disrespectful and harmful behavior. Through innuendo, rumors, and public discrediting, a hostile environment is created in which one individual gathers others to willingly, or unwillingly, participate in continuous malevolent actions to force a person out of the workplace").

withstand an attack on this scale, and the outcome is often personally and professionally devastating for the targeted person.[47]

These serial bullies are especially well practiced at the art of convincing superiors that their victims were at fault, or that the targeted person was an emerging danger to superiors and the institution. Their stories are often so convincing that serial bullies may actually be rewarded for destroying their victims. Even more perversely, serial bullies may be rewarded after they are discovered as serial bullies in the institution. Colleagues and supervisors may be terrified to confront them, being painfully aware of what happened to others who did. Busy with work, family, etc., few people have the time, energy, or courage needed to take on the serial bully who seems to have endless time, energy, and bravado to pursue targeted victims whether they are subordinates, peers, or superiors.[48] While this level of interpersonal conflict is exhausting and harmful to psychologically normal persons, the serial bully feeds on and is energized by emotionally charged conflict.

Faced with the potential professional and personal hell of dealing with such a relentless and venomous bully, bystanders' agendas often become just trying to avoid being the bully's next target. They abandon victims in order to save themselves. Supervisors, and even upper-level administrators, may realize how threatening these individuals are, and seek to appease them rather than to confront them. Once again, the serial bully is rewarded and not held accountable by the institution, further reinforcing the pathological behavior.

It is essential to understand, however, that serial bullies cannot be appeased. Efforts to appease workplace bullies just make them hungrier and bolder. Appeasing a bully is feeding a bully. The true serial bully will not, and probably cannot, stop his or her destructive behavior. The serial bully will devastate people and programs until the bully is removed or the institution is ruined.

The personality disorders that are at the root of many bullying behaviors are present at all personnel levels of an organization: Bosses, peers, subordinates, and clients. It's just that the problem is most likely to

---

[47] *See* Heinz Leymann & Annelie Gustafsson, *Mobbing at Work and the Development of Post-Traumatic Stress Disorders*, 5 EUR. J. WORK & ORGANIZATIONAL PSYCHOL. 252-54 (1996).

[48] A workplace bully may use an attack on a superior as a de facto means of elevating his/her status in the institution. By engaging the superior toe-to-toe, the bully attempts to appear to be on the same functional power level as the superior. If the superior backs-down or loses the battle, the bully will assume the status of a de facto superior. But if the bully loses, the bully will claim victim status and cry abuse of power by the superior, restarting the battle, and gaining yet another bite at the apple in attacking the superior.

become fully manifested in relationships where the bully has power over others. Research suggests that the majority of reported workplace bullies are bosses.[49] But bosses generally were and often still are peers and subordinates in the organizational structure. The personality disorder was always there and the problems won't go away until the bully does. It is just that giving power to a bully gives the bully an opportunity to abuse that power in ways that only a person with a personality disorder will do.[50] Power brings out the worst in workplace bullies. When they have no power they may go unnoticed, otherwise tending to be mediocre employees at best.

Exploring the Motivations of Workplace Bullies

What drives anyone to destroy their own workplace and the people around them? There are many types of bullies with varied motivations, but a common motivation is a hyper-selfish desire for personal power and prestige in the workplace. Workplace bullies may simply be seeking to destroy a perceived personal threat to their fragile egos and frighten other potential competitors into submission. Talented, hardworking people can elevate themselves honestly based on their own merits. Bullies, however, are attempting to "elevate" themselves by hammering others down, not understanding or caring what their actions do to the workplace and the people in it. What matters is getting what they want, and they believe their ends justify their means.

It is essential to recognize, however, that the targets workplace bullies are most likely to attack are also the people most needed for the long-term success of the institution. By attacking the most talented employees workplace bullies destroy the institution's current and future potential.

---

[49] Kaplan, *supra* note 10, at 148. *But see* Mao, *supra* note 3, at 687 ("One study by the National Institute for Occupational Safety and Health found that bullying by coworkers was more common than bullying by bosses. Another survey found that coworkers were bullies in forty-three percent of cases, compared to supervisor involvement in thirty-six percent of cases").

[50] *See generally* NAMIE & NAMIE, *supra* note 9, at 55 (describing personality disorders found in workplace bullies). It is essential to understand that true workplace bullies do not think and act like psychologically normal human beings. Workplace bullies generally don't feel remorse for the harm they inflict on their victims. Their victims "deserve" to be tormented if for no other reason than their perceived weakness. Psychologically normal people don't spend a lifetime plotting against the people around them and relishing in the pain they cause others, and then decide with firm conviction that they were fully justified in inflicting harm on others and that everyone else is the problem. For all of these reasons power given to a true workplace bully will be abused with disastrous consequences.

Talented, hardworking people are the key to institutional success. They are the essential lifeblood of successful institutions, but the first to leave when a workplace becomes dominated by workplace bullies. Workplace bullying serves only the short-term selfish interests of bullies at enormous costs to everyone.[51]

But many workplace bullies' motivations run far deeper that the misguided pursuit of self-interests. Kohut noted that a common motivation for workplace bullies is their inner fears of inadequacy and being "found out."[52] Bullying is used "to divert attention away from the inadequacies of the bully . . . this is how they keep their jobs."[53] Bullies are "mortally fearful of being viewed as they truly are—weak and often incompetent. *Those who can, do. Those who cannot, bully*."[54] Kohut concluded:

> All the different types of bullies are individuals who are resentful, bitter, angry, and jealous of the abilities of others because they know they can never "measure up." In fact, bullies are driven primarily by jealousy and envy, especially of their targets. To make sure their targets do not surpass them . . . bullies of all types must virtually destroy them. A bully's fear of being "discovered" often borders on paranoia. Since all of these feelings occur on a subconscious level, bullies truly believe in their worth and adequacy and refuse to consider otherwise. Since only feelings and behaviors that are acknowledged can be changed or relearned, it is very unlikely that any type of bully is capable of changing.[55]

Workplace bullies generally believe that aggression will be met with desired concessions and appeasement, because in their past experience, it usually has been. For most serial bullies, bullying has been a very lucrative venture yielding unearned rewards and power throughout their careers. So they are not likely to stop their workplace misconduct until a decisive force stops them. As Namie & Namie recognized: "Aggression

---

[51] *See* SUTTON, *supra* note 23, at 27. Clearly, institutional tolerance for workplace bullying is a disastrous policy. Aside from the serious legal, ethical, and moral problems related to institutional tolerance for workplace bullying, allowing the most talented and successful individuals to be run off, marginalized, or destroyed by bullies is at best a recipe for institutional failure. In the increasingly competitive world of higher education, failing academic units and institutions are unlikely to survive.

[52] KOHUT, *supra* note 25, at 152.

[53] *Id.*

[54] *Id.*

[55] *Id.*

and its rewards are communicated throughout the organization at lightning speed. The research findings from game theory unequivocally show that it is suicide for a cooperator to continue to choose a cooperative response, a submissive response, when competitor-opponents repeatedly choose aggression. What stops the aggressor is aggression."[56]

The Preferred Prey and Habitat of Workplace Bullies

There are many misconceptions about workplace bullies' preferred targets. Workplace bullies do not, for example, just seek out the weakest prey like a wolf circling a herd of sheep. To the contrary, workplace bullies strategically seek out high-value targets with strong professional achievement or potential in order to preempt threats to their own egos and status.[57] Jealous bullies use workplace harassment is an illicit means of destroying potential competitors.[58] Common characteristics of victims marked for harassment by workplace bullies are that those targeted are: Highly independent; ethical; competent; well-liked; and willing to challenge the bully and resist the bully's efforts to control others and enforce subservience.[59]

Bullies commonly target people with the highest potential for success. But their chosen victims may currently be vulnerable to the harassment because they are newer; untenured; lower in the institutional hierarchy; less well-connected, less social or verbal; or have other perceived weaknesses that can be usefully exploited by bullies. Although any person is a potential target, some research indicates that women, minorities, and newer workers may be at special risk of attack by workplace bullies.[60] In some workplace cultures they may be the canaries in the coal mine, the first to show signs of stress when a workplace bully becomes active in the organization. But bullies generally target their victims based on their own selfish objectives and perceived opportunities. Bias is usually not the

---

[56] NAMIE & NAMIE, *supra* note 9, at 78. It is important to note that aggression can also be stopped by providing no opportunity for aggression.

[57] SUTTON, *supra* note 23, at 200 ("feelings of insecurity and incompetence magnify the chances that superiors will bully subordinates").

[58] Yamada, *supra* note 12, at 483 ("bullies seek out agreeable, vulnerable, and successful coworkers, often motivated by the bullies' own feelings of inadequacy").

[59] *See, e.g.*, NAMIE & NAMIE, *supra* note 9, at 72 (A 2003 study by Namie & Namie found that the common profile for bullies' targets was that they "refuse to be subservient, are technically more skilled than their bully, are well liked, are ethical and honest, and abhor workplace politics").

[60] Yamada, *supra* note 12, at 489-490.

primary driving force in workplace bullying, although some groups may be more vulnerable in some circumstances.[61]

No workplace environment is safe from the determined workplace bully. But workplace bullies do prefer some habitats over others, and some habitats are easier for them to exploit. Namie and Namie found that the most serious incidents of workplace bullying were likely to occur in institutions with high percentages of altruists, including schools, hospitals, social services, etc.[62] Predators are naturally drawn to their prey. Altruists are the preferred prey for bullies, and bullies find more of them in altruistic institutions. These types of institutions also often have inadequate oversight by middle and higher level administrators, and instead may have a history of appeasing or even rewarding bad behavior to keep things quiet and under the radar of top officials or from public view.[63]

Every actor needs a stage. In higher education, faculty meetings are often the forum of choice for workplace bullies. Workplace bullies commonly use meetings they know targeted victims and intended audiences are required to attend as the theater for planned verbal beatings and public humiliations of their targets. Attacks are generally well scripted in advance by bullies; carefully orchestrated with allies and supporting minions; and all calculated to achieve maximum psychological impact on the targeted victim and observers.[64]

Workplace bullies are well aware that these types of public humiliations and displays of power are the most potent in inflicting psychological pain on victims and frightening others into passive submission. But workplace bullies may use any available means of harassment, *e.g*, passive-aggressive e-mail; un-witnessed hallway/elevator encounters; manipulated institutional reviews and processes; false anonymous reports; etc. Careful timing may also be used by the bully to

---

[61] *Id*. at 490 ("supervisory abuse . . . is most easily exercised over unskilled and semiskilled unorganized workers who comprise the bottom tier of the labor force. Blacks, Latinos, women, teenagers, and undocumented immigrant workers continue to be disproportionately represented in this bottom tier").

[62] NAMIE & NAMIE, *supra* note 9, at 73.

[63] *Id*. at 69 ("we've found some of the highest bullying rates in education"); *Id*. at 71 ("Sprinkle some narcissists and exploiters within a pool of people who believe it is a fair and benevolent world and the recipe is complete").

[64] *Id*. at 6 ("Methods escalate in abusiveness, and escape routes for targets are blocked. Bullies even recruit coworkers to further spread the misery. And as hatred progresses, the targeted individual grows sicker from multiple stress-related health complications. Workplace bullying is not merely hostile; it's abusive. And abuse is potentially traumatizing").

enhance the psychological impact on the victim, *e.g.*, the late Friday afternoon "bomb" to ruin the victim's weekend and deny any psychological rest from the harassment; veiled threats before important votes; hints of sabotaging pending opportunities; etc., continually accumulating the attacks to the level sufficient to cause enough psychological pain to drive away the targeted victim.[65] It is important to understand that: "The effects . . . are so devastating because they sap people of their energy and esteem mostly through the accumulated effects of small, demeaning acts, not so much through one or two dramatic episodes."[66] Workplace bullies thrive where this type of relentless harassment is tolerated.

Institutional Strategies for Dealing with Workplace Bullies

Although strictly manmade in origin, and not a natural disaster, the impact of workplace bullies on victims and the workplace can nonetheless prove personally disastrous for victims and disastrous for institutional programs.[67] For this reason institutional strategies for dealing with workplace bullies may be developed paralleling strategies for dealing with other disasters, including these essential steps:

> *Prevention-Mitigation*: Identifying all potential hazards and vulnerabilities and reducing the potential damage they can cause; *Preparedness*: Collaborating . . . to develop plans and protocols to prepare for the possibility that the identified hazards . . . will occur; *Response*: Working closely with . . . partners to effectively contain and resolve an emergency in, or around, a school or campus; and *Recovery*: Teaming with . . . partners to assist students and staff in the healing process, and restore a healthy and safe learning environment following an . . . event.[68]

---

[65] *See* KOHUT, *supra* note 25, at 198 ("the bully's objective is to remove you from the workplace; if you make this difficult, he or she may intensify efforts toward your destruction").

[66] SUTTON, *supra* note 23, at 29. Current U.S. employment law is focused on addressing extreme episodes of status based discrimination and fails in addressing the more subtle and multifaceted "pecked to death by ducks" tactics commonly used by workplace bullies.

[67] NAMIE & NAMIE, *supra* note 9, at 7-9 (describing how bullying can lead to incidents of violence in higher education institutions and noting in the cases reviewed that because of inadequate institutional responses: "Thirty-four people died who should not have").

[68] FEMA, GUIDE FOR DEVELOPING HIGH-QUALITY SCHOOL EMERGENCY OPERATIONS PLANS 2 (Feb. 17, 2014), http://rems.ed.gov/docs/REMS_K-12_Guide_508.pdf

The establishment of institutional policies and applied strategies for addressing workplace bullying, including stratagems for prevention, preparedness, response, and recovery, can help to create a holistic plan for effectively dealing with workplace bullies in higher education institutions.[69]

The most important workplace anti-bullying plan for any institution is a plan for prevention.[70] An institution can be best immunized against damages from workplace bullying through the establishment of preventative personnel policies and proactive personnel education programs. Prevention is always superior to remediation. The adoption and aggressive implementation of proactive personnel policies are at the center of effective anti-bullying efforts.[71] Workplace bullying occurs because workplace bullies are hired, retained, and tolerated. With wise planning and determined administration, institutional policies can help prevent the hiring, retention, and tolerance of workplace bullies.[72] Education programs can help personnel to understand the potential harms caused by workplace bullies; recognize emerging problems before significant damages occur; and encourage all personnel to take a proactive role in protecting the institution and its people from preventable harms related to workplace bullying.

An essential element in preventing harms from workplace bullying is diligently precluding known workplace bullies from gaining power in the institution. Giving power to known bullies is like allowing mischievous children to play with matches: The final result is as predictable as it is disastrous. Institutional power given to workplace bullies will be abused for selfish purposes and result in harm to the institution and its people. But as obvious as this outcome may be, workplace bullies aggressively

---

[69] Tepper & White, *supra* note 13, at 96-97 ("Without question, harassment can have a destructive effect on the academic environment . . . Preventive and educational efforts may yield better results than waiting for such conduct to occur").

[70] NAMIE & NAMIE, supra note 9, at 72 ("Employers can and should deliberately shape the workplace culture to prevent cutthroat behavior from ever developing").

[71] *Id.* at 74 ("If you want to drive out negative behavior, the consequences have to change").

[72] *Id.* at 72. The institution and its administrators must recognize the seriousness of workplace bullying and its danger to the institution and the people in it. Workplace bullying is another form of abuse, like child abuse, spousal abuse, elder abuse, etc. *See* Yamada, *supra* note 1, at 276 ("In terms of harm rendered, workplace bullying can be more akin to sexual assault or domestic abuse than to less severe forms of mistreatment"). Toleration only further empowers the abuser to harm the victim.

seek power, and it is commonly given to them by peers and superiors negligently or as appeasement.[73]

To achieve institutional preparedness, effective workplace anti-bullying policies and strategies should be established and operationalized in advance of a crisis.   An effective anti-bullying policy and its administration must communicate a clear and resolute policy message throughout the institution:

> Workplace bullying and harassment by any person will not be tolerated in this institution. It shall be the duty of all employees to prevent, report, and stop workplace bullying and harassment in this institution through all reasonable means including full compliance with this policy. Institutional administrators and other employees shall act in accordance with this clear policy statement: *Do not hire workplace bullies; do not retain workplace bullies; and do not tolerate workplace bullying.* Those who uphold these protective policies shall be appropriately supported by this institution for their vital aid in safeguarding the institution's people, mission, and resources. Those who violate these policies shall be appropriately sanctioned or terminated as institutional policy violators and unfit employees.[74]

Effective workplace anti-bullying policies can both prevent incidents of workplace bullying and prepare the institution for dealing with any incidents that do occur. Administrators must also be well prepared with effective applied strategies for dealing with workplace bullies and know that they have the full support of the institution in the lawful administration of institutional policies.

In responding to workplace bullies in the institution it is essential to recognize them early, understand what motivates them, and what stops them. As noted above, Namie and Namie found that: "What stops the aggressor is aggression."[75] A true workplace bully will only respond to superior institutional power applied with ready and certain personal consequences. In dealing with a workplace bully, however, institutional

---

[73] *See* SUTTON, *supra* note 23, at 69 (discussing the corrupting influence of power). Giving a workplace bully the power he or she wants today may seem easier than denying it and risking confrontation. But there will be a terrible price to pay in the future. Until a workplace bully can be removed from the institution the bully must be effectively defanged by denying power over others and opportunities for abuse whenever possible.

[74] *See infra* Appendix: Model Institutional Workplace Anti-Bullying Policy.

[75] NAMIE & NAMIE, *supra* note 9, at 78.

power must be resolutely but judiciously applied, recognizing that a favorite tactic of workplace bullies is provoking others into taking actions that bullies can use against them.[76]

To truly prevail over the bully it is essential to maintain the legal, ethical, and moral high ground at all times. Personnel responsible for the administration of workplace anti-bullying policies must know and follow institutional policies; know and follow applicable laws; and at all times maintain a professional demeanor and act with unimpeachable integrity.[77] To defeat a workplace bully, you must firmly hold the legal and ethical high ground. Ultimately all battles are about winning hearts and minds. By holding the moral high ground leaders can gain the support of the broad majority in ridding the institution of a troublesome bully.

True workplace bullies cannot be redeemed. They must be stopped by removing them from the institution or at least by limiting their abilities to harm others until they can be removed. Both contending with and trying to "cure" serial bullies are at best a waste of institutional time and resources that will likely only prolong the bully's ability to harm the institution and its people.[78] Serial bullies will not change, and probably cannot change. They generally have a life-long history of bullying, attesting to the fact that they are unwilling or unable to stop harassing others. Instead, serial bullies often have personality disorders that result in them seeing everyone else as the problem. Even though the bully is the

---

[76] KOHUT, *supra* note 25, at 202 ("if targets respond with aggressive, out-of-control behavior, bullies will use this response as another weapon"). In dealing with a bully it is tempting to fight fire with fire. But it is critical to understand that one doesn't really defeat a bully by adopting his or her tactics and becoming more like the bully. To the contrary, the ultimate victory for the bully is to change who the victim is; to turn a happy, productive, well-liked, and kind person into just another miserable bully; or even better for the bully, to provoke a targeted person into reactions that can be used by the bully against the targeted person.

[77] *Id.* One will likely have to stand up to the bully to protect the institution and people and stop the bully's misconduct. But it is critical to remember that winning a battle with the bully is not the goal: A healthy, productive workplace for everyone is the goal. Bullies are defined by their selfishness, inhumanity, and lack of ethics. In sharp contrast true professionals and leaders are defined by their altruistic dedication to the institutional mission and its people, they are unselfish, humane, and ethical in their conduct. An institution's mission and people can be protected by strong enforcement of altruistic and ethical workplace policies, including a well-crafted anti-bullying policy. In enforcing these policies administrators must remember that the real goal is advancing the institutional mission and protecting its people, and not fighting battles with bullies.

[78] *See* MARTIN LUTHER KING, JR., LETTER FROM BIRMINGHAM JAIL (1963) ("people of ill will have used time much more effectively than have the people of good will"). When abuse is ongoing and justice has been denied, every passing day without remedial action is yet another victory for perpetrators and yet another injury to victims.

clear aggressor by any objective measure, the bully will see no need for personal change and instead blame the victim.[79]

Systematic plans for recovery are a critically important but commonly neglected phase in dealing with incidents of workplace bullying. In severe cases of workplace bullying, personnel may be gravely traumatized and workplace cultures and programs may be badly damaged. Without an effective plan for recovery, personnel and programs may be unable to recover from the harms resulting from incidents of severe workplace bullying.

Damages to personnel may include low morale; loss of trust; unresolved anger; and stress related mental and physical health problems including post-traumatic stress disorder.[80] To restore morale and essential trust, institutional leaders must help personnel to see that the bully induced workplace nightmare is really over, and that there is a clear path forward to a more professional and productive future for everyone. Persons with stress related mental and physical health problems may require counseling and other support services while they heal from the workplace trauma.[81]

Damages to programs in higher education may include harms to public reputation and image; loss of key employees; loss of students; low productivity; dysfunctional culture; failed unit policies and operational systems; financial losses, and general mission failures. Any unit recovering from an incident of workplace bullying should be closely examined by administrators to diagnose how and why the harms occurred in order to prescribe a plan for recovery and the prevention of future damages. Some units, however, may require more extensive external assessments and professional consultations, personnel changes, reorganization, triage decisions, or program terminations to protect the institution. Guarding against damages to personnel and the institution

---

[79] KOHUT, *supra* note 25, at 37 (As Kohut recognized, workplace bullying behavior is often rooted in a bully's personality disorder: "Note that personality disorders at not mental illnesses, differentiating them from conditions like schizophrenia, panic disorder, or major depression. Rather, a personality disorder is a pervasive and enduring pattern of internal experiences and outward behaviors that deviate significantly from behavior that is expected from society. People with personality disorders are very rigid and inflexible in personal, social, and occupational situations . . . Since personality disorders are not mental illnesses, they cannot be 'cured.' Those affected can learn to modify and minimize their chaotic behavior, but treatment like this is seldom successful since personality disordered individuals are in deep denial that they are not the problem. To them, other people are the problem, and it is these others who need to change, not them").

[80] Kaplan, *supra* note 10, at 142 ("Many victims of bullying suffer psychological damage similar to post-traumatic stress disorder").

[81] NAMIE & NAMIE, *supra* note 9, at 24.

requires the establishment of sound institutional policies and practical applied strategies for prevention, preparedness, response, and recovery.[82]

The Evil Empire Strikes Back: Anticipating Counter-Attacks by Workplace Bullies

To avoid harms resulting from workplace bullying, institutions must adopt and aggressively enforce effective workplace anti-bullying policies. When an institutional anti-bullying policy is adopted, however, workplace bullies and their minions are likely to attempt to strike back at people and policies that threaten to stop their so far highly rewarding workplace misconduct. In an environment in which bullies were allowed to operate with impunity, bullies enjoyed power, privileged status, and the rewards of appeasement and tribute. They will not give these up voluntarily or easily.[83]

Namie & Namie noted common patterns among workplace bullies seeking to retain or regain their power over others.[84] Bullies commonly attempted to: 1) Convince higher-level leaders to abandon or undermine the anti-bullying policy; 2) Become the institutional leaders and kill the policy; 3) Pretend rehabilitation and seek to participate in policy construction and enforcement only to undermine both; 4) Have one of their supporters or minions put in charge of policy enforcement; 5) Falsely claim to be victims, using the policy as a sword and not as a shield, utilizing false complaints as their new tool for bullying; 6) Flood the system with frivolous but thoroughly documented and difficult to dismiss complaints; and/or 7) Attempt to hand-pick or influence the next leader to abandon or undermine the policy.[85]

Forewarned, however, is forearmed. Anticipation of counter-attacks by workplace bullies must be part of the effective administration of workplace anti-bullying policies. Those who seek to stop workplace bullies from harming institutions and people must be prepared to use all lawful and necessary means in defense of the institution and its people. They must act quickly and aggressively, playing by the rules, while understanding that bullies will not play by the rules. They must have their

---

[82] Tepper & White, *supra* note 13, at 106 ("Given the documented personnel and organizational costs of workplace harassment, a strong argument can be made that a university ought to adopt an anti-harassment policy before it is necessitated by law").

[83] NAMIE & NAMIE, *supra* note 9, at 77 ("recognize[e] the commitment of the pro-bullying forces ready to resist your campaign"). *See also* SUTTON, supra *note* 23, at 62 (2010) ("Assholes tend to stick together, and once stuck are not easily separated").

[84] NAMIE & NAMIE, *supra* note 9, at 155.

[85] *Id.* at 155-156.

priorities clear, putting protection of the pro bono institutional mission and its people first, even when that means exercising personal courage to take on the bullies for the common good.

When it becomes clear that an individual is a workplace bully harming the institution and its people, institutional anti-bullying policies must be enforced without delay. As Kohut recognized: "[S]erial bullies and mobbers are pathological people; their presence in the workplace is a liability to any organization. The smartest and most humane thing that upper level managers can do for their organization is to stop protecting bullies and tell them to either stop or get out."[86] Delay and secrecy are tools that tend to only benefit the bullies. Every unnecessary delay gives workplace bullies further opportunities to strike back and circumvent the enforcement of institutional policies. And the nefarious covert schemes of bullies are best diffused by making them overt, recognizing that as Justice Brandeis said "sunlight is said to be the best disinfectant."[87]

Recognize workplace bullies as policy violators and incompetent employees and take appropriate personnel actions as soon as practicable. Regardless of any other merits, bullies lack social competence which makes them incompetent employees regardless of any other skills.[88] Their costs always outweigh their benefits, because regardless of any contributions they may make, they will poison and ultimately destroy the social culture and reputation of the institution.[89]

It is regrettably common, however, for institutional administrators to tolerate or attempt to appease workplace bullies to avoid personal confrontations and personal costs.[90] For this reason, victims of attacks from workplace bullies must also be prepared to use all available lawful means to defend themselves, invoking external legal authorities and pushing reluctant administrators into action when necessary, understanding that superior legal or institutional powers are the only forces likely to stop true workplace bullies. The section below provides a

---

[86] KOHUT, *supra* note 25, at 252.

[87] Buckley v. Valeo, 424 U.S. 1, 67 n. 80 (*quoting* L. Brandeis, OTHER PEOPLE'S MONEY 62 (1933)). *See also* KOHUT, *supra* note 25, at 208 ("workplace bullies are like cockroaches; shine the light on them and they run for cover").

[88] SUTTON, *supra* note 23, at 88.

[89] *Id. See also* Kaplan, *supra* note 10, at 150 ("companies that make an effort to keep bullying to a minimum report higher productivity and greater profits, even when the bullies had supposedly increased production and brought in more money").

[90] *But see* NAMIE & NAMIE, *supra* note 9, at 73 ("When someone asks for relief from stress-inducing circumstances, to respond by doing nothing is to reject the legitimacy of the request").

review of potential remedies for persons subjected to attacks by workplace bullies.

Potential Legal Remedies External to the Institution

Formal legal action can be expensive, stressful, slow, and the outcome is often uncertain.[91] For these reasons legal action is generally a last resort turned to only when more efficient self-help and institutional remedies have proven futile.[92] Self-help remedies offer the advantages of being free or low-cost and the victim can retain significant control over the process.

It is important to note, however, that employee self-help remedies are not acceptable institutional substitutes for adequate employee supervision, effective personnel policies, and institutionally enforced remedies for workplace harassment. Institutions must provide proper supervision of employees and adequate systems for reporting and resolving allegations of workplace harassment.[93] There should be reasonable opportunities for reporting harassment, engaging in mediation when appropriate,[94] filing formal complaints, and obtaining institutionally enforced remedies in response to bona fide complaints of workplace harassment.[95] Effective institutional complaint adjudication systems can be free and relatively swift options for victims to resolve allegations and obtain remedies for workplace harassment.[96]

---

[91] *See* YAMADA, *supra* note 16, at 524 ("Despite the seeming abundance of potential legal protections for many American workers, effectuating one's employment-related rights can be a lengthy, expensive, and stressful undertaking. Legal process is costly and time-consuming for both employees and employers").

[92] *See* KOHUT, *supra* note 25, at 189 (reviewing self-help strategies). Self-help approaches may include, *e.g.*, strategic avoidance of known bullies to limit opportunities for abuse; standing up to bullies when this is likely to be safe and effective; or a well-planned and executed exit from a perpetually bully plagued unit.

[93] Faragher v. City of Boca Raton, 524 U.S. 775 (1998) ("An employer is subject to vicarious liability to a victimized employee for an actionable hostile environment created by a supervisor").

[94] Briana L. Seagriff, *Keep Your Lunch Money: Alleviating Workplace Bullying with Mediation*, 25 OHIO ST. J. ON DISP. RESOL. 575 (2010). It should be noted that institutional expectations for engaging in mediation prior to other remedies are not appropriate if the victim has already been severely traumatized or it is clear mediation is futile.

[95] Prohibitions against discrimination and harassment are core ethical principles among professionals in higher education. *See* AMERICAN ASSOCIATION OF UNIVERSITY PROFESSORS (AAUP), STATEMENT ON PROFESSIONAL ETHICS, para. 3 ("Professors do not discriminate against or harass colleagues"). Higher education institutions must have an effective means of enforcing these core principles.

[96] Kaplan, *supra* note 10, at 143 ("companies have recognized the problem and developed

Unfortunately, however, many institutions will not adopt and enforce effective workplace anti-bullying policies until they are required to do so by law.[97] Nonetheless, in certain circumstances, harassment victims may be able to force employers into providing necessary remedies by leveraging currently available external legal remedies,[98] or victims may be able to directly stop workplace bullies with court ordered civil or criminal remedies. The sections below review potential status based and non-status based legal remedies external to the institution.

Status Based Legal Remedies

Status based legal remedies may provide useful protections if the workplace bully is harassing the targeted victim based on a protected status under federal or state law, *e.g.*, race, color, religion, sex, national origin, age, or disability.[99] In practice, however, bias is generally not the bully's primary motivation for the harassment. In most cases, if the workplace bully is harassing a victim based on a protected status it is incidental to the broader goal of strategic harassment based on professional jealousies.[100]

---

their own policies against workplace bullying"). Before relying on institutional processes to remedy workplace harassment victims should investigate whether there is evidence of a bona fide remedial system in place, or whether the de facto function of the existing system is covering up institutional problems by delaying or denying remedies to victims. The latter will only further enable harassment and should be avoided in favor of more expeditious and effective remedies.

[97] NAMIE & NAMIE, *supra* note 9, at 34 ("Policies are typically crafted to comply with legislative mandates. Without laws, bullying policies in the workplace are not required"). *But see* Tepper & White, *supra* note 13, at 106 (arguing for adoption of a workplace bullying policy before it is required by law).

[98] NAMIE & NAMIE, supra note 9, at XVI (2011) ("the threat of litigation provides the leverage that convinces employers to take voluntary action").

[99] Status based legal remedies were a necessary reaction to the extreme injustice of U.S. practices of slavery, segregation, and discrimination. Nonetheless, to continue the movement toward greater social justice the focus must turn to remedies based on universal human dignity. *See* Jessica R. Vartanian, *Speaking of Workplace Harassment: A First Amendment Push Toward a Status-Blind Statute Regulating "Workplace Bullying"*, 65 ME. L. REV. 175, 213 (2012) ("Rosa Ehrenreich, for example, has argued that focusing excessively on the discriminatory context in which workplace harassment occurs has fostered the distorted view of sexual harassment as a special 'women's injury.' As she explains, sexual harassment is wrong, not because women are women, but because it is an affront to women's dignity as human beings"), *citing* Rosa Ehrenreich, *Dignity and Discrimination: Toward a Pluralistic Understanding of Workplace Harassment*, 88 GEO. L.J. 1, 3 (1999).

[100] Lawrence, *supra* note 1, at 26 ("federal and state anti-discrimination laws are only impacted in 20 per cent of workforce bullying cases").

Nonetheless, in some cases, status based legal protections may prove useful in dealing with workplace bullies. Victims of harassment may be able to obtain free support from federal and state employment law enforcement agencies and to leverage reluctant institutional officials into remedial action to stop the workplace harassment. This section reviews status based remedies including Title VII employment discrimination; age discrimination; discrimination based on disabilities; constitutional violations; and non-status based remedies including cease and desist remedies; defamation; assault and battery; false imprisonment; invasion of privacy; intentional infliction of emotional distress; and violations of criminal laws.

Title VII Employment Discrimination

Victims being discriminated against or harassed based on a legally protected status may be able to leverage remedial action to stop discrimination and harassment under Title VII and other applicable federal and state employment laws.[101] Title VII prohibits unlawful discrimination in the workplace, including harassment, based on "race, color, religion, sex, or national origin."[102] Employers may not discriminate based on race, color, religion, sex, or national origin, nor can they tolerate unlawful discrimination by employees under their supervision.[103] Title VII is enforced through the U.S. Equal Employment Opportunity Commission (EEOC), and discrimination based on any of these criteria can be reported to the EEOC for investigation and remedial enforcement. Further, an order from the EEOC or a court of law will likely force even the most reluctant institutional administrators into addressing the workplace harassment.

All invidious discrimination is offensive and unacceptable in the workplace. Sexual harassment, however, is a uniquely offensive type of discrimination that may be used by workplace bullies in an attempt to further demoralize and degrade a targeted victim. No one should be subjected to sexual harassment in the work place as a condition of making a living. Title VII, however, does not expressly address sexual harassment. But in *Meritor Savings Bank v. Vinson*, the U.S. Supreme

---

[101] State constitutions and statutes may also prohibit employment discrimination, strengthening and expanding protections for employees. Under federal law private schools are prohibited from employment discrimination by Title VII, and public schools are prohibited from employment discrimination both by Title VII and the Constitution.

[102] 42 U.S.C. § 2000e-2 (2011).

[103] Vance v. Ball State University, 133 S. Ct. 2434 (2013).

Court found that: "Without question, when a supervisor sexually harasses a subordinate because of the subordinate's sex, that supervisor 'discriminates' on the basis of sex."[104]

The Court has also noted, however, that Title VII is not a "general civility code."[105] Title VII does not extend to simple rudeness or other general inappropriate social conduct in the work place. Inappropriate social conduct may be addressed in institutional policies and by supervisors in employment reviews. But Title VII prohibits more specific and serious work place misconduct. In *Clark County v. Breeden*, the Court addressed the legal line for actionable misconduct under Title VII, stating "whether an environment is sufficiently hostile or abusive must be judged by looking at all the circumstances, including the frequency of the discriminatory conduct; its severity; whether it is physically threatening or humiliating, or a mere offensive utterance; and whether it unreasonably interferes with an employee's work performance."[106]

The Court also noted that "a recurring point in our opinions is that simple teasing, offhand comments, and isolated incidents (unless extremely serious) will not amount to discriminatory changes in the terms and conditions of employment."[107] The Court had noted in *Meritor* that: "For sexual harassment to be actionable, it must be sufficiently severe or pervasive to alter the conditions of the victim's employment and create an abusive working environment"[108] and that the "gravamen of any sexual harassment claim is that the alleged sexual advances were unwelcome."[109] If an employee can establish a prima facie case of discrimination, however, anti-discrimination laws are powerful tools in addressing workplace harassment.

Age-Based Discrimination in Employment in Violation of the ADEA

The Age Discrimination in Employment Act (ADEA), prohibits discrimination based on age against anyone 40 years of age or older.[110] The ADEA applies to all employers engaged in interstate commerce with 20 or more employees, including federal and state government

---

[104] 477 U.S. 57, 63 (1986).

[105] Oncale v. Sundowner Offshore Services, Inc., 523 U.S. 75, 81 (1986).

[106] 532 U.S. 268, 270-71 (2001), *quoting* Faragher v. Boca Raton, 524 U.S. 775, 787-88 (1998); Harris v. Forklift Systems, Inc., 510 U.S. 17, 23 (1993).

[107] Clark County v. Breeden, 532 U.S. 268, 271 (2001).

[108] Meritor Savings Bank v. Vinson 477 U.S. 57, 67 (1986).

[109] *Id.* at 68.

[110] 29 U.S.C. § 621 (2011).

institutions.[111]   Using age as a criteria in employment is not, however, prohibited "where age is a bona fide occupational qualification reasonably necessary to the normal operation of the particular business."[112]

Title VII prohibits all employment discrimination based on the "individual's race, color, religion, sex, or national origin" requiring employer neutrality concerning these factors. Title VII generally allows neither negative discrimination nor preferential treatment. In *General Dynamics v. Cline*, 540 U.S. 581 (2004), however, the U.S. Supreme Court held that the ADEA only prohibited negative discrimination against older workers, and did not, for example, prohibit a policy that provided more favorable employment conditions for employees over 50 than for employees under 50. A remedy under the ADEA would only be available for negative discrimination based on age for a victim over 40 years of age.

Discrimination in Employment Based on Disability in Violation of § 504 or the ADA

Section 504 of the Rehabilitation Act prohibits employers in institutions receiving federal funds from discriminating in employment against any otherwise qualified persons because of disabilities.[113] Employers must also provide reasonable accommodations for employees with disabilities.   Providing reasonable accommodations may mean restructuring physical access to work areas; modifying work schedules; redistributing tasks among workers; eliminating unnecessary job qualifications; and other reasonable accommodations so that otherwise qualified employees with disabilities have a fair opportunity to function effectively in their positions.   Section 504 does not, however, require employers to hire unqualified persons; to tolerate substandard job performance; or to refrain from addressing legitimate threats to health or safety.[114]

The Americans with Disabilities Act (ADA), extended § 504 type protections into the private sector and clarified obligations for public institutions.[115] Title I of the ADA prohibits employment discrimination by employers with 15 or more employees and who are engaged in interstate

---

[111] *But see* Kimel v. Florida Board of Regents, 528 U.S. 62 (2000) (barring monetary damages in ADEA suits against a state under the Eleventh Amendment unless the state waives immunity). Under Ex parte Young, 209 U.S.123 (1908), however, plaintiffs may still sue for injunctive relief for violations of federal law.

[112] 29 U.S.C. § 621 (2014).

[113] 29 U.S.C. § 794 (2014).

[114] *Id.*

[115] 42 U.S.C. § 12101 (2014).

commerce. Title II applies to public institutions including schools and other government institutions, and public transportation including school transportation systems. Title III requires non-discrimination, access, and reasonable accommodations.[116]

Constitutional Remedies

In public employment, if constitutionally prohibited harms are attributable to a state agent, constitutional remedies and damages under 42 U.S.C. § 1983 are possible remedies.[117] Potentially actionable issues include violations of the Equal Protection Clause, *e.g.*, discrimination based on race, color, gender, religion, national origin, etc., without a sufficient justification; First Amendment infringements, *e.g.*, Establishment Clause, Free Exercise Clause, Free Speech; etc.; unlawful search and seizure; or violations of the Due Process Clause, including procedural or substantive violations.[118] When government officials violate constitutional mandates, plaintiffs may be eligible for injunctive relief or monetary damages under 42 U.S.C. § 1983.

Non-status Based Legal Remedies

In the U.S. there are still very limited legal options for non-status based abuses in the workplace, *i.e.*, workplace bullying involving non-status based harassment. This lack of legal protections for victims of non-status based harassment is especially tragic because it leaves the vast majority of workplace bullying victims with no formal legal remedy, but with injuries just as serious as those incurred by victims of status based harassment. Further, this lack of legal remedies for victims of non-status based harassment further enables and emboldens harassers who can quickly learn that their victims have no legal protections from abuses. This section addresses possible legal options for victims of non-status based harassment from workplace bullies, including cease and desist remedies, tort claims, and criminal complaints.

---

[116] *Id.*

[117] *See* DAYTON, *supra* note 6, at 424 (describing constitutional torts under 42 U.S.C. § 1983).

[118] *Id.*

Cease and Desist Remedies

A low cost but sometimes useful option is a cease and desist letter or order from a court. A cease and desist letter is a formal letter served on the offending party warning that if the unlawful conduct does not cease, legal action will be taken. A cease and desist letter may be written by the victim of the wrongful conduct or a lawyer. A self-written letter has the advantages of being quick and free, but it may lack the deterrence impact on the bully of receiving a formal letter from a lawyer actively engaged in the practice of law and ready and willing to take the threatened legal action without delay.

An even more powerful option, however, is obtaining a cease and desist order from a court of law. A cease and desist *letter* carries with it only the power implied by the threat of subsequent legal action. In contrast a cease and desist *order* issued by a judge introduces the much stronger possibility of the workplace bully being found in contempt of court if a judge's order is violated. A judge may order fines and incarceration as remedies for contempt of court.

The unlawful conduct addressed in a cease and desist letter or order is generally some private cause of action under tort law or an alleged violation of criminal laws. Possible tort actions may include defamation; assault and battery; false imprisonment; invasion of privacy; and intentional infliction of emotional distress. Possible criminal acts are also addressed below.

Defamation

To defame someone is to unlawfully harm that person's public reputation. Slander is spoken defamation and libel is written defamation, but both are governed under the same laws of defamation. It is not enough for a defamation plaintiff to merely prove that the defendant said something negative about the plaintiff. The plaintiff must prove that the statement was untrue and that there was at least negligence by the defendant concerning the truth when the plaintiff is deemed a private figure. Those plaintiffs who are deemed to be public figures will find it much more difficult to prove a case of defamation because proof of reckless disregard for the truth or malice by the defendant is generally required. U.S. defamation law seeks to balance the individual's right to be free from untrue damaging public statements, with the rights of others to free speech and the public expression of their opinions, especially concerning public figures.

Nonetheless, while there is a broadly protected right to freedom of speech in the U.S., defamation is not protected speech. To establish a prima facie case of defamation, the plaintiff must show that the defendant's alleged defamatory declarations: 1) Contained untrue statements of fact concerning the plaintiff; 2) The statements were communicated to one or more persons other than the plaintiff; 3) The statements caused foreseeable prejudice towards the plaintiff; and 4) There are provable damages to the plaintiff.

As noted above the plaintiff's burden of proof also depends on whether the plaintiff is deemed a public or a private figure. Public officials are generally deemed public figures in defamation suits. According to the U.S. Supreme Court, in *Rosenblatt v. Baer*, public officials are those government officials that reasonably appear to the public to have substantial control over governmental affairs.[119] In *Hutchinson v. Proxmire*, however, the U.S. Supreme Court noted that the public figure designation does not extend to all public employees.[120] State courts have tended to hold that elected or higher-level appointed public education officials are public figures, including college presidents and deans, and that lower-level appointed education officials such as faculty and staff retain their citizen status as private figures even when they work for public institutions.[121]

Accordingly, to prove a case of defamation plaintiffs that are public figures must meet a higher burden of proof. In *New York Times v. Sullivan*, the U.S. Supreme Court required that to prove defamation as a public figure the plaintiff must prove "that the statement was made with actual malice . . . that is with knowledge that it was false or with reckless disregard of whether it was false or not."[122] In contrast plaintiffs that are private figures need only establish by a preponderance of the evidence that the defendant failed to use ordinary care to determine the truth or falsity of the statement concerning the plaintiff.[123]

A defamation plaintiff must prove all elements of a defamation claim by a preponderance of the evidence under the applicable standard for a public or private figure. A plaintiff that prevails in a defamation suit may seek monetary damages from the defendant, attorney's fees, and an

---

[119] 383 U.S. 75 (1966).

[120] 443 U.S. 111 (1979).

[121] *See* DAYTON, *supra* note 6, at 427 ("Mid-level appointed officials, such as . . . department chairs, have been a much closer call for courts, with some state courts holding that they are public figures and others holding that they are not public figures under state law").

[122] 376 U.S. 254, 279-280 (1964).

[123] DAYTON, *supra* note 6, at 427.

injunction against the defendant. In cases involving especially malicious behavior by the defendant punitive damages may also be awarded to the plaintiff.

Assault and Battery

Assault and battery are often discussed together, because an assault may be followed by a battery if a defendant carries through with a threat. Nonetheless, these two intentional torts are separate and distinct legal causes of action, and depending on the facts, the plaintiff may claim either or both of these intentional torts. An assault occurs when the defendant acts with the intent of causing apprehension of bodily harm or offense by the plaintiff, while battery is the actual and intentional infliction of harmful or offensive bodily contact. Assault and battery may also constitute a crime.

Proving a prima facie case of assault requires the plaintiff to establish by a preponderance of the evidence that there was an action by the defendant intended to cause apprehension and that it did in fact cause apprehension. For example, a defendant may have raised his fist and said he intended to strike the plaintiff. If the plaintiff can prove that the defendant's actions were taken with the intent to cause apprehension, and in fact did cause apprehension, the plaintiff has proven a prima facie case of assault and may argue for appropriate damages.[124]

Proving a prima facie case of battery requires the plaintiff to establish by a preponderance of the evidence that there was an action by the defendant intended to inflict harmful or offensive bodily touching and that it did in fact result in this bodily touching. For example, a defendant may have slapped the plaintiff, or a defendant may have approached the plaintiff with the intent to touch the plaintiff in an offensive way, *e.g.*, sexual contact or an affront to personal dignity such as ripping clothing, etc., and in fact the defendant did so. The plaintiff has proven a prima facie case and may argue for appropriate damages from the defendant.[125]

---

[124] DAYTON, *supra* note 6, at 428 ("Damages for assault may include compensation for emotional stress caused by the assault, physical injuries resulting from the distress, and other provable damages. Punitive damages may be appropriate where the defendant's actions were sufficiently malicious or outrageous").

[125] *Id.* at 429 ("Damages for battery may include compensation for physical injuries, damages to personal property, emotional distress, punitive damages, and other provable damages").

False Imprisonment

False imprisonment occurs when a plaintiff has been unlawfully confined by the defendant without consent. Proving a prima facie case of false imprisonment requires the plaintiff to establish by a preponderance of the evidence that there was an action by the defendant intended to cause confinement and that it did in fact cause unlawful confinement without the consent of the plaintiff.

Confinement may be caused by physical barriers; physical force; verbal orders or intimidation; or removing of the ability of the plaintiff to physically leave. For example, if the plaintiff can prove that the defendant unlawfully seized the plaintiff's car keys with the intent of confining the plaintiff to the area, and the plaintiff was in fact unable to leave without the car keys, the plaintiff has proven a prima facie case and may argue for appropriate damages.[126]

Invasion of Privacy

In the U.S., legal causes of action for invasion of privacy have been recognized in four general areas: 1) Invasion into the plaintiff's private life; 2) Public disclosure of the plaintiff's private facts; 3) Misappropriation of the plaintiff's name or likeness; and 4) Presenting the plaintiff in a false and offensive light.[127]   Like most tort actions, establishing a prima facie case of invasion of privacy generally tracks the basic elements of negligence and most other torts: Duty, breach, causation, and damages. There is a general duty to respect other persons' reasonable expectations of privacy. That duty is breached if the defendant's actions in invading the personal privacy of the plaintiff were serious and unreasonable. The defendant's actions must have caused foreseeable harm to the plaintiff. And there must be provable damages which may include serious emotional distress and mental suffering resulting from the invasion of privacy.[128]

---

[126] *Id.* ("Damages for false imprisonment may include compensation for any physical injuries resulting from the confinement, damages to personal property, emotional distress, punitive damages, and other provable damages").
[127] *Id.* at 430.
[128] *Id.*

Intentional Infliction of Emotional Distress

It is an unfortunate reality that some troubled individuals are motivated by jealousy, hatred, personal insecurities, a desire for power and control, etc., to intentionally inflict emotional distress on others. And it is not true that words can never hurt you. Words can cause serious emotional, psychological, financial, and even physical harm to victims of harassment. The tort of intentional infliction of emotional distress provides a remedy for wrongful emotional abuse intentionally inflicted on the plaintiff by the defendant.

With increased awareness of the connection between mental stress and physical health, and broader knowledge of the serious human and institutional consequences of harassment and bullying, U.S. courts are beginning to recognize the validity of claims of intentional infliction of emotional distress.[129] Nonetheless, the burden of proof for the plaintiff is still very high. Under current law the plaintiff must prove that the defendant engaged in extreme and outrageous acts intended to cause foreseeable harm to the plaintiff.[130] Damages may include compensation for the pain and suffering of emotional distress; consequential damages such as lost wages; counseling expenses; medical costs; and punitive damages where the defendant's actions were truly outrageous in nature.[131]

Violations of Criminal Laws

Workplace misconduct serious enough to violate criminal laws is serious indeed, but workplace bullies sometimes cross the line to criminality.[132] One advantage for the victims, however, is that if criminal activity has occurred these allegations are investigated and prosecuted by external law enforcement agents and proceedings are at no financial cost to the victim. A no cost remedy is especially beneficial to victims of

---

[129] *See* Raess v Doescher, 883 N.E.2d 790 (Ind. 2008) (allowing expert testimony by Dr. Gary Namie on workplace bullying and affirming a jury verdict in favor of the plaintiff).

[130] DAYTON, *supra* note 6, at 431.

[131] *Id.*

[132] *See* Susan Harthill, *Workplace Bullying as an Occupational Safety and Health Matter: A Comparative Analysis*, 34 HASTINGS INT'L & COMP. L. REV. 253, 265 (2011) ("The Federal Bureau of Investigation places workplace bullying on a continuum of workplace violence, a continuum that includes 'domestic violence, stalking, threats, harassment, bullying, emotional abuse, intimidation, and other forms of conduct that create anxiety, fear, and a climate of distrust in the workplace.'" FED. BUREAU OF INVESTIGATION, U.S. DEP'T OF JUSTICE, WORKPLACE VIOLENCE: ISSUES IN RESPONSE 13 (2004), available at www.fbi.gov/stats-services/publications/workplace-violence

workplace misconduct who may be under financial stress from medical expenses, missed work, or job loss. Further, any institutional officials who may have been covering up internal employment misconduct by bullies will likely not be able to cover up criminal activity in a police investigation.

Potential crimes involving workplace bullies may include criminal assault; battery; conspiracy; making false reports; hate crimes; wiretapping; voyeurism; mail tampering; terroristic threats; conversion; theft; destruction of property; vandalism; trespassing; and stalking. Cyber-bullying and cyber-stalking may also be areas in which criminal laws may be invoked to stop workplace related abuses.[133]

Needed Legal Remedies for Addressing Workplace Bullying

As other developed nations have already done,[134] the U.S. must enact protective legislation to stop the destructive practice of workplace bullying.[135] As Tepper & White recognized: "Many countries in Europe, including the United Kingdom, Sweden, France, Germany, Belgium, and Poland, have adopted some form of 'anti-bullying' legislation. Additionally, Canada has recognized the detrimental effects of bullying in the workplace and . . . require[s] employers to develop workplace-

---

[133] Hayley Ringle, *Parent Gets Back at School Official with Porn Site*, THE REPUBLIC (May. 24, 2012 9:53 PM), http://www.azcentral.com/community/gilbert/20120524higley-parent-porn-site-retaliation (defendant Esparza was angry over his belief that a school administrator, Frank Henricsen, took his son's iPod. In retaliation for the believed seizure and failure to return his son's iPod, Esparza set up a fake profile in Henricsen's name on an adult website including false nude photos of Henricsen. Henricsen only learned of the defamatory profile after he applied for a position and the employer found the website in his name through a GOOGLE search. Henricsen called the police, and law enforcement agents located Esparza by tracing access to the offending website back to Esparza's work computer. When confronted by police, Esparza first attempted to blame his son for creating the fake profile. But evidence showed a level of sophistication beyond that of a 13-year-old and that Esparza had used his work computer and accessed the website 25 times to slander Henricsen. Esparza confessed. Esparza was convicted of identity theft and computer fraud).

[134] Lawrence, *supra* note 1, at 27 ("Sweden was the first European country to implement legislation in 1993 specifically outlawing bullying at work"). Other nations have prohibited workplace bullying through constitutions, bills of rights, statutes, or common law. *Id.*, at 27-29.

[135] U.S. employers generally only implemented adequate protections against discrimination after they were required to do so by federal and state legislation. *See* DAYTON, *supra* note 6, at 386 (providing an overview of employment discrimination law and litigation in the U.S.).

violence-prevention policies, which provide protection from workplace bullying."[136] In the United States:

> Both federal and state statutory law currently provide remedies for such behavior where it is motivated by discriminatory animus and the target is a member of a protected class (such as gender or national origin). But no U.S. jurisdiction currently recognizes a cause of action against this sort of behavior when it is not linked to discrimination--in contrast to several European countries that provide remedies for workplace bullying untethered to discriminatory animus. Even though legislation to provide a remedy for such behavior has been introduced in several states, it has not been enacted, and it is often accompanied by strong opposition from employer interests. Courts have likewise been reluctant to expand the law to accommodate such claims.[137]

Statutory protections for K-12 students are being expanded to address non-status based bullying.[138] Legislation and institutional policies protecting against non-status based workplace bullying are also needed. Workplace bullying is an ongoing epidemic in the U.S., an epidemic that threatens the stability and success of U.S. businesses and institutions, and that poses a deadly serious risk to the health and safety of U.S. workers.[139]

The U.S. lags behind other Western Nations in responding to this serious and pervasive threat. Current legal remedies for workplace bullying in the U.S. are largely ineffective or non-existent. Short of criminal activity, extreme tortious conduct, or prohibited class-based discrimination, workplace bullying remains reprehensible but generally legal in the U.S. This puts U.S. businesses and institutions at a competitive disadvantage in international commerce and harms U.S. workers.[140] Employer opposition to protective legislation is misguided. Employers would greatly benefit from the increased productivity and morale, and the reduced conflict and costs that would result from workplace anti-bullying legislation.

---

[136] Tepper & White, supra note 13, at 93.

[137] Id. at 81-82.

[138] See John Dayton, Anne Proffitt Dupre & Ann Elizabeth Blankenship, Model Anti-Bullying Legislation: Promoting Student Safety, Civility, and Achievement Through Law and Policy Reform, 272 EDUC. L. REP. 19, 23 (2011).

[139] Yamada, supra note 1, at 273.

[140] Kaplan, supra note 10, at 142 ("Because workplace bullying results in lower productivity and higher rates of turnover, it costs companies millions of dollars each year").

Workplace protection legislation should be enacted at the federal and state levels to protect U.S. competitiveness and the health and safety of workers. In the meantime, however, private and public sector institutions should adopt strong workplace protection policies and vigorously enforce these policies. These policies are essential to protect the integrity and productivity of their institutions and the health and safety of their workers.

Workers should push lawmakers to enact appropriate legislation, and push institutions to adopt appropriate protective policies. Where these laws and policies have not yet been adopted, workers should press forward with all other available remedies to expose workplace bullying; expose institutions that condone or support workplace bullies; hold bullies personally accountable; and take all lawful actions to rid their workplace of abuse and harassment.

Child abuse, spousal abuse, elder abuse, racial discrimination, gender discrimination, and sexual harassment were not so long ago tolerated even though generally thought reprehensible. Victims were on their own: They were just expected to tolerate the abuse as an inevitable part of life. Changes in laws, policies, and social attitudes eventually protected these victims and put the abusers in retreat.

Similar protections for victims of workplace bullying must be enacted to protect workers and put workplace bullies in retreat.[141] The result would be a far more functional and productive workplace with healthier and happier workers, a result that would be better for everyone, including the bullies, who ultimately harm even themselves with their out-of-control workplace misconduct. Workplace bullies can no longer be allowed to maraud and attack unfettered. We know who they are; we know what they are doing; we know the serious damage it does; and we know we need to stop them. Until adequate federal and state protections are enacted, institutions should adopt strong workplace anti-bullying policies to project their people and institutions.[142]

When All Else Fails: Self-Help Strategies for Dealing with Workplace Bullies

Workplace bullying won't stop until there are effective and well enforced laws and policies in place prohibiting this workplace misconduct and consistently holding perpetrators and their institutional enablers accountable.[143] In the absence of adequate protective laws and policies,

---

[141] Yamada, *supra* note 1, at 276.

[142] Tepper & White, *supra* note 13, at 106.

[143] *See* SUTTON, *supra* note 23, at 2 (noting "the thousands of organizations that ignore,

the following are example strategies that may be used by individuals to develop personal plans for prevention, preparedness, response, and recovery in dealing with workplace bullies:

> *Educate Yourself Concerning Workplace Bullying*: A growing body of research seeks to understand and address the problem of workplace bullying. By studying this research, bullies, and their tactics, you can learn to recognize early warning signs and emergent schemes of workplace bullies and take preventive actions before becoming their victim and sustaining significant personal and professional damages.

> *Educate Others Concerning Workplace Bullying*: Educating colleagues about workplace bullying and prevention is a key step in keeping your workplace bully free. Further, if you need support from colleagues in dealing with a bully, it will be much easier to gain support if colleagues understand workplace bullying and the serious dangers workplace bullies present to everyone in the workplace.

> *Push for the Enactment of Workplace Anti-Bullying Laws and Policies*: Work with others to enact workplace anti-bullying policies in your institution, and to pass protective laws in your state and nation. Even if you don't need these workplace protections in the future, others most certainly will. Stopping workplace bullying is in everyone's best interests, and every additional advocate's efforts will bring us all closer to enacting necessary workplace protections.

> *Build a Strong Network of Professional and Personal Support*: A strong network of support is always beneficial. But if you find yourself in the crisis of a full scale attack by workplace bullies, you will weather this attack far better with a strong network of professional and personal support in your workplace, institution, community, and extended professional network. Bullies try to make their victims feel isolated and helpless. To defend against

---

forgive, or even encourage nastiness"). Workplace bullies are not the only parties responsible for the damage done to people and institutions. Often they are either actively or passively enabled by administrators aware of the problem. To stop workplace bullying institutional administrators must be held accountable for the effective enforcement of anti-bullying policies.

these tactics, work to further strengthen your professional and personal support systems. And always do what you can to provide professionally and personally support to others who are under attack from workplace bullies.

Take Early Warnings Seriously: Like a shark, workplace bullies commonly "bump" their prospective targets to gauge their vulnerabilities prior to a full-scale attack. Understand the seriousness of the situation: Genuine workplace bullies seek total professional and personal destruction of their targets. Understand they will not play by the rules in achieving their goals. At the first sign of a pending threat from a workplace bully start strengthening your defenses and preparing an effective response strategy.

Examine Your Own Conduct: Take a long, hard, honest look at anything you may be doing that could make it easier for workplace bullies to attack you. Are you allowing them to have too much control over your life; putting your trust in the wrong people; continuing relationships that need to be ended; allowing them to treat you disrespectfully or to take unfair advantage? Is your professional or personal conduct making you more vulnerable to attacks? Bullies will be searching for any and all vulnerabilities to exploit. Modify your conduct as necessary to provide workplace bullies with as few opportunities as possible for attacks. Expect that all known vulnerabilities will be exploited. Take action to mitigate potential damages before workplace bullies can exploit opportunities.

Document the Bully's Misconduct: Keep thorough, accurate, and objective records documenting acts of misconduct by workplace bullies. This documentation may be necessary to prove misconduct or to rebut false claims by bullies. Bullies commonly lie. If you don't have solid evidence to rebut these lies, the lies may be believed. When documenting misconduct keep in mind that your records may be the key evidence in disciplinary hearings, dismissals, and litigation. Solid documentation wins disputes.

Don't Take the Harassment Personally: Understand that the bully's behavior is all about the bully, and not about you, so don't take the bully's criticisms and attacks personally. Bullies are pathologically egocentric. Bullies do not perceive others as real persons or human equals in the way that psychologically normal persons do. To the bully you are just another object in the bully's way; a symbol of something the bully hates; and/or simply the most recent target in an unending line of victims for the release of the bully's dark pathologies. Although harassment seems very personal when it's happening, it is only personal because it's happening to you right now instead of someone else. Understand that bullies commonly have a long line of targets, past, present, and future, none of whom they really care anything about. Taking bullies' harassment personally gives them too much emotional credit and is a pointless waste of your emotional energy.

Take Back Your Power: If you are under attack by a workplace bully, it is imperative that you get control of your own emotions, thoughts, and life. Stop playing the bully's game. Don't allow the bully to manipulate you emotionally or to define the rules of engagement. Become pro-active and not just reactive. Take a deep breath, clear your mind, and think through your best options for getting your life and career moving ahead again in the direction you have chosen regardless of what the bully does. Strategically review your best options, construct an effective plan for moving forward, and execute that plan with confidence and determination. You have as much power and control over your life as you are willing to exercise, and the bully only has as much power and control over you as you are willing to allow. You could have no greater victory over bullies than to strengthen your personal and professional power, happiness, and success in spite of their attacks.

Take Away the Bully's Power: The bully's power is based on instilling fear in victims and bystanders. When the fear is gone, so is the bully's power. Expose arrogant bullies for who they really are: Incompetent, fearful, bitter, and vengeful persons who selfishly seek power, profit, and prestige through the intimidation and abuse of others; people who can only elevate themselves by pounding down others; serious threats to the healthy function of the institution and everyone in it. You do not have to be confrontational: You need only speak the truth that everyone already knows openly and courageously to shatter the false facades of bullies, exposing them, and neutralizing their power.

Stay in Control of Your Own Career and Life: If you want to stay in your current workplace, find a way to stay with dignity and peace. But only leave your current workplace and life because you decided to, and you believe the move is better for you professionally and personally. You don't have to stay in an unhealthy workplace, and you shouldn't stay if the environment is toxic and it is unlikely to change. But never allow bullies to drive you out from a place you wish to stay, or to otherwise harm your career and life. You, and only you, are in control of your career and life.

Remain Happy and Productive: Bullies are trying to make you miserable enough to leave and/or fail. You can thwart bullies simply by remaining happy and productive in your life and work. Further, if you decide you want to leave your current workplace you will need good health and a solid record of workplace success to make a strong move forward and upward in your career. The key to your future success is being happy and productive now. That is also the key to frustrating bullies.

Protect Your Health as Your Highest Priority: When under attack from workplace bullies, closely monitor and protect your mental and physical health. The constant drumbeat of harassment from workplace bullies takes a toll on even the strongest individuals. But no job is worth compromising your health and happiness. Be proactive in protecting your health, even if that means finding a healthier workplace.

Be Determined to Endure and Learn from Your Experiences: You have free will, and you are ultimately in control of your own destiny. Never allow anyone to take that control from you. Decide your own future; be determined to endure through necessary challenges; and from those challenges learn to improve yourself and your future, so that those who sought to destroy you are in fact only making you wiser and stronger. It is said that your enemy can be your greatest teacher. Life's most difficult experiences often teach us the most valuable lessons, while deepening our understanding and compassion for others who may be suffering. You can learn to practice the alchemy of turning bad experiences into good lessons and deeds by learning from negative events and sharing what you have learned to help others to endure and learn.

Conclusion

The U.S. must join the rest of the developed world in seriously addressing the problem of workplace bullying.[144] To continue to ignore this problem is to callously dismiss the suffering of victims, enable their further abuse by perpetrators, and harm everyone in the process. It is time to recognize that the problem is serious, it is widespread, and effective legal and institutional remedies are necessary to protect people and institutions.[145]

Victims of workplace bullying and harassment experience increased anxiety, depression, and stress related physical and mental illnesses.[146] In a bully dominated workplace job satisfaction and productivity plummets. And bullying and harassment are so emotionally charged that they can create a psychological black hole in the workplace consuming the time and energy that should have been focused on productive work. The result is demoralized and emotionally exhausted employees. In extreme cases victims pushed beyond their psychological limits and desperate to end severe and prolonged harassment may ultimately respond with workplace violence against the perpetrator and others they believe supported or allowed the abuse, creating the possibility of negligence claims and wrongful death suits against employers.[147] As institutions increasingly adopt and enforce workplace anti-bullying policies, those that do not protect employees against this type of workplace harassment are increasingly likely to be found negligent.[148]

---

[144] *See* Lawrence, *supra* note 1, at 29 (2013) (an international review of the problem of workplace harassment, summarizing legal remedies, and finding: "What is clearly apparent is that legislative intervention is necessary, as is establishment of anti-bullying and anti-harassment policies within workplaces").

[145] Vartanian, *supra* note 99, at 178-179 ("In many ways, the stage is set for regulating workplace harassment broadly in the United States, as many European countries have done for years").

[146] *See* Susan Harthill, *The Need for a Revitalized Regulatory Scheme to Address Workplace Bullying in the United States: Harnessing the Federal Occupational Safety and Healthy Act*, 78 U. CIN. L. REV. 1250, 1298-99 (2010) (arguing that OSHA should address workplace bullying because it is "likely to cause serious physical harm" under the general duty clause of the Act). *See also* Kaplan, *supra* note 10, at 142 ("Many victims of bullying suffer psychological damage similar to post-traumatic stress disorder").

[147] NAMIE & NAMIE, supra note 9, at 7-9 (*quoting* Oliver Wendall Holmes, Jr., "Beware how you take away hope from any human being" and describing how bullying can turn deadly when perceived injustices are not addressed).

[148] DAYTON, *supra* note 6, at 436 ("As the circumstances change, so does what is reasonable under those circumstances").

Every worker has a fundamental human right to work in a safe and respectful workplace, a workplace where the individual can focus on productive work and not be made into an involuntary participant in a workplace bully's blood-sport version of office politics.[149] But even if the ethical and moral imperatives of protecting people and institutions are not sufficient motivations for necessary changes in laws and policies to protect against the senseless harms of workplace bullying, economic necessity will increasingly demand these changes for institutions to remain viable in an increasingly competitive market for recruiting and retaining top faculty and students, and operating economically efficient institutions. Workplace bullies drive off the best people; damage institutional reputations and productivity; and can cost institutions enormous amounts of money, big losses with no institutional benefits.

Higher education institutions must adopt needed changes to meet new challenges and to protect and perpetuate their greatest traditions. The academic environment has always been one in which individual autonomy, academic freedom, and free speech were valued and protected. These great values must always be protected. It must be recognized, however, that workplace bullying is not individual autonomy, academic freedom, or free speech, but is instead highly destructive of these values.[150]

Workplace bullies should never be hired, retained, tenured, or allowed to continue to disrupt and damage institutions and the people in them. Fair warning is due however: If you are a workplace bully, stop it. Because if you do not you will be stopped and held accountable. It is just a matter of time. The process of establishing effective legal remedies and accountability for workplace misconduct in the U.S. has already begun.[151]

---

[149] *See* U.N. Charter art. 23, para. 1 ("Everyone has the right . . . to just and favourable conditions of work"). *See also* Yamada, *supra* note 16, at 562 ("Workplace bullying is a profound violation of the 'right to be let alone'"); *id.* at 567 ("workers should not have to check their dignity at the office or factory door").

[150] Tepper & White, *supra* note 13, 102 ("Conflict based upon competing ideas is often part of the creative process; conflict based upon relentless personal attacks is not").

[151] *See* THE U.S. CAMPAIGN FOR WORKPLACE BULLYING LAWS (Feb. 17, 2014), http://www.bullyfreeworkplace.org/id29.html

Appendix: Model Institutional Workplace Anti-Bullying Policy[*]

John Dayton, J.D., Ed. D.

Statement of Institutional Policy

It is recognized by this institution that all persons have a right to a safe and respectful workplace. It shall be the policy of this institution to safeguard that right fully and impartially.

It is further recognized that workplace order, efficiency, and civility are essential to the achievement of a safe and respectful workplace. It shall be the policy of this institution to uphold order, efficiency, and civility in the workplace.

It is further recognized that order, efficiency, and civility in the workplace are essential to recruiting and retaining the highest quality personnel to support the advancement of the institutional mission and to maximize and protect institutional resources. It shall be the policy of this institution to only recruit and retain the highest quality personnel.

It is further recognized that employment misconduct in the form of workplace bullying presents an ongoing threat to this institution's people, mission, and resources. Employees that engage in employment misconduct in the form of workplace bullying are not the highest quality personnel and should not be hired, retained, or tolerated. It shall be the policy of this institution to enact and enforce personnel policies to address workplace misconduct in the form of workplace bullying and remove employees engaged in this misconduct as policy violators and unfit employees.

Therefore, under the lawful authority of this institution this workplace anti-bullying policy is hereby enacted and shall be fully enforced.

---

[*] This is a model policy intended for academic purposes and as a general guide in constructing an effective institutional policy. Modify this model policy as needed to fit the unique needs of your institution. Nothing in this document is intended as legal advice and should in no way be interpreted as legal advice which can only be obtained from an attorney licensed to practice law in your jurisdiction and knowledgeable concerning your state's laws and institutional policies.

Workplace bullying and harassment by any person will not be tolerated in this institution. It shall be the duty of all employees to prevent, report, and stop workplace bullying and harassment in this institution through all reasonable means including full compliance with this policy. Institutional administrators and other employees shall act in accordance with this clear policy statement: *Do not hire workplace bullies; do not retain workplace bullies; and do not tolerate workplace bullying.* Those who uphold these protective policies shall be appropriately supported by this institution for their vital aid in safeguarding the institution's people, mission, and resources. Those who violate these policies shall be appropriately sanctioned or terminated as institutional policy violators and unfit employees.

Policy Definitions and Interpretation

To safeguard and advance individual rights and the institutional mission, it is the purpose of this policy to uphold order, efficiency, and civility in the workplace through preventing and stopping workplace bullying. Provisions of this policy shall be liberally interpreted to achieve this stated purpose.

Employee: Any person working for this institution including full-time, part-time, and temporary personnel. Further, all parties doing business with this institution or on institutional property are expected to comply with the anti-harassment provisions of this policy.

Policy Violation: Any act by an employee found to be in contravention of this policy after the provision of adequate due process consistent with institutional personnel policies and applicable laws. A policy violation may serve as the basis for personnel action including termination of employment.

Workplace Bullying: A pattern of harassment by an employee directed at another employee that under the totality of the circumstances a reasonable person would find was intended to: Wrongfully interfere with the targeted person's work performance or conditions; inflict unjustifiable distress; degrade, defame, intimidate, or threaten; create a hostile work environment; or any other pattern of intentional abuse that a reasonable person would find objectively offensive and professionally unacceptable in the workplace including conspiring with others to engage in any of the proceeding prohibited acts. Workplace bullying does not include acts that were welcomed, intentionally provoked, or involved mutual retaliation by the complainant; nor does workplace bullying include professional critiques; ordinary employee supervision; reasonable performance evaluations; valid disciplinary actions; disagreements; or misunderstandings provided these were conducted in good faith and not intended as acts of harassment, abuse, or conspiracy in violation of this policy.

Workplace Bullying Prohibited

Workplace bullying as defined by this policy is expressly prohibited in this institution.   Violations of this policy are subject to employment sanctions up to and including termination.   All employees hold their positions subject to good faith compliance with this and other applicable institutional policies.

Reporting of Policy Violations Mandated

Any employee having reasonable cause to believe that a violation of this policy has occurred shall report the alleged violation to his or her supervisor, or an appropriate alternative administrator if the supervisor is reasonably believed to be involved in or concealing activities prohibited under this policy. It shall be the duty of all employees to know this policy, fully comply with this policy, and to report violations of this policy as soon as practicable, but in no case more than 5 working days after acquiring reasonable cause to report under this policy. Failure to make a required report shall be considered an act of insubordination subject to employment sanctions.

Any person making a good faith report under this policy shall be immune from institutional sanctions related to that good faith report. Anonymous reports may be made to supervisors and other institutional administrators. This shall not, however, be construed to permit any formal disciplinary action based solely on an anonymous report. An anonymous report shall serve only as a basis for further investigation concerning a potential violation of this policy.

Protection of Rights

Through promoting order, efficiency, and civility in the workplace, and prohibiting harassment and retaliation, it is the intention of this policy to protect the rights of all persons, including all lawful rights to free speech and academic freedom. It is recognized that workplace bullying impairs employees' rights of free speech and academic freedom. Conduct that violates this policy is not protected speech or academic freedom and is subject to reasonable time, place, and manner restrictions for legitimate employment purposes.

Enforcement Mandates

It is the duty of all employees to fully comply with this policy and to cooperate in its administration. Necessary and appropriate administrative procedures not already provided in this policy shall be developed and implemented to enforce the purposes and mandates of this policy.

Annual Notice of Policy Mandated

All employees shall receive annual notice of this policy. This policy shall be available online and remain open for inspection at all times. All employees shall annually confirm receipt of this policy; that they fully understand this policy; and that they agree to fully comply with this policy.

Pre-employment Screening Mandated

Prior to hiring of any new employee it shall be the responsibility of the hiring supervisor to: 1) Thoroughly check personal references and any other probative and lawful available resources to assure that the applicant does not have a prior history of employment misconduct prohibited under this policy; and 2) Discuss with search committee members and any other persons who had significant personal contact with the applicant during the interview process whether there are any reasonable grounds to believe that the applicant is likely to engage in employment misconduct prohibited under this policy. If discovered evidence or unbiased professional opinions would lead a reasonable person to believe that the applicant is likely to engage in employment misconduct prohibited under this policy, that applicant is ineligible for employment in this institution.

Training in Policy Compliance and Reporting Mandated

All new employees shall successfully complete a training session on the promotion of workplace order, efficiency, and civility and compliance with this policy including mandated reporting.

Annual Policy Compliance Review for All Employees Mandated

An assessment of compliance with this policy shall be part of every employee's annual performance review. This policy applies to all employees at all levels of this institution with equal force and without exception. An employee's record of compliance with this policy shall be considered in all employment decisions including decisions on contract renewal, promotion, and tenure. An assessment of compliance with this policy is required prior to appointing any person to an administrative position.

Mandated Administrative Duties in Policy Compliance

All institutional administrators shall have an affirmative duty to proactively address workplace bullying and harassment through effective education and prevention efforts; a duty to thoroughly and objectively investigate complaints under this policy; and a duty to take appropriate remedial actions in a timely manner. An evaluation of the performance of these duties shall be part of every administrator's annual performance review. Any administrator who has failed to comply with this policy shall not be promoted to any higher administrative position and willful non-compliance with this policy constitutes grounds for employment sanctions including termination of employment.

Resolution of Complaints

Allegation of Policy Violation

Any person may make a good faith report alleging a violation of this policy. Any person making an allegation as a purported victim of workplace bullying and requesting an institutional remedy must present to the reviewing administrator evidence of good faith resolution efforts prior to receiving remedial assistance from the institution, unless there is clear and convincing evidence of a policy violation by the alleged perpetrator and further informal resolution efforts are clearly not in the best interests of the parties or the institution.

Evidence of Good Faith Resolution Efforts

Whenever reasonable possible, all employees are expected to make good faith efforts to informally and collegially resolve conflicts and to minimize any negative impacts of interpersonal conflicts on other personnel and the institution. All reasonable informal resolution efforts should generally be attempted in good faith prior to initiating formal personnel proceedings.

Evidence of good faith resolution efforts may include oral or written statements and any other relevant evidence concerning reasonable attempts to resolve misunderstandings or negotiate informal resolutions of disputes at the employee level prior to requesting institutional assistance. If there is insufficient evidence of good faith resolution efforts, the reviewing administrator may encourage further resolution efforts prior to endorsing institutional support for an informal adjustment or a formal complaint.

If sufficient evidence of good faith resolution efforts has been provided, or found unnecessary under the circumstances by the reviewing administrator, the complainant may request institutional assistance with an informal adjustment or file a formal complaint.

In those instances when there is clear and convincing evidence of a policy violation; willful refusal by the alleged perpetrator to cooperate with reasonable resolution efforts; conflicts threaten harm to persons or the institution; or there is particularly egregious misconduct, formal institutional proceedings shall be initiated without delay.

Informal Adjustments

All parties to disputes under this policy may make requests to the reviewing administrator for informal adjustments for the purpose of reasonably resolving disputes. Administrators may grant requests that promote the purposes of this policy and that are in the best interests of the institution. *Under no circumstances, however, may an alleged perpetrator be granted any informal adjustment that may be perceived by reasonable persons as institutional appeasement or reward for misconduct in violation of this policy.* Informal adjustments may include, for example, temporary or permanent reassignment of duties, supervisors, or placements; supervised meetings; memorandums of understanding; mediation; etc. In order to protect order, efficiency, and civility in the workplace, and prevent harassment and retaliation, a reviewing administrator may also act *sua sponte* in making informal adjustments in employees' work assignments or other reasonable informal adjustments that are clearly in the best interests of the institution.

Filing Formal Complaints

Any purported victim of workplace bullying alleging a violation of this policy by a named alleged perpetrator may file a formal complaint at any time. If the complainant has not already made a showing of good faith resolution efforts and attempted informal adjustments, the complainant must attest clearly in the formal complaint that informal resolution efforts are futile in this case, and present sufficient supporting evidence for this claim.

A form for filing official complaints shall be available to all employees. The form shall request the name of the alleged victim of the policy violation; name of the alleged policy violator; a concise description of the alleged policy violation(s) including a summary of relevant events; times and dates, names of witnesses; any corroborating evidence; and any other information or evidence that will assist in the investigation of the complaint. The instigating administrator may request additional evidence and statements from any employee, and it shall be the duty of all employees to cooperate fully in any good faith investigation. A formal complaint must be filed within 45 days of the most recent event included in the complaint unless the reviewing administrator finds that there was sufficient cause for delay in filing the complaint.

Investigations and Probable Cause

Upon receiving a formal complaint alleging a violation of this policy the reviewing administrator/investigator shall conduct a prompt, thorough, and objective investigation to determine whether there is probable cause to believe that an employee has violated this policy. Investigation proceedings shall be conducted as confidential personnel matters to the extent allowed by law and institutional policy. The investigator shall create a case file including a copy of the initial report of the alleged violation; a summary of the investigation process including evidence reviewed and persons interviewed; and a summary of findings, evidence supporting those findings, and a clear statement concerning whether there is probable cause to believe that an employee has violated this policy.

If no probable cause is found the complaint shall be dismissed without prejudice. If probable cause is found the case shall be scheduled for a hearing and formal notice shall be served to any person alleged to have violated this policy. Any other violation of civil law or institutional policy discovered in this investigation shall be promptly reported to appropriate institutional officials. Any criminal act discovered in this investigation shall be promptly reported to appropriate institutional officials and law enforcement agents.

Hearings

An employee alleged to have violated this policy shall receive written notice in accordance with institutional procedures for personnel hearings, including notice of the charges, evidence, rights of parties, and notice of the time, place, and nature of the hearing. If the result of the hearing is a finding that the charged party has violated this policy, a written summary of the findings shall be sent to the Director of Personnel for appropriate personnel action.

Personnel Actions

Personnel actions may include sanctions for violations of this policy up to and including termination of employment. Unless otherwise prohibited by law or institutional policy hearing findings shall be considered final. Appropriate personnel actions shall be executed without delay, subject only to certification presented to the Director of Personnel of a successful institutional appeal or a valid court order staying the execution of personnel actions.

Appeals

A party found in violation of this policy and subjected to employment sanctions has a right to appeal those findings and any resulting sanctions. The process for appeal shall be in accordance with institutional policies for appeals in personnel matters.

Policy Sanctions

Compliance with this policy is a required job duty for all employees. This policy is in force at all times on all institution property; in all institution controlled media and forums; and at all institution sponsored events. Violations of this policy are subject to employment sanctions including termination of employment.

Aggravating Circumstances

In considering appropriate sanctions for policy violations, proof of aggravating circumstances shall result in more severe sanctions. Aggravating circumstances under this policy shall include but not be limited to: Willful refusal to cooperate with reasonable and lawful proceedings under this policy; knowingly repeating a prohibited act after a written warning was issued by a reviewing administrator; and violations of this policy involving concomitant breaches of other valid institutional policies or laws. Repeated violations shall be subject to progressively severe sanctions. Anytime there is clear and convincing evidence in a quantum sufficient to convince a reasonable person that a repeat offender under this policy poses an ongoing risk of serious harm to other employees through continued violations of this policy, institutional administrators shall initiate employment termination proceedings without delay.

Disqualifications Resulting from Sanctions

An employee who has been formally sanctioned under this policy for workplace bullying shall be ineligible to hold any administrative position in this institution; may not participate in the administration or amendment of this policy; or participate in the employee recruitment, hiring, or tenure process beyond any minimal participation that may otherwise be required for faculty members under current institutional policy.

Additional Sanctions

In addition to institutional sanctions for non-status based violations of this policy, harassment based on race, color, religion, sex, national origin, age, disability, or other criteria prohibited by law shall also be addressed under applicable federal or state laws. Actions constituting crimes shall be immediately reported to appropriate law enforcement agents consistent with federal and state laws and institutional policy.

False and Frivolous Complaints

Any person who recklessly, knowingly, or purposely files a false complaint shall be subject to employment sanctions. Further, a clear pattern of filing frivolous complaints for the purpose of harassment or other nefarious intents shall constitute a violation of this policy. Good faith complaints that prove unfounded shall not be subject to sanctions.

Retaliation and Related Misconduct Prohibited

There shall be no act of retaliation against any person who makes a good faith report, complaint, or otherwise acts in compliance with this policy. Any misconduct by employees related to proceedings under this policy is expressly prohibited including any act of retaliation; intimidation of witnesses; destruction of evidence; false statements; interference with process; or willful refusal to cooperate with lawful proceedings; and shall be subject to employment sanctions including termination.

Policy Amendments

This policy and its administration shall be reviewed annually to assure that it is advancing its stated purposes in a fair, efficient, and effective manner. This policy may be amended consistent with ordinary procedural rules of institutional governance except that proponents of an amendment must show clear and convincing evidence that the proposed amendment will advance the stated purposes of this policy in a more fair, efficient, and effective manner. Any employee who has been formally sanctioned under this policy for workplace bullying shall be ineligible to participate in the review or amendment of this policy.

Workplace Bullying Resolution Process

© Dayton 2014

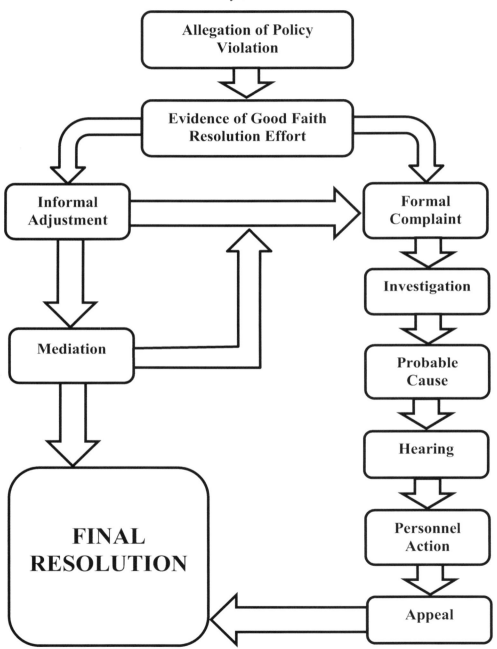

Tax Credit Scholarship Programs: A Model Statute for a Better Program

Hillel Y. Levin, J.D.[*]

Advocates for school choice have long supported well-known and diverse causes like charter schools, magnet schools, home schools, and private school vouchers.[1]   In recent years, they have achieved substantial success in pushing states to adopt a new way of funneling public funds to private schools, namely tax credit scholarship programs.[2]

In broad terms, tax credit scholarship programs allow taxpayers to receive tax credits for contributing to student scholarship organizations ("SSOs").[3]   SSOs then disburse the funds as scholarships for children to attend private schools. Such programs have now been adopted by a dozen states.[4]

---

[*] Hillel Y. Levin is Associate Professor of Law at the University of Georgia School of Law. He is grateful to Robert Jacques for his excellent work in helping to prepare this article for publication.

[1] *See* Bruce R. Van Baren, Comment, *Tuition Tax Credits and* Winn*: A Constitutional Blueprint for School Choice*, 24 REGENT U. L. REV. 515, 526 (2012) (declaring that "[t]he phenomenon of school choice has swept across the country" so that "[c]harter schools, virtual schooling, homeschooling, vouchers, and many other options are now available to parents seeking an alternative to the educational status quo.").

[2] *See generally* Hillel Y. Levin, *Tax Credit Scholarship Programs and the Changing Ecology of Public Education*, 45 ARIZ. ST. L.J. 1033 (2013) (comparing tax credit programs to assess common problems in their structure and implementation).

[3] Such organizations go by different names in different states. *E.g.*, ARIZ. REV. STAT. ANN. § 43-1602 (2012) (permitting nonprofit organizations to apply for certification as a "school tuition organization"); GA. CODE ANN. § 20-2A-1(3) (West 2012) (defining "[s]tudent scholarship organization"); FLA. STAT. ANN. § 1002.395(2)(f) (West 2012) (defining "[e]ligible nonprofit scholarship-funding organization"); IND. CODE ANN. § 20-51-3-3 (West 2012) (stating requirements of "scholarship granting organization[s]"); 72 PA. CONS. STAT. ANN. § 8702-F (West 2012) (defining "[e]ducational improvement organization" and "[p]re-kindergarten program"). I refer to them all as SSOs for the sake of uniformity.

[4] Those states are: Alabama, Arizona, Florida, Georgia, Indiana, Iowa, Louisiana, New Hampshire, Oklahoma, Pennsylvania, Rhode Island, and Virginia. Bill Chappell, *Alabama's Governor Signs Education Bill Allowing School Choice*, NPR (Mar. 14, 2013, 12:23 PM), http://www.npr.org/blogs/thetwo-way/2013/03/14/174297267/alabamas-governor-signs-education-bill-allowing-school-choice (last visited Mar. 23, 2013); Emily Workman, *Vouchers, Scholarship Tax Credits, and Individual Tax Credits and Deductions* 9-13, Oct. 2012, *available at*

Tax credit scholarship programs, which have withstood constitutional challenges at the federal and state level,[5] have received surprisingly little scrutiny from the education law and policy community of scholars.[6]   In a recent article[7] in the Arizona State Law Journal, I cast a careful eye on these programs.[8]   The article assesses their place within the changing ecology of publicly-funded education, accounts for their recent and rapid rise in prominence among advocates for school choice and policymakers, and compares different states' programs.   I demonstrate that states' programs differ in critical ways and thereby have substantially different effects.   Perhaps most importantly, that article identifies some serious problems with extant programs and recommends a set of guidelines to improve them.[9]   This article proposes a model statute designed to implement those recommendations.

The Goals of the Statute and Its Broad Contours

Before presenting the proposed statute, it may be helpful to briefly discuss its primary goals and means of achieving those aims, paying particular attention to ways in which my proposal differs from extant models.

The Goals of the Statute

Articulating the purpose of a tax credit scholarship program is the most important step in developing such a program.   Doing so allows us to identify means of achieving its purposes and ways to assess the program's

---

http://www.ecs.org/clearinghouse/01/04/76/10476.pdf.

[5]*See* Ariz. Christian Sch. Tuition Org. v. Winn, 131 S. Ct. 1436, 1449 (2011) (declining to give standing for want of causation and redressability because tax credits are distinct from government expenditures); Meredith v. Pence, 984 N.E.2d 1213, 1230 (Ind. 2013) (upholding Indiana's scholarship program under the state constitution); Bush v. Holmes, 919 So.2d 392, 408, 412 (Fla. 2006) (invalidating the state's transferring "tax money earmarked for education to private schools" but limiting the decision only to programs involving the direct transfer of public money); Kotterman v. Killian, 972 P.2d 606, 624–25 (Ariz. 1999) (en banc) (upholding Arizona's tuition tax credit against a challenge of its federal and state constitutionality). *But see* Griffin v. Cnty. Sch. Bd., 377 U.S. 218, 233 (1964) (holding that closing public schools while providing a property tax credit for donations to a segregated private school denied equal protection of the laws).

[6] Levin, *supra* note 2 at 1050.

[7] *Id.*

[8] *See generally id.* (comparing the state tax credit regimes and how they compare to their stated goals).

[9] *Id.* At 1061-73.

success. Broadly speaking, a tax credit scholarship program may have either of two different purposes. On the one hand, the goal may be to provide public funding for private schools in order to reduce the cost of private schooling for any student, regardless of means; on the other hand, the goal may be to direct scholarship funding to children who otherwise would not have the means of attending private schools and/or those who are not being well-served by the public schools to which they are assigned.[10]

My model statute assumes that the goal of a tax credit scholarship program is the latter. In a sense, this choice is ideological and thus contestable. However, putting aside any ideological motivations, this assumption is warranted for three reasons. First, proponents of such programs explicitly advocate their adoption as a means of assisting poor students, students in poor public schools, and struggling students.[11] Second, although the empirical research assessing the educational benefits of alternatives to traditional public schools is equivocal, the evidence suggests that underprivileged children enjoy the most benefit from them.[12]

Third, and perhaps most importantly, if the purpose of such programs is simply to channel public funds to private schools, there are far more

---

[10] *See id.* At 1061-75 (reviewing competing theories and concluding that honesty about a tax credit's purpose is necessary, regardless of what motive predominates a bill's enactment).

[11] *See* Martha Minow, *Confronting the Seduction of School Choice: Law, Education, and American Pluralism*, 120 YALE L.J. 814, 829 (2011) ("[A]dvocates for poor children of color joined forces with free-market supporters and endorsers of public aid for parochial schools to seek publicly funded school choice programs that would include private religious schools."); Scott W. Somerville, *The History and the Politics of School Choice*, 10 GEO. MASON U. C.R. L.J. 121, 132 (1999) ("[M]ost home schoolers are for school choice plans like Arizona's, because they provide real opportunity for poor families now, without jeopardizing free minds or free markets.").

[12] *See* RONALD G. CORWIN & E. JOSEPH SCHNEIDER, THE SCHOOL CHOICE HOAX 24 (2005) (noting that a randomized study found improved results for African-American students); Paul E. Peterson, William G. Howell, Patrick J. Wolf & David E. Campbell, *School Vouchers: Results from Randomized Experiments*, in THE ECONOMICS OF SCHOOL CHOICE 107, 131 (2003) (concluding from an analysis of voucher programs in three cities that there were effects "only on the average test performance of African American students," who after two years scored 6.3% higher on the Iowa Tests of Basic Skills than African Americans remaining in public school); Krista Kafer, *School Choice in 2003: An Old Concept Gains New Life*, 59 N.Y.U. ANN. SURV. AM. L. 439, 454–55 (2003) (discussing government and academic studies finding significant academic gains for African American students); William N. Evans & Robert M. Schwab, *Finishing High School and Starting College: Do Catholic Schools Make a Difference?*, 110 Q. J. ECON. 941, 971 (1995) (finding that attending Catholic schools increases the likelihood of graduating and attending college, especially for urban students).

straightforward means of doing so than adopting a tax credit scholarship program. For example, a state could offer vouchers,[13] provide direct tuition tax credits,[14] or simply offer tax credits for donations to private schools. The only rational reason to impose the intermediating institution of SSOs is to provide a means of channeling the public funds to some limited class of people. Thus, if a state chooses to adopt a tax credit scholarship program, then it ought to do so for the purpose of providing opportunities for students who would not otherwise have the means to do so to attend private school. Simply put, if a state has a different goal, then it should not adopt a tax credit scholarship program.

To achieve this primary goal, my model statute imposes two critical requirements. First, it limits eligibility for scholarships in a novel way that provides states with the flexibility necessary to achieve their goal. Second, as a means of assessing the program's success, the model statute requires participating private schools to administer the same standardized tests to students that are required for students in the public schools. To be sure, there are other choices that states must make in designing a tax credit scholarship program, many of which are addressed by my model statute, but these two are the most significant.

Scholarship Eligibility

With respect to scholarship eligibility, I propose that scholarships be means-tested. Some states have imposed such a restriction, but their method of doing so has been too crude and limiting.[15] My model statute

---

[13] Twelve states and the District of Columbia have a voucher system. The states are: Arizona, Colorado, Florida, Georgia, Indiana, Louisiana, Maine, Ohio, Oklahoma, Utah, Vermont, and Wisconsin. Becky Vevea, *What is a School Voucher?*, *available at* http://www.greatschools.org/school-choice/7200-school-vouchers.gs (last visited Feb. 10, 2013). In 2002, the Supreme Court upheld Ohio's voucher program against an Establishment Clause challenge. Zelman v. Simmons-Harris, 536 U.S. 639, 662–663 (2002).

[14] No state provides direct tuition tax credits, but interest in adopting such a program has increased. For example, a bill pending in the Wisconsin legislature would allow parents to earn a refundable tax credit of up to $1,000 for each elementary pupil or $1,500 for each secondary pupil attending a school that does not receive more than $3,000 per pupil in state aid or property tax revenue. Assemb. B. 195, 2013 Leg. (Wis. 2013), *available at* https://docs.legis.wisconsin.gov/2013/related/proposals/ab195 (last visited May 16, 2013).

[15] Means-testing eligibility ties eligibility to a students' household income, which is an effective way to direct scholarships to students who could not otherwise afford private schooling. Levin, *supra* note 2, at 1066-68. In addition, it may mitigate the problem of parents directing their own contributions to their children's benefit. *Id.* This approach

provides for a graduated means-testing approach. Students residing in households earning up to 200% of the federal poverty guidelines may receive scholarships up to the total tuition cost of the private school that the student attends.[16] Students residing in households earning greater than 200% and up to 400% of the federal poverty guidelines receive scholarships up to 50% of the private school's total tuition cost.[17] Finally, students residing in households earning greater than 400% and no more than 600% of the federal poverty guidelines may receive scholarships up to 25% of the private school's total tuition cost.[18] Students from higher-earning households are ineligible for scholarships from SSOs.

Further, SSOs should be obligated to spend at least 70% of their scholarship funding on children otherwise zoned for failing public schools or to students who are performing poorly in otherwise acceptable public schools.[19] This requirement ensures that scholarship organizations direct a substantial amount of their funding to students who require it due to poor public options or their own educational needs.[20]

---

suffers, however, from problems of potential over-inclusion or under-inclusion. *Id.* An over-inclusive program would serve children with access to excellent public schools, thereby limiting funds for more needy students in underperforming areas. *Id.* On the other hand, because private schooling tends to be quite expensive, some states' limits might be far too low. *Id.* For example, a family of four with $47,100 in annual income — two times the federal poverty level — is far from wealthy. *See* Annual Update of the HHS Poverty Guidelines, 78 Fed. Reg. 5,182, 5,183 (Jan. 24, 2013) (providing a $23,550 poverty threshold for a family of four in the contiguous United States). Yet, some states proscribe such a family's children from accessing scholarships. *See* FLA. STAT. ANN. § 1002.395(3) (West 2012) (limiting scholarships to students who qualify for the free or reduce-price lunch program); Child Nutrition Programs; Income Eligibility Guidelines, 78 Fed. Reg. 17,628, 17,630 (Mar. 29, 2013), *available at* http://www.fns.usda.gov/cnd/governance/notices/iegs/IEG_Table-032913.pdf (last visited May 17, 2013) (setting a family of four's reduced-price and free lunch thresholds in the contiguous United States to $43,568 and $30,615, respectively).

[16] *See infra* Part III, § 2(b)(g)(1).

[17] *See infra* Part III, § 2(b)(g)(2).

[18] *See infra* Part III, § 2(b)(g)(3).

[19] *See infra* Part III, § 2(b)(f).

[20] *See* Levin, *supra* note 2, at 1066-70 (proposing that SSOs should be obligated to spend at least 70% of their funding on such children as a way to ensure expenditures for those most in need and prevent abuse from wealthier individuals while allowing some flexibility to assess students' educational needs).

Assessment and Accountability: Standardized Testing

Standardized testing requirements are deeply controversial in the field of educational law and policy,[21] and I have serious doubts about the degree to which policymakers have fetishized high-stakes testing. Reflecting the contentiousness of the issue, states with tax credit scholarship programs have taken different approaches to the question of assessment. Some require no testing.[22] Others require those students awarded scholarships from SSOs to be tested.[23] And still others require all participating private schools to administer standardized tests to all students.[24]

Despite my reservations, my model statute provides for mandatory testing at participating private schools.[25] If state and federal legislators have concluded that the best way to assess educational achievement, teacher performance, and the success of schools is through standardized testing, then I see no alternative but to subject private schools receiving public funds to the same requirements. This requirement will be useful in several ways. Most obviously, we can use test results to compare public school education to that offered by participating private schools. Testing would thus help us decide whether this method of providing for school choice is a good use of taxpayer funds. Second, by making the aggregate test results publicly available, parents could make informed choices in choosing private schools for their children.

Finally, by imposing this requirement, more parents may be incentivized to participate in public debates about the value of standardized testing. Currently, those people whose children attend private schools—often the most affluent and politically powerful and motivated among the population—have little at stake in this social debate.

---

[21] Andrea Rodriguez, Comment, *Revealing the Impurities of Ivory Soap: A Legal Analysis of the Validity of the Implementation of the No Child Left Behind Act*, 10 SCHOLAR: ST. MARY'S L. REV. ON MINORITY ISSUES 75, 96 (2007); Motoko Rich, *Holding States and Schools Accountable*, N.Y. TIMES, Feb. 10, 2013, at A25.

[22] Six states lack a testing mandate: Arizona, Georgia, New Hampshire, Oklahoma, Pennsylvania, and Rhode Island.

[23] Three states require testing for scholarship recipients: Florida, Louisiana, and Virginia. FLA. STAT. ANN. § 1002.395(8)(c)(2) (West 2012); LA. REV. STAT. ANN. § 47:6301(B)(2)(a)(ii) (2012); VA. CODE ANN. § 58.1-439.28(D) (West 2013).

[24] Three states require testing for all students at participating schools: Alabama, Indiana, and Iowa. Alabama Accountability Act of 2013, § 9(c)(2)(a)(1) (Mar. 14, 2013), *available at* http://algop.org/wp-content/uploads/2013/03/AL-Accountability-Act-Full-Text.pdf; IND. CODE ANN. § 20-51-1-4.7 (West 2012); IOWA CODE ANN. § 422.11S(5)(b) (West 2013).

[25] *See infra* Part III, § 1(c).

By applying the same rules to their children as apply to children in public school, these parents too will have skin in the game. Those who believe that testing is useful and beneficial will be pleased; those who disagree will be motivated to advocate for change.

The Model Statute

An Act to Provide Tax Credits for Contributions to Student Scholarship Organizations.

Section 1. Definitions.

(a) An *eligible student* is any child in this state entering any grade from kindergarten through twelfth grade and who resides in a household earning up to 600% of the federal poverty guidelines.

(b) A *qualifying eligible student* is any eligible student who attended any public school in the state in the previous academic year and who scores at a grade level of one or more below the grade at which the eligible student would be assigned based on age in math or reading. In addition, a *qualifying eligible student* is any eligible student who was previously designated as a qualifying eligible student unless, after two years of benefiting from funding from a student scholarship organization, the student does not improve by one or more grade level in math or reading relative to the student's grade.

(c) An *eligible private school* is any private school in this state that complies with all laws applicable to private schools in this state and that subjects all of its students to the standardized tests required for public school students in this state.

(d) A *student scholarship organization* is an organization that is created to receive donations from taxpayers and to disburse scholarship funds for the benefit of eligible students at eligible private schools.

Section 2.

(a) Tax credit availability:

(1) A taxpayer who files a state income tax return and is not a dependent of another taxpayer may claim a credit for a contribution made to a student scholarship organization. The cumulative amount of tax credits issued pursuant to this Section shall not exceed _____ million dollars ($__,000,000) annually.[26] The Department of Revenue

---

[26] Different states have capped their tax credits for this program at wildly different levels. For example, Rhode Island caps total tax credits at $1 million; Indiana at $5 million;

shall develop a procedure to ensure that this cap is not exceeded and shall also prescribe the various methods by which these credits are to be issued.

(2) The tax credit may be claimed by an individual taxpayer or a married couple filing jointly in an amount equal to the total contributions made to a student scholarship organization for educational scholarships during the taxable year for which the credit is claimed, not to exceed _____ thousand dollars ($_,___) per taxpayer or married couple filing jointly.[27]

(3) The tax credit may be claimed by a corporate taxpayer in an amount equal to the total contributions made to a student scholarship organization for educational scholarships during the taxable year for which the credit is claimed up to __ percent (__%) of the tax liability of the taxpayer.[28]

Alabama at $25 million; Georgia at $58 million; Pennsylvania at $100 million; Florida at $229 million; and no cap at all for Louisiana. R.I. GEN. LAWS ANN. § 44-62-3(b) (West 2012); IND. CODE ANN. § 6-3.1-30.5-13 (West 2012); Alabama Accountability Act of 2013, § 9(a)(3) (Mar. 14, 2013), *available at* http://algop.org/wp-content/uploads/2013/03/AL-Accountability-Act-Full-Text.pdf; GA. CODE ANN. § 48-7-29.16(f)(1) (West 2012); 72 PA. CONS. STAT. ANN. § 8706-F(a)(1) (West 2012); FLA. STAT. ANN. § 1002.395(5)(a) (West 2012). Because different states face vastly different budgetary constraints and have substantially different socioeconomic and educational circumstances from one another, each state must decide for itself how much to divert from the public programs that would otherwise receive these tax revenues for this program. I suggest beginning with a conservative number but allowing the number to grow if the program proves successful in achieving its goals. *See* Levin, *supra* note 2 at 1072-73 (introducing a framework to conservatively implement programs by gauging the goals with actual effects).

[27] Here, again, states differ substantially—allowing anywhere from $500 to $50,000 in tax credits for individuals—and states must decide on an individual basis how much to allow. *Compare* ARIZ. REV. STAT. ANN. § 43-1089(A) (2012) (allowing individuals to receive up to $500 in a dollar-for-dollar tax credit) *with* VA. CODE ANN. § 58.1-439.26(A) (West 2013) (capping individual tax credits at $50,000 per year).

[28] Here, again, states differ substantially and must decide on an individual basis how much to allow. In addition, some states impose a firm dollar cap for tax credits for corporate entities, while others impose a limit based on a corporate entity's total tax liability. *Compare* 72 PA. CONS. STAT. ANN. § 8705-F(d) (West 2012) (imposing a $750,000 cap for corporations) *with* Alabama Accountability Act of 2013, § 9(a)(2) (Mar. 14, 2013), *available at* http://algop.org/wp-content/uploads/2013/03/AL-Accountability-Act-Full-Text.pdf (limiting a corporation's tax credit to up to 50% of its total tax liability).

(4) A corporate taxpayer, an individual taxpayer, or a married couple filing jointly may carry forward a tax credit under the tax credit scholarship program for __ years.[29]

(b) Student scholarship organizations must do all of the following:

a. Notify the Department of Revenue of their intent to provide educational scholarships for the benefit of eligible students.

b. Demonstrate to the Department of Revenue that they have been granted exemption from the federal income tax as an organization described in Section 501(c)(3) of the Internal Revenue Code.

c. Distribute periodic educational scholarship payments as checks made out and mailed to the eligible private schools where the benefiting eligible students are enrolled.

d. Provide a Department of Revenue approved receipt to taxpayers for contributions made to the student scholarship organization.

e. Ensure that at least 95 percent of their revenue from donations is spent on educational scholarships for the benefit of eligible students, and that all revenue from interest or investments is spent on educational scholarships for the benefit of eligible students.

---

[29] Once again, states differ in whether to allow tax credits to carry forward and, if so, for how long. *See* Alabama Accountability Act of 2013, § 9(a)(4) (Mar. 14, 2013), *available at* http://algop.org/wp-content/uploads/2013/03/AL-Accountability-Act-Full-Text.pdf (allowing taxpayers to carry forward tax credits for three years); ARIZ. REV. STAT. ANN. § 43-1183(E) (2012) (permitting corporate taxpayers to carry forward unused credits for five years); FLA. ADMIN. CODE r. 12-29.002(6) (2013) (permitting unused tax credits to be carried forward for five years); GA. CODE ANN. § 48-7-29.16(e) (West 2012) (prohibiting the use of a tax credit against prior years' tax liability while allowing unused credits to be used against the succeeding five years' tax liability); IND. CODE ANN. § 6-3.1-30.5-9.5 (West 2013) (expanding the use of tax credits earned after 2012 to up to nine years after the year of the donation); IOWA ADMIN. CODE r. 701-52.38(422) (2013) (granting the right to carry forward unused tax credits for five years); LA. REV. STAT. ANN. § 47:6301(A)(1) (2012) (authorizing carry forwards in perpetuity); 72 PA. CONS. STAT. ANN. §§ 8706-F(d) (West 2012) (proscribing tax credits from being carried forward or carried back); VA. CODE ANN. § 58.1-439.26(B)(2) (West 2013) (allowing tax credits to be carried forward for five years).

f. Spend each year no less than 70 percent of their expenditures on educational scholarships for the benefit of any combination of:

1. eligible students zoned for failing public schools; *or*

2. qualifying eligible students.

g. Provide scholarships to benefit eligible students according to the following guidelines:

1. Eligible students residing in households earning up to 200% of the federal poverty guidelines may benefit from scholarships up to the total tuition cost of the eligible private school that the eligible student attends;

2. Eligible students residing in households earning greater than 200% and no more than 400% of the federal poverty guidelines may benefit from scholarships up to 50% of the total tuition cost of the eligible private school that the eligible student attends.

3. Eligible students residing in households earning greater than 400% and no more than 600% of the federal poverty guidelines may benefit from scholarships up to 25% of the total tuition cost of the eligible private school that the eligible student attends.

h. Cooperate with the Department of Revenue to conduct criminal background checks on all of their employees and board members and exclude from employment or governance any individual who may reasonably pose a risk to the appropriate use of contributed funds.

i. Ensure that educational scholarships are portable during the school year and can be used at any eligible private school for the benefit of the eligible student according to the wishes of the parent or guardian. If an eligible student benefiting from a scholarship transfers to another eligible private school during a school year, the educational scholarship amount may be prorated.

j. Publicly report to the Department of Revenue by June 1 of each year, or on such other date directed by the Department of Revenue, all of the following information prepared by a certified public accountant regarding their grants in the previous calendar year:

1. The name and address of the student scholarship organization.

2. The total number and total dollar amount of contributions received during the previous calendar year.

3. The total number and total dollar amount of educational scholarships awarded during the previous calendar year, the total number and total dollar amount of educational scholarships awarded during the previous year for eligible students zoned for failing public schools, and the total number and total dollar amount of educational scholarships awarded during the previous year for qualifying eligible students.

k. Ensure and certify to the Department of Revenue that educational scholarships are not provided for students to attend a school with paid staff or board members, or relatives thereof, in common with the student scholarship organization.

l. Ensure and certify to the Department of Revenue that scholarships are provided in a manner that does not discriminate based on the gender, race, or disability status of the scholarship applicant or his or her parent or guardian.

m. Ensure and certify to the Department of Revenue that all private schools receiving funds are in compliance with subsection (c) of this section.

(c) Any eligible private school that receives funding from any student scholarship organization must do all of the following:

a. Make a report of aggregate standardized test scores available to all persons upon request. Such a report must provide parents or guardians with a reasonable means of comparing the academic achievement, success, or progress of children in the eligible private school with other children in the state.

b. Provide all parents or guardians who seek or receive scholarship funding on behalf of an eligible student from a student scholarship organization a report of aggregate standardized test scores prior to the enrollment of the eligible student in the eligible private school. Such a report must provide parents or guardians with a reasonable means of comparing the academic achievement, success, or progress of children in the eligible private school with other children in the state.

c. Provide all parents or guardians of students receiving scholarships from student scholarship organizations, and all student scholarship organizations that have provided the school with scholarship funding, with a report containing all standardized test scores of their own children. Such a report must provide parents or guardians with a reasonable means of assessing their children's academic progress in comparison with other children in the same grade in the school and in comparison with other children in the same grade in the state.

Teacher Evaluation at the Intersection of Age and Disability Discrimination: A Case Law Analysis

Mark Paige, J.D., Ph.D. & Perry A. Zirkel, J.D., Ph. D.[*]

Recently the New York City schools denied tenure to almost half of its teachers because they failed to meet performance expectations.[1] School officials attributed the drop to rigorous teacher evaluation systems that purportedly identify underperforming teachers.[2] The City's schools, like others across the nation, reportedly have been using teacher evaluation to "end tenure as we know it."[3] Another New York newspaper reported more bluntly that the City's goal was to "boot those performing badly."[4]

But is it that easy? Are evaluations so precise that they can leave no doubt about a teacher's performance and clearly support a teacher's dismissal? Moreover, do teachers who receive poor evaluations, and consequently lose their employment, leave quietly, without recourse? In some cases, the answer is likely "yes." However, many teachers do not summarily accept the district's decision. This paper analyzes legal cases in which teachers challenged a school district's employment action as violating the Americans with Disabilities Act (ADA), its sister statute Section 504 of the Rehabilitation Act (§ 504), or the Age Discrimination in Employment Act (ADEA). These statutes prohibit an employer from discriminating against an employee because of their disability or age, respectively.

---

[*] Mark Paige is an Assistant Professor at the University of Massachusetts-Dartmouth, specializing in Law and Education, Public Finance, and Collective Bargaining. Perry A. Zirkel, is a University Professor of Education and Law at Lehigh University, with expertise in Special Education Law, General Education Law, and Current Labor Arbitration issues.

[1] Al Baker, *Many New York Teachers Denied Tenure in Policy Shift,* N.Y.TIMES (Aug. 17, 2012), http://www.nytimes.com/2012/08/18/nyregion/nearly-half-of-new-york-city-teachers-are-denied-tenure-in-2012.html?pagewanted=all&_r=0.

[2] *Id.*

[3] *Id.*

[4] Adam Lisberg & Meredith Koldoner, *Bloomberg Vows to Tenure only Good Teachers and Boot Bad Ones,* THE DAILY NEWS (Sept. 27, 2010), http://www.nydailynews.com/new-york/mayor-bloomberg-vows-tenure-good-teachers-boot-bad-article-1.443446.

Evaluations assume center stage in these cases. On the one side, administrators argue that evaluations supported their actions. On the opposing side, teachers contend that they mask a discriminatory motive. In the final analysis, the judge, not the administrator, decides the fate of the teacher. Thus, as school districts across the country prepare to strike their "boot" to underperformers, it is an appropriate time to survey the existing case law concerning teacher challenges to such dismissals that arise under civil rights statutes. Thus, this study synthesizes the case law where teachers have challenged adverse employment actions[5] based on performance evaluations as violating § 504/ADA and/or the ADEA.

A pair of developments makes it a particularly appropriate time to address these questions. First, as the comments from the New York City officials reflect, school districts are applying teacher evaluations with a renewed vigor, especially as a way to terminate allegedly incompetent teachers. Second, the number of teachers covered by these civil rights statutes is growing. More specifically, in 2008, Congress passed the Amendments to the ADA, consequently expanding the definition of "disability" under both the ADA and § 504.[6] Concomitantly, the teaching population is aging, thereby demographically extending the ADEA's coverage.[7] Thus, it seems to be the "perfect storm" for tracking the litigation where § 504/ADA and the ADEA intersect with performance-based employment actions, such as dismissals.

This article is organized as follows: The first section consists of the literature review; section two describes the applicable civil rights laws and the elements a plaintiff must demonstrate to succeed; section three canvasses the applicable rulings under these laws decided since 2000; and the fourth section provides policy guidance for administrators based on case law analysis.

---

[5] In many instances this includes claims pertaining to dismissals. The term "dismiss" is used in this paper in the generic sense, encompassing both non-renewal and termination. But the paper also discusses other employment actions, such as failure to hire, failure to promote, and constructive discharge.

[6] 42 U.S.C. § 12102 (2006 & Supp. VI 2012); *see also* Kania v. Potter, 358 F. App'x 338, 341 (3d Cir. 2009) (noting that the expanded definition of disability under the ADA also expands the class of employees entitled to protection under the Rehabilitation Act).

[7] THOMAS CARROLL, WHO WILL TEACH OUR CHILDREN? EXPERIENCE MATTERS (2010) (noting, *inter alia*, that the teaching workforce is the oldest it has been in the history of the country; the number of teachers over the age of 50 has more than doubled since 1988; the median age of a teacher is 41, meaning that roughly half of the current teaching population is within the protected class covered under the ADEA).

Literature Review

The quality of a teacher is the single most important in-school factor in a student's education,[8] and teacher evaluation is the central mechanism by which to improve the quality of our teachers.[9] Rigorous evaluation systems identify a teacher's strengths and weaknesses, thereby contributing to their professional development.[10] In extreme instances, it also provides documentation to dismiss an employee,[11] as well as other adverse employment actions. Regardless of their use, improving teacher evaluation is viewed as pivotal to improving teacher quality.[12]

Scholars and researchers, however, have amply criticized teacher evaluation in its present form. According to Weisberg and others, teacher evaluation, as currently practiced, does not recognize degrees of quality and, instead, treats all teachers equally.[13] In their view, teacher evaluation

---

[8] JENNIFER E. RICE, TEACHER QUALITY: UNDERSTANDING THE EFFECTIVENESS OF TEACHER ATTRIBUTES v (2003). To be sure, the authors recognize that substantial out of school factors impact a student's learning opportunities. *See* PRUDENCE L. CARTER & KEVIN G. WELNER (EDS.), CLOSING THE OPPORTUNITY GAP: WHAT AMERICA MUST DO TO GIVE EVERY CHILD AN EVEN CHANCE (2013) (arguing, in essence, that meaningful educational opportunity can only be provided when policy also addresses issues related to poverty, housing, etc., not just those related to education).

[9] *Id.* See also Steven M. Kimball & Anthony Milanowski, *Examining Teacher Evaluation Validity and Leadership Decision Making within a Standards-Based Evaluation System, 45* EDUC. ADMIN. Q. 34 (2009).

[10] LINDA DARLING-HAMMOND, EVALUATING TEACHER EFFECTIVENESS 5 (2010).

[11] KELLY FRELS & JANET L. HORTON, A DOCUMENTATION SYSTEM FOR TEACHER IMPROVEMENT OR TERMINATION (2007). The authors recognize that the recent trend to use evaluation systems as a means to terminate teachers is closely linked to accountability reforms in the legislative and political contexts. The federal initiative Race to the Top, which demands that states reform their evaluation system as a precondition of funds, reflects this concept. Likewise, changes to collective bargaining statutes mirrors this trend. *See, e.g.,* Mark A. Paige, *Applying the "Paradox" Theory: A Law and Policy Analysis of Collective Bargaining Rights and Teacher Evaluation Reform from Selected States,* 2013 BYU EDUC. & L.J. 21 (2013) [hereinafter *Applying the "Paradox" Theory*] (highlighting reforms in several states' collective bargaining statutes related to teacher evaluation); Mark A. Paige, *Using VAM in High Stakes Employment Decisions.* 94 PHI DELTA KAPPAN 3 (November 2012) [hereinafter *Using VAM*] (contending that using value added measures in teacher evaluations for purposes of high-stakes employment decisions should be avoided.); Mark A. Paige, *Teacher Evaluation Reform: Finding the Forest Through the Trees,* TEACHERS COLL. RECORD (November 4, 2011), http://www.tcrecord.org/Content.asp?ContentId=16582.

[12] *See, e.g.,* DANIEL WEISBERG THE WIDGET EFFECT: OUR NATIONAL FAILURE TO ACKNOWLEDGE AND ACT ON TEACHER DIFFERENCES 2 (2009).

[13] *Id. See also* ROBIN CHAIT, REMOVING CHRONICALLY INEFFECTIVE TEACHERS: BARRIERS AND OPPORTUNITIES 2 (2010); Erik E. Hanushek & Steven G. Rivkin, *The Distribution of Teacher Quality and Implications for Policy,* 4 ANN. REV. OF ECON. 131,

fails to distinguish talent, a shortcoming that the private sector would never tolerate,[14] and rewards teachers without regard for impact on student learning.[15] As a result, it has become a perfunctory, relatively useless process.[16]

Because of the current listlessness of teacher evaluation, some policymakers and practitioners have engaged in an effort to reform it. A thorough discussion of that specific debate extends beyond the scope of this article,[17] but it is fair to say that many critics agree that evaluation can be a vehicle to dismiss under-performing teachers.[18] More specifically, they contend that teacher evaluation provides demonstrative evidence to support a district's decision.[19]

Of course, dismissals have legal consequences in many instances. To begin with, state statutes require that a tenured teacher receive a hearing to

---

153-154 (2012) (arguing that there exists a substantial variation between teacher contributions to achievement).

[14] WEISBERG, *supra* note 12, at 2.

[15] *Id.*

[16] *Id.*

[17] For example, there is considerable disagreement with respect to what evaluative methods should be used to measure teachers, with value-added modeling being one contested alternative. *See, e.g.,* Erik R. Hanushek, *Generalizations about Using Value-Added Measures of Teacher Quality*, 100 AM. ECON. REV. 267 (2010); Heather Kupermintz, *Teacher Effects and Teacher Effectiveness: A Validity Investigation of the Tennessee Value Added Assessment System*, 25 EDUC. EVALUATION & POL'Y ANALYSIS 287 (2003) (arguing that value added modeling may be an innaccruate measure of a teacher's impact on learning); William Sanders, *Research Findings from the Tennessee Value-Added Assessment System Database: Implications for Educational Evaluation and Research,* 12 J. PERS. EVALUATION IN EDUC. 3 (1998) (generally affirming the accuracy of the use of student test scores for purposes of measuring teacher quality); Steven Sawchuk, *Wanted: Ways to Measure Most Teachers,* EDUC. WEEK, Feb. 2, 2011, at 2 (providing an overview of the debate and arguments involved in reforming teacher evaluation).

[18] *See, e.g,* CHAIT, *supra* note 13, at 22-23 (noting that districts must invest "significant time and resources" in improving evaluations and using them as a means to dismiss teachers); WEISBERG, *supra* note 12, at 2 (noting that "most commentary" on teacher evaluation reform has been concerned with using it as a means for dismissal.)

[19] CHAIT, *supra* note 13, at 22-23 (generally arguing throughout that the evaluation system must be rigorous and developed to support dismissing teachers); *cf.* Hanushek & Rivkin, *supra* note 13, at 152 (decrying the alleged failure of administrators to consider teacher effectiveness in lay off and personnel decisions). *But cf. Applying the "Paradox" Theory, supra* note 11 (arguing that the rush to reform teacher evaluation may have unintended consequences, and, in fact, undercut reform efforts); *Using VAM, supra* note 11 (contending that use of value added measures for high-stakes employment decisions should be avoided).

contest a termination.[20] Although non-tenured teachers do not receive due process in most states,[21] they do enjoy legal protections under more limited circumstances.[22]   A district may not end an employment relationship with any teacher—regardless of tenure status—based on his or her disability, age, or in violation of other established civil rights laws.

To date, the literature concerning the law of teacher evaluation is underdeveloped. First, existing literature is stale and requires accounting for recent case developments.[23] Second, the literature elevates form over legal substance, emphasizing process as the essential ingredient to legally sound teacher evaluations.[24] For instance, one early article on teacher evaluation sets forth the "accepted procedure" for evaluating teachers (*e.g.*, using direct observation of the teacher) and equates this procedure with legal due process,[25] while another provides a "documentation system"—complete with sample letters and memos for the personnel file––for terminating teachers.[26] Third, the literature lacks comprehensive and systematic analysis of rulings in which teacher evaluations played a critical role in the case. For example, in concluding that "based on several court cases [school districts] must adhere to statute and board

---

[20] *See, e.g.,* N.H. REV. STATS. ANN. § 189:14-A, II (2011); MASS GEN. LAWS ch. 71, § 42 (2011).

[21] This is the general rule. However, at least one state, Connecticut, allows a non-tenured teacher a hearing to contest their non-renewal. CONN. GEN. STAT. ANN. § 10-151 (West 2011).

[22] For instance, a union and a school district may negotiate a collective bargaining agreement that confers additional rights to non-tenured teachers concerning a non-renewal.

[23] This literature dates back at least to the early 1980s. *See, e.g.,* Donovan Peterson, *Legal and Ethical Issues of Teacher Evaluation,* 7 EDUC. RES. Q. 6 (1983) (outlining, in incredibly general terms and without reference to any recognized legal authority, requirements of a teacher evaluation system).

[24] *See, e.g.,* LARRY ROSSOW & JAMES TATE, THE LAW OF TEACHER EVALUATION (2003); Joseph Beckham, *Ten Judicial "Commandments" for Legally Sound Teacher Evaluation,* 117 EDUC. L. REP. 435 (1997); Joseph Beckham, *Legally Sound Criteria, Processes and Procedures for the Evaluation of Public School Professional Employees,* 14 J.L. & EDUC. 529 (1985); Peterson, *supra* note 23; Leah Ballard & Davis Gullat, *Choosing the Right Process for Teacher Evaluation,* 26 AM. SECONDARY EDUC. 13 (Mar. 1998); Gary Hartzel, *Avoiding Evaluation Errors: Fairness in Appraising Employee Performance,* 79 NASSP BULL. 40 (Jan. 1995); Donald Langlois & Mary Rita Colarusso, *Don't Let Teacher Evaluation Become an Empty Ritual,* 1988 EXEC. EDUCATOR 32 (May 1988).

[25] Peterson, *supra* note 23 (framing a due process inquiry as determining whether "established rules [concerning how to conduct evaluations] must be followed to protect individual rights").

[26] KELLY FRELS & JANET HORTON, A DOCUMENTATION SYSTEM FOR TEACHER IMPROVEMENT OF TERMINATION (2007).

requirements,"[27] Downey and Frase cited only three court decisions.[28] Fourth, this same source[29] and others[30] confuse or conflate legal requirements with best practices.

Finally, and significantly, the literature omits a discrete discussion of teacher evaluation in the specific context of civil rights litigation and this study addresses that gap. Although scholars have broadly assessed cases in this area,[31] they have not yet engaged in a "deep dive" into particular statutes. As an initial exploration and illustration, this comprehensive case review of teacher evaluation's intersection with § 504/ADA and the ADEA is particularly appropriate in light of the expansion of the scope of coverage under both these statutes and the renewed emphasis on teacher evaluation as a dismissal vehicle.

Legal Framework of the ADA/§ 504 and the ADEA

The ADA/§ 504 and the ADEA primarily protect a teacher[32] in two

---

[27] Larry Frase & Carolyn Downey, *Teacher Dismissal: Crucial Substantive Due Process Guidelines from Court Cases,* 4 NAT'L APPLIED EDUC. RES. J. 13 (1990-1991). Their conclusion states the obvious: School officials should always follow legal requirements.

[28] *Id.* at 21.

[29] *Id.* at 20.

[30] *See, e.g.,* Beckham, *supra* note 24, at 529 (concluding, purportedly from a review of case law, that evaluations should be related to job requirements and evaluation procedures should be clearly articulated and followed). *But see* Perry A. Zirkel, *Teacher Evaluation: A Case of "Loreful Leadership,"* 13 PRINCIPAL LEADERSHIP 46 (2013) (distinguishing between best practices and legal standards).

[31] Perry Zirkel, *Legal Boundaries for Performance Evaluation of Public School Professional Personnel,* 172 EDUC. L. REP. 1 (2003) (providing an annotation of the case law of teacher evaluation across a wide range of topics, including challenges under the Constitution, state and federal civil rights law, and collective bargaining agreements). However, one recent study provides an empirical, rather than narrative, perspective on this intersection. *See* Mark Paige & Perry Zirkel, *Teacher Termination Based on Performance Evaluations: Age and Disability Discrimination?*, EDUC. L. REP. (forthcoming 2014) (providing a quantitative review of the nearly 100 rulings in cases where teachers disputed adverse employment actions based on performance since 2000 on the grounds that the district violated § 504/ADA and/or the ADEA).

[32] For purposes of this paper, rulings involving public school teachers form the unit of analysis because the debate over evaluation reform is exclusively concerned with this group. However, the ADA and ADEA apply to employment in the private sector, not just public employees, and therefore extend to private schools. 42 U.S.C. § 12111 (5) (2006 & Supp. VI 2012) (defining an employer with 15 or more employees as a "covered entity" under the Act) and 29 U.S.C. § 623 (2006 & Supp. VI 2012) (making it unlawful for an "employer" to discriminate against someone based on their age). In contrast, § 504's coverage is more limited than that of the ADA and ADEA; it applies to recipients of federal financial assistance. 29 U.S.C. § 794(a) (2006 & Supp. VI 2012). It can apply

regards. First, they prohibit "direct discrimination," *i.e.*, an employer may not terminate a teacher because of their disability or age. Second, they prohibit retaliation, *i.e.*, an employer may not terminate a teacher because s/he exercised statutory rights. The following overview frames the specific bases for these enumerated prohibitions.

Overall Framework of the ADA/§ 504 and the ADEA

Section 504 provides as follows:
:

> No otherwise qualified individual with a disability in the United States… shall, solely by reason of her or his disability, be excluded from the participation in, be denied the benefits of, or be subjected to discrimination under any program or activity receiving Federal financial assistance or under any program or activity conducted by any Executive agency or by the United States Postal Service.[33]

In addition, § 504 prohibits school districts from retaliating against teachers who exercise their rights under the statute, and an employer cannot discriminate against an employee because s/he exercised rights conferred under § 504.[34] Section 504's prohibitions apply to recipients of "federal financial assistance."[35] However, its protections specifically extend to public school districts (local education agencies).[36] Thus, school districts may not directly discriminate against teachers for employment purposes, either through a direct means or by retaliation.[37]

---

to private school teachers under certain circumstances. *See, e.g.,* Dupre v. Roman Catholic Church of the Diocese of Houma-Thibodaux, et al, 1999 WL 694081, at *4 (E.D. La. Sept. 2, 1999) (ruling that § 504 applies to Catholic school because school was a considered a "program or activity" that received federal financial assistance).

[33] 29 U.S.C. § 794(a) (2006 & Supp. VI 2012). Moreover, it is worth noting that these statutory protections are not specific to teachers.

[34] *See* Reinhardt v. Albuquerque Pub. Sch. Bd. of Educ., 595 F.3d 1126, 1132 (10th Cir. 2010) (applying the prohibition against retaliation under the ADA to cases arising under the Rehabilitation Act). Thus, § 504/ADA prohibit an employer from discriminating against an employee because the employee made "a charge, testified, assisted, or participated in any manner in an investigation, proceeding, or hearing under [the ADA]"). 42 U.S.C. § 12203(a) (2006 & Supp. 2012).

[35] 29 U.S.C. § 794(a) (2006 & Supp. VI 2012).

[36] 29 U.S.C. § 794(b)(2)(B) (2006 & Supp. VI. 2012) (defining "program or activity" to include all the operations of local educational agencies).

[37] *See, e.g.,* 29 U.S.C. 794(d) (2006 & Supp. VI 2012) (noting that the standards used to

The ADA prohibits employers (as opposed to just those who receive federal financial assistance under § 504) from discriminating against individuals with disabilities in the employment context.[38] Specifically, the ADA reads:

> [N]o covered entity shall discriminate against a qualified individual on the basis of disability in regard to job application procedures, the hiring, advancement, or discharge of employees, employee compensation, job training, and other terms, conditions, and privileges of employment.[39]

In addition to the prohibition against direct discrimination, under the ADA it is unlawful for an employer to retaliate against an employee for exercising his or her rights under the statute.[40] An employer with 15 or more employees is a "covered entity" and subject to the ADA's prohibitions set forth above.[41]

Both § 504 and the ADA define disability in terms of three alternative prongs:

1. A physical impairment that substantially limits a major life activity, or
2. Having a record of such an impairment, or
3. Being regarded as having such an impairment.[42]

Importantly, Congress amended the ADA in 2008 by passing the ADA Amendments Act ("ADAAA"), which expanded the first pong of the definition of disability in two ways.[43] First, the Amendments expanded

---

assess employment discrimination claims under the ADA shall be applied to assess such claims brought under § 504).

[38] 42 U.S.C. § 12112(a) (2006 & Supp. VI 2012). Thus, as a point of clarification, these statutes are designed to protect employees generally and are not specific to teachers.

[39] *Id. See also* 42 U.S.C. § 12112(b)(1)-(7) (2006 & Supp. VI 2012) (defining the various prohibited discriminatory actions under the ADA).

[40] 42 U.S.C. § 12203(a) (2006 & Supp. VI 2012). Specifically, the ADA prohibits an employer from discriminating against an employee because the employee "made a charge, testified, assisted, or participated in any manner in an investigation, proceeding, or hearing under this Act." *Id.*

[41] 42 U.S.C. § 12111(2) (2006 & Supp. VI 2012).

[42] 42 U.S.C. § 12102(1) (2006 & Supp. VI 2012); *see also* Mays v. Principi, 301 F.3d 866, 869 (7th Cir. 2002) (explaining that the definition of a disability is the same under the ADA and the Rehabilitation Act).

[43] ADA Amendments Acts of 2008, Pub. L. No. 110-325, 122 Stat. 3553, 3553 (2008).

the scope of examples constituting major life activities, including activities such as concentration, eating, and major bodily functions.[44]   Second, the law prohibits consideration of ameliorative effects of mitigation measures (*e.g.*, medication or assistive devices) regarding the "substantially limits" determination.[45]   In addition, the definition of disability should be construed in favor of coverage and "to the maximum extent permitted" under the Act.[46] The Amendments went into effect on January 1, 2009.[47]

Importantly, to receive protection under both § 504/ADA a person with disabilities must also be "qualified."[48]   A qualified individual "can perform the essential functions of the employment position" with or without reasonable accommodations.[49]   A reasonable accommodation may include making facilities accessible to individuals with disabilities, restructuring the job, or modifying work schedules, to name a few.[50]   The law does not require accommodations that present an undue hardship on the employer.[51]

For purposes of this paper, claims under § 504/ADA are closely related in two important respects.   To begin with, the 2008 Amendments to the ADA that broadened the definition of disability apply also to that definition in the context of § 504 claims.[52]   Additionally, in assessing employment discrimination claims, courts generally apply the same

---

[44] 42 U.S.C. § 12102(2)(A) (2006 & Supp. VI 2012).

[45] 42 U.S.C. § 12102(4)(E)(i)(I)-(IV) (2006 & Supp. VI 2012). A notable exception is the consideration of the ameliorative effects of ordinary eyeglasses is permitted. 42 U.S.C. § 12102(4)(E)(ii)(2006 & Supp. VI 2012).

[46] 42 U.S.C. § 12102(4)(A) (2006 & Supp. VI 2012).

[47] ADA Amendments Act of 2008, Pub. L. No. 110-325, § 8, 122 Stat. 3553, 3559 (2008); *see also* Nyrop v. Indep. Sch. Dist., 616 F.3d 728, n. 4 (8th Cir. 2010).

[48] 42 U.S.C. § 12112(a) (2006 & Supp. VI 2012) and 29 U.S.C. § 794(a) (2006 & Supp. VI 2012).

[49] 29 U.S.C. § 12111(8) (2006 & Supp. VI 2012); 34 C.F.R. 104.3(l)(1) (2011); *see also* 29 U.S.C. § 794(d) (2006 & Supp. VI 2012) (noting that the standards used to determine whether § 504 has been violated in a complaint alleging employment discrimination shall be the standards applied under Title I of the Americans with Disabilities Act of 1990).

[50] 29 U.S.C. § 12111(9) (2006 & Supp. VI 2012).

[51] *See* Filar v. Bd. of Educ. of City of Chicago, 526 F.3d 1054, 1068 (2008) (plaintiff must demonstrate that the accommodation is "reasonable in the sense of both efficacious and of proportional to costs") (citations omitted). It is worth noting that these statutory protections do not come with federal financial support to assist in providing for required accommodations.

[52] 29 U.S.C. § 705(20)(B) (2006 & Supp. VI. 2012) (referencing Section 504's definition of "individual with a disability" as that term is defined under the ADA); *see also* 42 U.S.C. § 12102(1) (2006 & Supp. VI 2012).

standards under § 504 and the ADA.[53]   Thus, as a practical matter, courts analyze each claim in tandem, a practice this paper parallels.

The ADEA prohibits employment discrimination on the basis of age.[54] It provides as follows:

> It shall be unlawful for an employer—
>
> 1. to fail or refuse to hire or to discharge any individual or otherwise discriminate against any individual with respect to his compensation, terms, conditions, or privileges of employment, because of such individual's age;
> 2. to limit, segregate, or classify his employees in any way which would deprive or tend to deprive any individual of employment opportunities or otherwise adversely affect his status as an employee, because of such individual's age; or
> 3. to reduce the wage rate of any employee in order to comply with this chapter.[55]

In addition, the ADEA prohibits employers from discriminating against an employee by retaliating against him or her for exercising rights under this law.[56]   School districts must comply with the ADEA because they are specifically identified as an "employer."[57]   The Act protects individuals over the age of 40.[58]

---

[53] 29 U.S.C. § 794(d) (2006 & Supp. VI. 2012) (noting that the standards used to determine whether this section [504] has been violated in a complaint alleging employment discrimination under this section shall be the standards applied under ADA); *see also* Dryek v. Garvey, 334 F.3d. 590, 597 n.3 (7th Cir. 2003) (noting that "[w]hile the ADA does not apply to federal agencies, *see* 42 U.S.C. § 12111(5)(B) (2006), the standards set out in the ADA are used in determining whether a violation of the Rehabilitation Act occurred in the employment context").

[54] 29 U.S.C. §§ 621 *et seq.* (2006).

[55] 29 U.S.C. § 623(a)(1)-(3) (2006 & Supp. VI. 2012).

[56] 29 U.S.C. § 623(d) (2006 & Supp. VI 2012). Specifically, it is unlawful for the employer to discriminate against an employee that "has made a charge, testified, assisted, or participated in any manner in an investigation, proceeding, or litigation under" the ADEA. *Id.*

[57] 29 U.S.C. § 630(b) (2006 & Supp. VI 2012) (defining employer covered under the Act as any agency or instrumentality of a State or a political subdivision of a State).

[58] 29 U.S.C. § 631(a) (2006 & Supp. VI 2012).

Elements of Direct Discrimination Claims under § 504/ADA and the ADEA

Derived from the template that the Supreme Court established in *McDonnell Douglas Corp. v. Green*[59] for cases under Title VII, or the Equal Employment Opportunities Act, the lower courts employ a multi-step, burden-shifting analysis to assess direct discrimination claims brought under § 504/ADA or the ADEA.[60] To establish a *prima facie* case under a § 504/ADA claim, the plaintiff must show that s/he:

1. is a member of the protected class (*i.e.*, has a disability);
2. is "otherwise qualified" to perform the essential tasks of the job;
3. was subject to an adverse employment action; and
4. sought reasonable accommodation that the employer refused.[61]

Similarly, to establish a *prima facie* case under the ADEA, an employee must show the following:

1. s/he is a member of the protected class (over 40);
2. s/he was qualified for the position;
3. s/he suffered an adverse employment action;
4. the circumstances surrounding the adverse employment action give rise to an

---

[59] 411 U.S. 792, 802 (1973).
[60] *See, e.g.,* Doe v. Fallsburgh Cent. Sch. Dist., 63 F. App'x 46, 48 (2d Cir. 2003) (reiterating that claims under the ADA and Rehabilitation Act all proceed under the "familiar burden-shifting analysis articulated under *McDonnell Douglas* and its progeny"); *see also* Dryek v. Garvey, 334 F.3d 590, 597 n.3 (7th Cir. 2003) ("[T]he standards set out in the ADA are used in determining whether a violation of the Rehabilitation Act occurred in the employment context"); Missick v. New York City, 707 F. Supp. 2d 336, 347 (E.D.N.Y. 2010) (applying the *McDonnell-Douglas* test in the context of employment discrimination claim in both ADA and ADEA contexts).
[61] *Missick,* 707 F. Supp. 2d at 347.

inference of discrimination.[62]

Per the Supreme Court's model under *McDonnell-Douglas*,[63] if the employee establishes a *prima facie* case, the employer must demonstrate they had legitimate reasons for the termination and, if that occurs, the burden shifts back to the employee to demonstrate the reasons were pretextual.[64]

Elements of Retaliation Claims under § 504/ADA and ADEA

Like the direct discrimination claims, but with slight variation as to the precise elements, retaliation claims under 504/ADA and the ADEA follow the aforementioned[65] *McDonnell-Douglas* burden-shifting framework.[66] For the *prima facie* step, the plaintiff must show that:

1. s/he engaged in protected activity;
2. the employer was aware of the activity;
3. the employer took adverse action against the employee; and
4. a causal connection between her protected activity and the adverse employment action[67]

Assuming a plaintiff establishes a *prima facie* case, the defendant must proffer legitimate reasons for the adverse employment action, and then the

---

[62] *Id.* The precise wording of the final prong of the *prima facie* test relating to whether an inference of discrimination can be drawn varies slightly across jurisdictions. *See, e.g.,* Galabya v. New York City Bd. of Educ., 202 F.3d 636, 640 (2d Cir. 2000) (requiring the employee to put forth facts that indicate circumstances that would give rise to an inference of discrimination); *but cf.* Sanchez v. Denver Pub. Sch. 164 F.3d 527, 531 (10th Cir. 1998) (requiring employee to demonstrate that she was treated "less favorably than others not in the protected class" to satisfy final *prima facie* prong).

[63] *See supra* note 60 and accompanying text.

[64] *See, e.g., Doe,* 63 F. App'x at 48; *Missick,* 707 F. Supp. 2d at 347.

[65] *See supra* note 60 and accompanying text.

[66] *See* Horwitz v. Bd. of Educ. of Avoca Sch. Dist. No. 37, 260 F.3d 602, 613 (10th Cir. 2010) (identifying and applying the *prima facie* elements in a retaliation claim brought under ADEA); Reinhardt v. Albuquerque Pub. Sch. Bd. of Educ., 595 F.3d 1126, 1131 (10th Cir. 2010) (applying the *McDonnell-Douglas* standard to retaliation claims brought under § 504 and noting that the standard for retaliation claims under the Rehabilitation Act is the same as the standard for retaliation claims under the ADA).

[67] *See, e.g., Horwitz,* 260 F.3d at 613 (*McDonnell Douglas* as applied in an ADEA claim); Frank v. Lawrence Union Free Sch. Dist., 688 F. Supp. 2d 160, 172 (E.D.N.Y. 2010) (applying the *McDonnell-Douglas* burden-shifting analysis for retaliation claims brought under § 504/ADA).

plaintiff must demonstrate that those reasons are pretextual.[68]

The Case Rulings

This section summarizes first the direct discrimination and then the retaliation case rulings in the § 504/ADA context, with each of these groups organized according to a streamlined *McDonnell Douglas* framework.[69] Next, the synthesis addresses the direct discrimination and retaliation rulings under ADEA in a parallel sequence.

§ 504/ADA Direct Discrimination: An Analysis of Court Rulings

Prima Facie Case

In several cases, school districts successfully asserted that the plaintiff-teacher had not satisfied the first element of the *prima facie* burden—proffering evidence, beyond his or her own opinion, of meeting the definition of an individual with a disability.[70] As a leading example, the plaintiff-teacher in *McCrary v. Aurora Public Schools*[71] did not provide

---

[68] *See, e.g., Horwitz*, 260 F.3d at 612; *Reinhardt*, 595 F.3d at 1131.

[69] For the sake of simplicity, the second and third steps are treated as one category-- "Legitimate, Non-Pretextual Reasons."

[70] *See, e.g., Frank*, 688 F. Supp. 2d at 170-171 (ruling that obesity is not a disability under the ADA, but there was an issue as to whether plaintiff was "regarded as" disabled; plaintiff's claim survived summary judgment on other grounds); Missick v. City of New York, 707 F. Supp. 2d 336, 352 (E.D.N.Y. 2010) (ruling that teacher was not disabled because medical doctor indicated that she was in fact fit to teach and teacher admitted her purported disability did not hinder her ability to teach); Boyd v. Dallas Indep. Sch. Dist., 2010 WL 1687665, at *7 (N.D. Tex. April 27, 2010) (holding that repetitive stress disorder that allegedly affects ability to write without pain is not a disability under the ADA); Levine v. Smithtown Cent. Sch. Dist., 565 F. Supp. 2d 407, 428 (E.D.N.Y. 2008) (finding that teacher was not disabled where, in part, she did not produce any medical evidence that her ailments, including bipolar disorder and Lyme disease, substantially limited a major life activity); Ramirez v. New York City Bd. of Educ., 481 F. Supp. 2d 209, 220 (E.D.N.Y. 2007) (concluding teacher's high blood pressure and episodes of arrhythmia did not constitute disability under ADA, and neither did depression because it did not substantially interfere with a major life activity); Adoo v. New York City Sch., 2006 WL 5838977, at *8 (E.D.N.Y. Dec. 18, 2006) (finding no limitation to a major life activity merely because she cannot walk long distances or readily traverse a flight of stairs).

[71] 57 F. App'x 362, 371-372 (10th Cir. 2003) (holding that plaintiff failed to establish her Attention Deficit Disorder (ADD), sleep apnea, or pulmonary disease substantially limited any major life activity where medical evidence suggested that her cognitive functioning was average to above average, her sleep apnea has been ameliorated, and there was no medical evidence that the pulmonary disease substantially limited teacher's

sufficient evidence that her attention deficit disorder, sleep disorder, or alleged pulmonary condition substantially limited a major life activity.[72] Lack of medical evidence, or even evidence that contradicts a teacher's claim, can be fatal to a claim.[73] At their outer limits, however, this line of cases warrants caution in light of the ADAA Amendments of 2008.[74]

As an initial matter, a negative evaluation alone does not constitute an adverse action that is required for a teacher to satisfy the second *prima facie* element.[75] An interesting line of cases exists whereby teachers argue they satisfy this element under a constructive discharge theory. Here, teachers contend that the district made working conditions so intolerable that they had no choice but to resign.[76] Teachers have contended (generally, unsuccessfully) that administrators created intolerable conditions by failing to accommodate for their disability[77] or the misuse of

---

ability to breath).

[72] *Id.*

[73] *See, e.g.,* Farina v. Branford Bd. of Educ., 458 F. App'x 13, at *14 (2d Cir. 2011) (rejecting teacher's claim that she was disabled where she provided only conclusory statements that her fatigue and insomnia prevented her from standing for extended periods and she was not under any medical restrictions during relevant times); Ragusa v. Malverne Free Sch. Dist., 381 F. App'x 85, 88 (2d Cir. 2010) (finding that plaintiff is not disabled where the record contains no medical evidence other than a doctor's note which cleared the plaintiff to work); *McCrary,* 557 F. App'x at 371 (noting that teacher's deficits were within the average range and a physician testified that she generally functioned above-average); *Missick,* 707 F. Supp. 2d at 352-353 (finding that plaintiff's evidence of disability was "unsupported" and school board's medical examination concluded teacher was fit to teach).

[74] *See supra* notes 43-47 and accompanying text.

[75] *See, e.g., Farina,* 458 F. App'x at 17.

[76] Constructive discharge requires a plaintiff to present evidence that the employer deliberately created intolerable working conditions as perceived by a reasonable person, and the employer did so with the intention of forcing the employee to quit. *See* Pozsgai v. Ravenna City Sch. Bd. of Educ., 2012 WL 1110013, at * 8 (N.D. Ohio March 30, 2012) (citations omitted).

[77] In many of the cases dealing with constructive discharge, teachers were unable to establish facts that would lead to an inference that the working conditions were so intolerable that they left the teacher with no other choice but to leave the position. *See, e.g.,* Eckstrand v. Sch. Dist. of Somerset, 583 F.3d 972, 978 (7th Cir. 2009) (ruling that teacher could not support a constructive discharge claim where record showed that the district had, in fact, made many of the reasonable accommodations for the teacher and, as such, the circumstances were not intolerable); *Pozsgai,* 2012 WL at *8 (ruling that teacher failed to state a claim of constructive discharge because she could not demonstrate she suffered an adverse employment action where, although she resigned, the district attempted to provide her with reasonable accommodations pursuant to the ADA and offered her a different position with equivalent wages and benefits and, therefore, demonstrated an intent to maintain the employment relationship).

personnel evaluation system.[78]   Chances of success on a constructive discharge claim are especially weak in instances where school districts attempt to accommodate the teacher's disability.[79]

Yet a district's failure to make reasonable accommodations that, in fact, aggravates a teacher's disability lends support to a teacher's constructive discharge argument.[80]   In one egregious case, the school district denied "outright" a teacher's various accommodation requests, including her request that she work less (she had a voice condition that made it difficult for her to speak for extended periods).[81]   Oddly, they refused to allow the teacher to employ accommodations (a sound system) that she provided at her own expense.[82]   Moreover, the *Chavez* court questioned the district's motives in using the evaluation process. Viewing the facts most charitably to the plaintiff, the court found that a neutral fact-finder could infer that the district embarked on a course of action intended to "harass" the teacher which included numerous unannounced visits to her classroom, an action inconsistent with past practice.[83]

Litigation under the third element of the § 504/ADA *prima facie* case requiring the teacher to demonstrate s/he is "otherwise qualified" has also surfaced.   Perpetual absenteeism, especially where the teacher does not communicate an expected return to work, renders a teacher not otherwise qualified.[84]   Interestingly, some districts have argued that a teacher's poor

---

[78] *See, e.g.,* Cigan v. Chippewa Falls Sch. Dist., 388 F.3d 331, 332-3 (7th Cir. 2004) (finding that a teacher who retired could not demonstrate that superintendent's recommendation that she not be renewed amounted to creating the type of "unendurable environment" required to sustain a constructive discharge claim); Becker v. Elmwood Local Sch. Dist., 2012 WL 13569, at *8 (N.D. Ohio Jan. 4, 2012) (holding that plaintiff's resignation to avoid a non-renewal is not a constructive discharge when the resignation was motivated by belief that a non-renewal would affect his future employment chances).

[79] *See, e.g., Poszgai,* 2012 WL at * 8 (noting that school district engaged in an iterative process to find reasonable accommodations for the teacher under the ADA and such actions, in part, undercut teacher's claim that she suffered an adverse employment action of constructive discharge).

[80] *See* Chavez v. Waterford Sch. Dist., 720 F. Supp. 2d 845, 851 and 859 (E.D. Mich. 2010) (ruling that allegation of constructive discharge could proceed where district's failure to accommodate the teacher's requests to teach fewer classes were outright denied and district prohibited her from using a microphone and projector that were purchased by the teacher herself); *cf.* Baker v. Riverside Cnty. Bd. of Educ., 584 F.3d 821 (9th Cir. 2009) (finding that teacher had standing under § 504 and the ADA to argue that she was constructively discharged for advocating for a special needs student).

[81] *Chavez*, 720 F. Supp. 2d at 859.

[82] *Id.* at 851.

[83] *Id.* at 849, 859.

[84] *See* Howard v. Magoffin City Bd. of Educ., 830 F. Supp. 2d 308, 315 (E.D. Ky. 2011) (noting that where employee gave no indication of when she would return to work she

performance as documented in an evaluation system, itself, makes the individual unqualified.[85]   Courts have had mixed responses to these arguments and, as one court suggested, no legal authority exists for the proposition that poor job performance alone renders a person unqualified for ADA purposes.[86]

School districts have defeated numerous claims asserting that they failed to provide a reasonable accommodation, the final *prima facie* element in direct discrimination claims arising under § 504/ADA. Rulings in this context pivot on whether the employee and employer engaged in a collaborative process to determine a reasonable accommodation, as required.[87]   For instance, in one case a teacher failed to provide medical documentation regarding her disability requested by the district; consequently, the court dismissed her ADA claim.[88]   Of course, the "interactive process requirement" to find a reasonable accommodation is a two-way street, and when a district fails to engage in this analysis, a court may rule in favor of the teacher.[89]   Refusing to provide accommodations

---

was not otherwise qualified); Ramirez v. New York City Bd. of Educ., 481 F. Supp. 2d 209, 222 (E.D.N.Y. 2007) (finding that excessive absences make employee unqualified); Harris v. Proviso Area for Exceptional Child., 581 F. Supp. 2d 942, 959 (N.D. Ill. 2008) (ruling that where substitute teacher could not perform the essential function of coming to work, she was not otherwise qualified).

[85] Dass v. Chicago Pub. Sch., 2010 WL 4684034, at *13 (N.D. Ill. Nov. 12, 2010) (noting that negative performance evaluation made teacher not otherwise qualified where teacher also admitted having struggled to perform her duties and pointing out that the focus of the analysis is on the employee's performance at the time of dismissal). *But cf. Chavez*, 720 F. Supp. 2d at 856-857 (noting that school district cited no authority that allegedly deficient performance on the job renders a person unqualified under the ADA).

[86] *Chavez*, 720 F. Supp. 2d at 856-857 (noting also, in *dicta,* that under a summary judgment standard, the court must assume the facts in a light most favorable to the plaintiff which requires that they adopt the teacher's version of her performance).

[87] *See, e.g.,* 42 U.S.C. § 12112(b)(5)(A) (2006 & Supp. VI 2012) (requiring that the mental or physical limitation be "known" to the employer to trigger the reasonable accommodation requirement); *see also* Thompson v. City of New York, 2002 WL 31760219, at *8 (S.D.N.Y. Dec. 9, 2002) (finding that pertinent regulations require that both the employee and employer engage in a process that is "flexible,[and] interactive") (citations omitted).

[88] *Thompson,* 2002 WL at * 7 (finding for school district where plaintiff did not adequately communicate her alleged disability and rather assumed that the employer should have provided her with a paraprofessional on their own initiative); *cf.* Beck v. Univ. of Wisconsin Bd. of Regents, 75 F.3d 1130, 1134 (7th Cir. 1996) (noting that an employee has the initial duty of informing the employer of his disability before ADA liability is triggered).

[89] *See, e.g.,* Whitney v. Bd. of Educ. of Grand Cnty., 292 F.3d 1280, 1287 (10th Cir. 2002) (finding a genuine issue of material fact existed with respect to whether or not

that were purchased and supplied by the disabled teacher is a failure to engage in this process.[90] Indeed, such refusals may be viewed not only as a failure to accommodate, but also as engaging in proactive harassment.[91]

Legitimate, Non-Pretextual Reasons

Teacher claims at this stage generally allege that negative performance evaluations mask discriminatory motives.[92] Thus, two competing visions of a teacher's performance are pitted against one another—the teacher's and the administrator's. The court determines which controls. Teachers have had little success in this battle of opinions, primarily because their evidence is largely confined to their personal opinion regarding performance.

Generally speaking, a subjective differing opinion about the nature of performance does not trump that of the administrator.[93] In one representative case, a teacher argued that her supervisors were incompetent and, therefore, her opinion with respect to teacher

---

teacher posed a direct threat to her students and, if so, whether the threat could be addressed with a reasonable accommodation).

[90] *See, e.g.,* Chavez v. Waterford Sch. Dist., 720 F. Supp. 2d. 845, 849 and 858 (E.D. Mich. 2010) (teacher supplied a sound system to address her need to amplify her voice, but principal refused to allow its use).

[91] *Id.*

[92] *See, e.g.,* Fall v. New York State United Teachers, 289 F. App'x 419, 421 (2d Cir. 2008) (finding that the record is replete with evidence supporting that legitimate basis for termination and plaintiff cannot demonstrate pretext); Doe v. Fallsburgh Cent. Sch. Dist., 63 F. App'x 46, 47 (2d Cir. 2003) (ruling that a district's recommendation for non-renewal, in part, because she was rated as not "excellent" and there were "significant gaps in curriculum and evaluation of students" were not pretextual); Duggins v. Appoquinick Sch. Dist., 2013 WL 472283, at *4 (D. Del. Feb. 5, 2013) (principal has no evidence in the record to contradict negative review of her performance, and therefore cannot demonstrate pretext); *cf.* Ryan v. Greater Lawrence Technical Sch., 896 F. Supp. 2d 117, 133 (D. Mass. 2012) (noting that, in the context of a gender discrimination claim, school officials' proffered nondiscriminatory reason for terminating teacher because his job performance was consistently below the level necessary to obtain professional teacher status; teacher's teaching deficiencies were consistently detailed by school officials in the six teacher evaluations completed by the assistant principal during the teacher's first two years of teaching, and observed by her during classroom walk-throughs in his third year of teaching, and comparable deficiencies were recorded by another school administrator in the teacher's third-year evaluations).

[93] *See, e.g.,* Becker v. Elmwood Local Sch. Dist., 2013 WL 472283, at *4 (6th Cir. May 3, 2013) (finding that plaintiff's opinion of his performance was not as positive as he asserted when read in light of the documented negative evaluations); *Fall*, 289 F. App'x at 421 (finding that the record was replete with evidence supporting a legitimate basis for termination and the plaintiff cannot demonstrate pretext).

performance controlled.[94]   Moreover, such assertions juxtaposed against a well-developed record documenting the teacher's poor performance do not demonstrate pretext.[95]   These holdings comport with a general judicial aversion to second-guessing employer personnel decisions.[96]

§ 504/ADA Retaliation Rulings

Prima Facie Burden

The cases under a retaliation theory generally revolved around the second required *prima facie* element of "adverse employment action."[97] Courts have ruled that the following are not adverse employment actions: Negative employment reviews (by themselves);[98] excessive scrutiny

---

[94] *Fall*, 289 F. App'x at 421.

[95] *Id.*

[96] *See, e.g.,* Mesnick v. General Elec. Co., 950 F.2d 816, 825 (1st Cir. 1991) (noting, in the context of an ADEA claim, that "[c]ourts may not sit as super-personnel departments, assessing the merits or even the rationality of employer's non-discriminatory business decisions") (citations omitted).

[97] By way of reminder, there are four elements to a *prima facie* retaliation claim. An employee must demonstrate that: (1) the employee was engaged in an activity protected by the ADA, (2) the employer was aware of that activity, (3) an employment action adverse to the plaintiff occurred, and (4) there existed a causal connection between the protected activity and the adverse employment action. Frank v. Lawrence Union Free Sch. Dist., 688 F. Supp. 2d 160, 172 (E.D.N.Y. 2010).

[98] *See, e.g.,* Pozsgai v. Ravenna, 2012 WL 1110013, at *9 (N.D. Ohio Mar. 30, 2012) (finding that negative performance evaluations were *de minimis* and in the context of both the FMLA and state law disability retaliation claims did not constitute adverse employment action); Missick v. City of New York, 707 F. Supp. 2d 336, 349 (E.D.N.Y. 2010) (ruling that negative evaluations were the product of legitimate, non-discriminatory motives and not retaliatory); Holley v. Pritchett, 2004 WL 2757871, at *17 (S.D. Ind. Sept. 30, 2004) (holding that negative poor performance evaluations were legitimate and non-discriminatory actions, but there was an issue of fact regarding whether the accommodation of an assistant was effective because the assistant was not trained); Scafidi v. Baldwin Union Free Sch. Dist., 295 F. Supp. 2d 235, 239 (E.D.N.Y. 2003); Wiemann v. Indianola Cmty. Sch. Dist., 278 F. Supp. 2d 968, 976 (S.D. Iowa 2003) (in context of state disability discrimination claim, negative performance evaluation is not an adverse employment decision); *cf.* Thompson v. City of New York, 2001 WL 31760219, at *6 (S.D.N.Y. Dec. 9, 2002) (in context of Title VII retaliation complaint, negative performance reviews were not retaliatory where the employee had a long record of poor performance prior to filing complaint under Title VII). *But cf.* Frank v. Lawrence Union Free Sch. Dist., 688 F. Supp. 2d 160, 173 (finding that negative reviews amounted to adverse employment action where teacher received harshest reviews immediately after he informed his employer that he believed he was being discriminated against and intended to seek counsel).

concerning an employee's job performance;[99] placement on a performance improvement plan;[100] or a teacher's perception that there exists an "attitude of dislike" towards her from school administrators.[101] But courts have ruled that, although most transfers do not equate to an adverse employment action,[102] one that aggravates a teacher's disability may satisfy this *prima facie* prong.[103]

Legitimate, Non-Pretextual Reasons

In most instances, well-documented poor performance defeats a retaliation claim at this stage. Similar to the cases decided in a direct discrimination context,[104] a teacher's difference of opinion with a school administrator regarding their job performance generally will not defeat this argument.[105] Teachers have advanced arguments—without much

---

[99] *Scafidi*, 295 F. Supp. 2d at 239 (finding that increased scrutiny over employee's job performance does not constitute an adverse employment action, if no negative employment consequences flow from such scrutiny).

[100] Henry v. Unified Sch. Dist. No. 503, 328 F. Supp. 2d 1130, 1159 (D. Kan. 2004) (failing to find adverse action for retaliation claim under the ADA where the principal discussed putting teacher back on plan of assistance to address concerns about classroom safety and teaching methods, and principal said his contacts with teacher would have to be "formal" because teacher had involved lawyers and union in district's dealings with teacher).

[101] Trepka v. Bd. of Educ., 28 F. App'x 455, 462 (6th Cir. 2002) ("Teacher's perception of an attitude of dislike among certain administrators against her . . . is not even close to the adverse *action* required to constitute retaliation").

[102] *See, e.g.,* McCrary v. Aurora Pub. Sch., 57 F. App'x 362, 369 (10th Cir. 2003) (ruling that even though proposed transfer was against her will, since teacher would have received same salary and benefits in other position, her seniority would not have been affected by transfer, and she failed to show that her job responsibilities would have changed); Salmon v. West Clark Cnty. Sch., 64 F. Supp. 2d 850 (S.D. Ind. 1999) (a transfer that does not result in a material loss of pay or benefits is not an adverse employment action); *see also infra* note 106 and accompanying text.

[103] *See, e.g.,* Scafidi, 295 F. Supp. 2d at 238-239 (finding that a transfer of a teacher's office to several places, including a storage closet, amounted to an adverse employment action).

[104] *See supra* notes 97-101 and accompanying text.

[105] *See, e.g.* Scott v. Kneeland Cmty. Sch. Dist., 898 F. Supp. 2d 1001, 1009 (N.D. Ill. 2012) (nothing in the record submitted by teacher could demonstrate that teacher's dismissal which, in part, based on poor performance and failure to attend work, was pretextual); *see also* Larkin v. Methacton Sch. Dist., 773 F. Supp. 2d 508, 532 (E.D. Pa. 2011) (rejecting teacher's argument that she had more experience than another candidate for a position that was ultimately selected by administrators). *But cf.* Frank v. Lawrence Union Free Sch. Dist., 688 F. Supp. 2d 160, 174 (E.D.N.Y 2010) (noting that opinions of teacher's supervisors/administrators differed with respect to the performance of the employee).

success—that the timing between the protected activity and the adverse employment action demonstrates a discriminatory motive.[106] Even a close temporal link alone between protected activity and a dismissal will generally not demonstrate pretext.[107] The record must reflect something more, beyond timing.[108]

A number of representative examples exist in which timing combined with other factors substantiates a teacher's retaliation claim at the pretext stage. For instance, when school officials altered a teacher's schedule to increase the burden on her only one month after she requested accommodations, her retaliation claim survived summary judgment.[109] Likewise, when a teacher received his harshest criticism along with numerous unannounced visits "just a few days" after he filed a discrimination complaint, a court found evidence of pretext.[110] When school districts create inaccurate records that lead to the teacher not receiving a contract, pretext can be found.[111]

ADEA Direct Discrimination Rulings

Prima Facie Burden

In terms of litigation regarding ADEA direct discrimination claims,

---

[106] Hess v. Rochester Sch. Dist., 396 F. Supp. 2d 65, 77 (D. N.H. 2005) (ruling that teacher could not demonstrate a link between termination and his request for accommodation that was made four years prior to termination and school district had legitimate reasons for termination because teacher failed to supervise students); *cf.* Moser v. Indiana Dep't of Corr., 406 F.3d 895, 905 (7th Cir. 2005) ("[S]uspicious timing alone rarely is sufficient to create a triable issue"); *cf.* Clark Cnty. Sch. Dist. v. Breeden, 532 U.S. 268 (2001) (for purposes of Title VII alleging retaliation, the temporal proximity between the alleged retaliatory act and protected activity must be "very close") (citations omitted).

[107] *See e.g.,* Cassimy v. Bd. of Educ. of the Rockford Pub. Sch. Dist. # 205, 461 F.3d 932 (7th Cir. 2006) (nothing in the record suggests that the decision to reclassify the employee was motivated by any other than the legitimate reasons set forth).

[108] *Id.*

[109] Villanti v. Cold Spring Harbor Sch. Dist., 733 F. Supp. 2d 371, 383 (E.D.N.Y. 2010).

[110] *Frank*, 688 F. Supp. 2d at 173.

[111] *See* Reinhardt v. Albuquerque Pub. Sch. Bd. of Educ., 595 F.3d 1126, 1135 (10th Cir. 2010) (noting that teacher established pretext when her contract was not extended allegedly because she did not service enough students as a speech language pathologist, but a state investigation discovered that the school district maintained inaccurate records concerning the number of students serviced under special education); *cf. Frank*, 688 F. Supp. 2d at 168 (noting that where school district destroyed administrator's notes concerning teacher's performance, teacher is entitled to an inference that the notes favored his position).

several patterns emerge concerning the second prong (adverse employment action). Reflecting the rulings on this prong in the § 504/ADA context,[112] courts ruled the following to not be adverse employment actions: Negative performance evaluations, alone;[113] a transfer that does not change the pay or benefits of the employee;[114] or increased criticisms about performance.[115] In the case of *McCrary v. Aurora Public Schools,* the court rejected a teacher's argument that placement on an improvement plan amounted to an adverse employment action, because the teacher suffered no tangible economic loss.[116] Yet

---

[112] *See supra* note 76 and accompanying text.

[113] *See* Sotomayor v. City of New York, 862 F. Supp. 2d 226, 254 (E.D.N.Y. 2012) (noting that criticism of an employee in the course of evaluating and correcting her work is not an adverse employment action); Weimann v. Indianola Cmty. Sch. Dist., 278 F. Supp. 2d 968 (S.D. Iowa May 6, 2003) (finding that negative performance evaluations and written reprimands did not amount to an adverse employment action where there was no tangible change in working conditions); *cf. Solomon v. Southampton Union Free Sch. Dist.,* 2011 WL 3877078, at *9 (E.D.N.Y. Sept. 1, 2011) (holding that teacher failed to make out a prima facie case under Title VII as she "failed to provide *any* evidence that her negative evaluation affected her employment in any way, and therefore it is not an adverse employment action."). *But cf.* Shapiro v. New York City Dep't of Educ., 561 F. Supp. 2d 413, 423 (S.D.N.Y. 2008) (finding adverse action where negative performance rating resulted in loss of opportunity to receive summer school employment and reduced pension benefits).

[114] McCrary v. Aurora Pub. Sch., 57 F. App'x 362, 369 (10th Cir. 2003) (ruling that even though proposed transfer was against her will, since teacher would have received same salary and benefits in other position, her seniority would not have been affected by transfer, and she failed to show that her job responsibilities would have changed); Galabya v. New York City Bd. of Educ., 202 F.3d 636, 640 (2d Cir. 2000) (transfer to school with allegedly inferior facilities and for the purposes of teaching a different grade level is not an adverse employment action); Howard v. Magoffin Cnty. Bd. of Educ., 830 F. Supp. 2d 308, 315 (E.D. Ky. 2011) (noting that transfer of instructional assistant is not adverse employment action because employee retained same job classification and responsibilities); Stofsky v. Pawling Cent. Sch. Dist., 635 F. Supp. 2d 272, 298 (S.D.N.Y. 2009) (transferring underperforming school psychologist to another school building did not constitute adverse employment action). *But cf. Shapiro,* 561 F. Supp. 2d at 423 (noting that, while transfers are not ordinarily adverse employment actions, transfer to facility that was not a school and widely viewed by peers as punishment did constitute adverse employment action).

[115] *See, e.g.,* Dressler v. New York City Dep't of Educ., 2012 WL 1038600, at *7 (S.D.N.Y. Mar. 29, 2012) (ruling that supervisor's harsh criticisms do not rise to adverse employment action).

[116] 57 F. App'x 362, 369 (10th Cir. 2003) (essentially adopting the district court's finding that the remediation plan is not an adverse employment action because it does not constitute a significant change in employment status); *see also* Sanchez v. Denver Pub. Sch., 164 F.3d 527, 532 (10th Cir. 1998) (ruling that a "mere inconvenience or alteration of job responsibilities" is not an employment decision) (quotations and citation omitted).

when a negative evaluation caused an employee to be excluded from employment in extracurricular positions, opportunities to work in summer school, and reduced pension benefits, an adverse employment action was found.[117]

Legitimate, Non-Pretextual Reasons

In most court rulings on this issue, poor performance as documented in evaluations will demonstrate legitimate, non-discriminatory reasons for taking an adverse employment action, such as termination.[118] When a difference of opinion exists between a teacher and the administrator concerning an evaluation, courts defer to the administrator's opinion.[119] In one noteworthy case, a teacher's consistent and repeated rebuttals to evaluations only supported the administrator's assessment that, ironically,

---

[117] *Id.* As an additional note, this does raise the question of whether negative evaluations associated with various alternative compensation proposals that have become increasingly popular may be considered adverse, if litigated. *See also Stofsky*, 635 F. Supp. 2d at 298 (noting, in *dicta,* that an adverse employment action can be found where transfer results in an assignment that is materially "less prestigious.").

[118] *See, e.g.,* Valtchev v. City of New York, 400 F. App'x 586, 592 (2d Cir. 2010) (explicitly distinguishing an adverse employment action from negative performance evaluations); Wingate v. Gage Cnty. Sch. Dist. 34, 528 F.3d 1074 (8th Cir. 2008) (district decision to hire younger teachers who had better performance ratings than plaintiff were legitimate and non-pretextual reasons); Dirusso v. Aspen, 123 F. App'x 826, 828-829 (2d Cir. 2004) (the record contained nothing to suggest that principal's negative assessments were not legitimate); Gilles v. Pleasant Hill Elementary Sch. Dist. No-69, 2011 WL 5005995, at *7 (C.D. Ill. Oct. 20, 2011) (holding that plaintiff could not demonstrate district's performance concerns were pretextual where evidence was undisputed that principal was dissatisfied with teacher's failure to prepare lesson plans, unprofessional interactions with students, among other issues); Skiff v. Colchester Educ., 514 F. Supp. 2d 284, 299 (D. Conn. 2007) (failing marks on teacher's performance based on classroom observations were legitimate, non-discriminatory and non-pretextual). *But cf.* Gladwin v. Pozzi, 403 F. App'x 603, 606 (2d Cir. 2010) (noting that, in the context of a gender discrimination claim, plaintiff was "never given" a negative performance evaluation, and the record shows she was deemed by co-workers as very effective, committed, and very efficient) (internal quotations omitted).

[119] *See, e.g,* Wingate v. Gage Cnty. Sch. Dist., 528 F.3d 1074, 1080 (8th Cir. 2008) (finding that plaintiff's disagreement with administration's opinion of her teaching does not create a triable issue of fact); Dirusso v. Aspen Sch. Dist. No. 1, 123 F. App'x 826, 833 (10th Cir. 2004) (finding that the record contains nothing to suggest principal's assessments of teacher's performance were not legitimate); Schmeers v. Montgomery, 511 F. Supp. 2d 1128, 1137 (M.D. Ala. 2007) (noting that "[t]he inquiry into pretext centers upon the employer's beliefs, and not the employee's own perceptions of his performance."); Skiff v. Colchester Educ., 514 F. Supp. 2d 284, 299 (D. Conn. 2007) (teacher's argument that administrator's assessment was "subjective" did not defeat argument that the negative performance evaluations were legitimate and non-pretextual).

concluded that the teacher was averse to self-reflection and professional growth.[120]   Consistency among administrators regarding a teacher's performance strengthens the school district's case.   Indeed, similar performance ratings from multiple evaluators support a finding that the evaluations are legitimate and non-pretextual.[121]   Increased frequency of evaluations and scrutiny by administrators do not suggest evidence of a discriminatory motive.[122]   Rather, courts suggest administrators are fulfilling their professional duties when they more closely examine a teacher's performance.[123]

To be sure, inconsistency between formative evaluations and summative recommendations may create an inference of pretext.   In one case,[124] for instance, a school administrator recommended dismissal, in part because of poor performance, but the actual evaluation, which was completed by the same administrator recommending dismissal, noted that the teacher "exceeded expectations" in most domains.[125]

The ADEA Retaliation Rulings

Prima Facie Burden

The cases in the ADEA retaliation context fall along the first (engagement in protected activity) and fourth (causal link between the

---

[120] *Skiff*, 514 F. Supp. 2d at 299.

[121] *See, e.g.,* Missick v. City of New York, 707 F. Supp. 2d 336 (E.D.N.Y. 2010).

[122] *See, e.g., id.* at 350; *see also* Soleyn v. Bd. of Educ. of the City of New York, 1999 WL 983872, at *1-3 (S.D.N.Y. Oct. 28, 1999); Castro v. New York City Bd. of Educ. Pers. Dir., 1998 WL 108004, at *1-4 (S.D.N.Y. Mar. 12, 1998).

[123] Johnson v. New York City Bd. of Educ., 2000 WL 1739308, at *8 (E.D.N.Y. Oct. 10, 2000) (writing that "[i]t is logical, proper, and natural to infer that the reason for Defendant's heightened scrutiny of Plaintiff's performance" is that Defendant was concerned about its students and Plaintiff's ability to teach them satisfactorily" in light of past performance issues).

[124] Garcia v. Corpus Christi Indep. Sch., 866 F. Supp. 2d 646 (S.D. Tex. 2011) (finding pretext established where school district's stated reason that teacher was being terminated, in part, because she was a poor performer; evidence of pretext established in light of the fact that teacher had a positive evaluation in prior year, was cleared of any wrongdoing concerning a particular incident involving inappropriate use of a force against a student, and administrator made remarks suggesting plaintiff should retire); *cf.* Frank v. Lawrence Union Sch. Dist., 688 F. Supp. 2d 160 (E.D.N.Y. 2010) (finding, in context of ADA claim, teacher satisfied pretextual burden where his supervisors had conflicting opinions about his performance and whether or not he should be awarded tenure and administrators destroyed evidence critical to teacher's case.)

[125] *Garcia*, 866 F. Supp. 2d at 653.

activity and termination) prongs of the prima facie case.[126]   With respect to the first prong, courts have ruled the following as not being recognized protected activity under the ADEA: Filing grievances that challenge poor performance evaluations and transfers that do not result in reduction of pay, among others.[127]   With respect to the fourth prong, courts have also found that when numerous performance related reasons were given for a teacher's termination, there was no causal link between the protected activity and the termination.[128]   Likewise, when the timing between the adverse action and alleged protected activity was attenuated, a teacher failed to establish the necessary causal link.[129]

Legitimate, Non-Pretextual Reasons

Rulings at this stage mirror those issued regarding retaliation under other civil rights laws discussed herein. Prior satisfactory reviews do not demonstrate pretext.[130]   Indeed, in one case, with a fact pattern common in many schools, a teacher had relatively effective teaching skills in the past, but was criticized for her inability to work with colleagues and declining performance over time.[131]   The court noted her general positive history, but found that the administration had documented their concerns in light of present developments and, therefore, no evidence of pretext was found.[132]   In a variation on this theme, placement on an improvement plan following a teacher's filing of a discrimination complaint does not amount to pretext, especially when a district has documented performance concerns.[133]   Similarly, and as one might intuitively expect, when the adverse employment event and its underlying reasons occur before a

---

[126] *See supra* note 70 and accompanying text.

[127] *See e.g.,* McCrary v. Aurora Pub. Sch., 57 Fed. App'x 363, 371 (7th Cir. 2003) (ruling that teacher's grievances concerning her poor performance ratings did not constitute protected activity under the ADEA); *see also Garcia*, 866 F. Supp. 2d at 658 (finding that teacher did not engage in ADEA protected activity when she challenged her termination on the grounds that the district did not have "good cause"); *see also* Stofsky v. Pawling Cent. Sch. Dist., 635 F. Supp. 272, 302 (S.D.N.Y. 2009) (noting that teacher's complaint that alleged that she was retaliated against for "opposing conduct" that was prohibited under the ADEA was insufficient to establish that she engaged in protected activity).

[128] Horwitz v. Bd. of Educ. of Avoca Sch. Dist. No. 37, 260 F.3d 602, 614 (7th Cir. 2001).

[129] *Id.* at 613; *see also Garcia*, 866 F. Supp. 2d at 658.

[130] *Horwitz*, 260 F. 3d at 614.

[131] *Id.* at 615-616.

[132] *Id.*

[133] *See, e.g,* Phillis v. Harrisburg Sch. Dist., 2010 WL 1390663, at *15 (M.D. Pa. March 31, 2010).

plaintiff files an age discrimination complaint, pretext has not been found.[134]

One case, *Phillis v. Harrisburg School District*,[135] deserves attention because it may present a typical fact situation wherein teachers contend that the classroom dynamics (*e.g.*, a particularly difficult group of children) explains poor performance. In *Phillis* the teacher argued, in part, that the district's failure to account for her particularly challenging students demonstrated pretext. The court rejected this argument and noted that her low teaching evaluations were based on specific, objective accounts of her interactions with students and other teachers.[136] Even assuming that the students were difficult to control, the record supported the fact that the teacher lacked professionalism in dealing with classroom situations.[137]

Policy Recommendations

This comprehensive and in-depth analysis of the applicable case law yields significant policy recommendations. First, where administrators act egregiously and use the evaluation system as a means to carry out unsupported claims, courts will be displeased and draw inferences against the school districts.[138] For instance, *Frank v. Lawrence Unified School District*, involved an administrator's destroyed evaluation notes and records that, according to the teacher, would have contradicted the poor performance rating he received.[139] As a preliminary matter, these actions increase a school district's risk exposure in a litigation context regarding civil rights claims such as those discussed in this article. But, more importantly, from a systemic perspective they undercut the integrity in the evaluation system as a whole. Indeed, it feeds a common sentiment among many teachers that administrators use evaluation as a "gotcha" tool, rather than a means to improve performance. Although it should go without saying, administrators should follow the data and observations

---

[134] Papasmiris v. Dist. 20 of New York City Dep't of Educ., 299 F. App'x 97, 99 (2d Cir. 2008) (finding that employee received negative performance evaluations before he filed complaint of age discrimination and therefore could not establish retaliation); *see also* Garcia v. Corpus Christi, 866 F. Supp. 2d 646, 658 (S.D. Tex. 2011) (alleged retaliatory acts occurred before plaintiff filed complaint with EEOC).

[135] *Phillis*, 2010 WL at *15.

[136] *Id.*

[137] *Id.*

[138] *See, e.g.*, Frank v. Lawrence Union Free Sch. Dist., 688 F. Supp. 2d 160, 168 (E.D.N.Y. 2010).

[139] *Id.*

where they lead. If the record does not reflect poor performance, then administrators should avoid making a termination decision.[140] While this recommendation may be self-evident to most, there are signs that school districts are using evaluation inappropriately.[141]

Second, multiple administrator perspectives—a "triangulation" of observation—can be useful in a number of respects. To begin with, multiple opinions likely comport with best practices. Indeed, in assessing a teacher, especially in a high-stakes employment decision, administrators would be wise to seek opinions of neutral evaluators, assuming the collective bargaining agreement permits such action. But assessments from different evaluators may manage litigation risk. Indeed, it would seem logical that when an administrator intends to make a high-stakes termination decision, s/he would seek counsel of a colleague(s). These additional insights may reaffirm—or provide additional questions—about the evaluation of an employee. And, as discussed, the practice supports a district's decision when challenged.

Third, administrators must be aware that § 504/ADA envisions an interactive process when a teacher requests a reasonable accommodation. Indeed, administrators should start from the positive premise that a reasonable accommodation can be reached assuming that the educator is qualified with a disability. Starting from this premise will, most importantly, help ensure compliance with the law and, additionally, reflect positively on the administration, should this issue arise in the context of litigation.

Fourth, administrators need continued training regarding employee rights and employer responsibilities in the area of § 504/ADA. Of course, the law evolves and courts are constantly interpreting these statutes, thus, any practical advice that flows from case law must be transmitted to administrators. And, as this paper suggests, cases in this area—civil rights laws and teacher evaluation—may be on the rise given recent statutory and demographic shifts.[142] However, this training is needed to ensure that new administrators (many of whom come from the classroom and have no experience in this area) are cognizant of these statutory protections. To the extent possible, educator and administrator preparation programs

---

[140] *See, e.g.,* Garcia v. Corpus Christi Indep. Sch., 866 F. Supp. 2d 646, 652 (S.D. Tex. 2011) (finding pretext where district's ultimate termination decision was not supported in evaluations that, in many domains, ranked teacher as "exceed[ing] expectations").

[141] Al Baker, *Bumpy Start for Teacher Evaluation Program in New York Schools,* N.Y. TIMES (Dec. 22, 2013), http://www.nytimes.com/2013/12/23/nyregion/bumpy-start-for-teacher-evaluation-program-in-new-york-schools.html.

[142] *See supra* notes 6-7 and accompanying text.

should also address this need.[143]

Fifth, administrators should follow their professional judgment and, to the extent possible, reduce any focus with how a court may view the wisdom of their actions. This advice may seem contradictory, given this article's call for increased attention to the law of teacher evaluation. However, many of the cases discussed here reflect a consistent theme: Courts defer to administrators' opinions when it comes to performance of a teacher.[144] Courts hesitate to find in favor of an employee when such a decision puts them sitting as "super-personnel" boards rather than courts of law.[145] Thus, while administrators should never use the evaluation process unfairly, they should not hesitate to even-handedly apply it for fear of litigation.

Finally, a note of caution is in order. The world of teacher evaluation is shifting. State regulations on the subject are imposing new requirements (*e.g.*, value-added modeling) or mandating a specific number of classroom visits. It remains to be seen how these changes impact court rulings, if at all, in the context of challenges brought under civil rights statutes.

---

[143] *See, e.g.*, Mark A. Paige, *The Case for School Law in Teacher Preparation Programs*, TEACHERS COLL. RECORD (Oct. 26, 2009) (noting that one reason to emphasize instruction on education law topics in teacher preparation programs relates to the fact that many teachers become administrators).

[144] *See, e.g.*, Morse v. Frederick, 551 U.S. 393, 428 (2007) (Breyer, J. dissenting) ("[Yet] no one wishes to substitute courts for school boards, or to turn the judge's chambers into the principal's office").

[145] Mesnick v. General Elec. Co., 950 F.2d 816, 825 (1st Cir. 1991) (noting, in the context of an ADEA claim, that "[c]ourts may not sit as super-personnel departments, assessing the merits or even the rationality of employer's non-discriminatory business decisions") (citations omitted).

Education Law 2.0: Improving Access, Equity, and Literacy and the Potential Impact of the Online Open Access Legal Movement

Kevin P. Brady, Ph. D. & Justin M. Bathon, J.D., Ph. D.[*]

> Because technology creates change, it is usually resisted, and often ridiculed or mocked. When it succeeds in its primary drive--to improve upon something we currently have--it only does so after being gradually, grudgingly accepted.[1]

Presently, both the U.S. legal profession and legal education are at critical crossroads. Since the invention of the legal case method over one hundred forty-four years ago in 1870 at Harvard Law School by legal pioneer, Christopher Columbus Langdell, American law schools as well as the legal profession have remained relatively unchanged and a longstanding symbol of status quo ante.[2] Beginning with the economic downturn of 2007, however, the legal profession and the country's accredited law schools have continued to face unprecedented decreases in law school enrollments and sizable downsizing of attorney positions nationwide. According to the American Bar Association (ABA), today's law school enrollments are at 1977 levels, when the U.S. had far fewer ABA-accredited law schools.[3] In 2013, for example, two-thirds of the nation's 202 accredited law schools reported declines in first-year student enrollment.[4] According to recent data from the Law School Admission Council (LSAC), U.S. law school applicants for the fall 2013 class have decreased 15.9 percent from applicants in fall 2012 and the number of overall law school applications has decreased 20 percent.[5] U.S. Bureau of

---

[*] Kevin Brady is an Associate Professor in the Department of Leadership, Policy and Adult and Higher Education, North Carolina State University. Justin Bathon is an Assistant Professor in the Department of Educational Leadership Studies, University of Kentucky and Director of the Center for the Advanced Study of Technology Leadership in Education (CASTLE), University Council for Educational Administration (UCEA).
[1] ROBERT FRIEDEL, A CULTURE OF IMPROVEMENT: TECHNOLOGY AND THE WESTERN MILLENNIUM (2007).
[2] *Status quo ante* is a Latin phrase and translates to "the ways things were before."
[3] Jennifer Smith, *U.S. Law School Enrollment Fall: Lack of Jobs Has Students Steering Away From Legal Career*, WALL ST. J., Dec. 17, 2013.
[4] *Id.* Of those U.S. law schools accredited by the American Bar Association (ABA) that experienced declines in their first-year enrollment, a significant number of those declines were at a level of 10 percent or higher.
[5] *Id.*

Labor Statistics forecast the labor market will have a demand for only 22,000 net lawyer jobs per year over the next decade.[6]   Faced with significant and potentially irreversible declines in legal education and the profession, the U.S. legal community has uniformly acknowledged the dire need for major transformative changes, including considering a two year law degree curriculum program, fewer accredited law schools, and the need for today's lawyers to combine legal expertise with current technological competencies.[7]

To remain relevant, today's U.S. legal community must accept rapidly changing technological innovations, especially those innovations that potentially enhance legal access, equity, and literacy.   Ironically, the educational law and policy community, as a whole, has been relatively slow to integrate technology as a useful tool to help keep pace with the continual and important legal and policy changes impacting elementary through postsecondary education in the U.S.

This article proceeds in four parts. In Part I, the traditional model of print legal information is discussed to develop a historical foundation of how print legal information was distributed prior to the development of the Internet and how this type of distribution limited the access of legal information.   Part II discusses the development of online digital legal information and the origins of the open access movement involving primary and secondary legal materials.   Part III examines how the educational law community is currently being influenced by the online, open access movement. Finally, in Part IV, implications on the future of educational law and policy research and scholarship are explored.

The Traditional Print Model of Legal Information Access

In 2013, worldwide Internet usage was estimated at nearly 2.4 billion users and still growing.[8] In the U.S., Internet usage is at an all-time high with nearly 86 percent of Americans surveyed revealing that they use the Internet on a fairly regular basis.[9] Clearly, we have entered the modern digital age based on society's significant online presence. Interestingly, however, the positive impact of the digital age and related "Web 2.0"

---

[6] *Id.*

[7] *Id.*

[8] Jessica Kril, *Statistics and Data on Internet Usage Worldwide*, STATISTA (2013), http://www.statista.com/topics/1145/internet-usage-worldwide/.

[9] Jeffrey O. Cole, Michael Suman, Phoebe Schramm, Liuning Zhou, & Andromeda Salvador, *The Digital Future Project 2013: Surveying the Digital Future-Year Eleven*, CENTER FOR THE DIGITAL FUTURE (2013), http://www.digitalcenter.org/wp-content/uploads/2013/06/2013-Report.pdf.

technologies impacting how today's legal information is created, disseminated, and accessed by the general public is far from being utilized to its full potential.[10] As Harvard University's Chris Dede stated, Web 2.0 represents "a shift from the presentation of material by website providers to the active co-construction of resources by communities of contributors."[11]

Despite the rapid and revolutionary expansion of Internet usage, the traditional print model of legal information is still alive, especially as it relates to the dissemination of important secondary legal information. A recent report by the American Bar Association's (ABA) *Legal Technology Resource Center* (LTRC), shows that certain types of secondary legal information, including legal treatises, law reviews/periodicals, and selected legal forms continue at least a partial adherence to traditional print publishing.[12] Yet with the advent and continuing growth of e-books coupled with today's shrinking budgets at many law firms, and financial directives to law school libraries to substantially limit the purchase of traditional print legal materials, it is expected that traditional print versions of legal treaties, law reviews/periodicals, legal forms, and other secondary legal materials will continue to decline.[13]

Nevertheless, as the old adage says, "traditions die hard." The print model of legal information is historically steeped in tradition. The distribution of print legal information has followed an established pattern and structure for many years that was neither predicated on increased user access or a low or no-cost model for the user(s) of the legal information. In the U.S., legal information dissemination and retrieval originated with private publishing companies, such as West Publishing Company, who not only published important legal information but also created the structure necessary to conduct legal research using their published legal information, including the various West case reporters and the West *Key*

---

[10] Often heard in the news as well as in the popular news media, the term "Web 2.0" was first coined in 2004 by Dale Dougherty and Tim O'Reilly. Specifically, Web 2.0 refers to technology-based trends and businesses that focus on the principals of an Internet system that is both participatory and collaborative. The core value of the open access movement is increased access to online, digitalized information, especially for individuals that have been previously excluded from access to this information.

[11] Chris Dede, *A Seismic Shift in Epistemology*, 43(3) EDUCAUSE REV. 80, 80 (2008).

[12] Carole A. Levitt & Mark E. Rosch, *Finding the Right Case: Online Legal Research 2013,* AMERICAN BAR ASSOCIATION (2013), http://www.americanbar.org/publications/techreport/2013/finding_the_right_case_online _legal_research_in_2013.html.

[13] *Id.*

Number Digest.[14]   When West's *Key Number Digest* acquired official recognition from the American Bar Association (ABA), it became an indispensable component of accepted legal authority.[15] In addition to case reporters, legal digests, annotated legal codes, encyclopedias, and law reviews, were all other essential types of legal information maintained by privately published sources that acquired judicial authority over time.[16]

One of the most significant criticisms of the traditional print model of legal information distribution was the limited boundaries surrounding access to these important legal materials.   In order to access these materials, individuals not only needed to be directly affiliated with the legal profession but also trained in how to conduct legal research, which was primarily provided by accredited law schools to students pursuing formal training.   As of result of significantly limited access to legal information under the traditional print model, many groups, including unrepresented racial minorities and other disfavored groups, were impaired in retrieving and understanding the complexities of the U.S. legal system and use it as a means to address injustices.[17]

Another criticism of the U.S. traditional print model of legal information was that certain major legal indexes, including West's *Key Number Digest* system, were seen as too conservative and as "reinforc[ing] dominant ideologies."[18] Legal information access tools, such as West's *Key Number Digest* system, limited certain legal fields of research inquiry and firmly established other categories of legal information that reinforced laws' conservative nature in the U.S.[19] Some defenders of the traditional print model of legal information contend that those studying legal information must have an established classification system for organizing complex legal subjects.[20] Ultimately, advocates of the traditional print model of legal information argue that this traditional system offers enhanced practicality to a largely pragmatic legal profession,

---

[14]WILLIAM MARVIN, WEST PUBLISHING COMPANY: ORIGIN, GROWTH, LEADERSHIP (1969).

[15] Richard Delgado & Jean Stefancic, *Why Do We Ask the Same Questions? The Triple Helix Dilemma Revisited,* 99 LAW LIBR. J. 307, 313 (2007).

[16]Robert C. Berring, *Legal Information and the Search for Cognitive Authority,* 88 CAL. L. REV. 1675, 1676-77 (2000).

[17] Richard Delgado & Jean Stefancic, *Why Do We Tell the Same Stories? Law Reform, Critical Librarianship, and the Triple Helix Dilemma,* 42 STAN. L. REV. 207 (1989).

[18] Steven M. Barkan, *Deconstructing Legal Research: A Law Librarian's Commentary on Critical Legal Studies,* 79 LAW LIBR. J. 617, 632 (1987).

[19] *Id.*

[20] Spencer L. Simons, *Navigating Through the Fog: Teaching Legal Research and Writing Students to Master Indeterminacy through Structure and Process,* 56 J. LEGAL EDUC. 356, 359-63 (2006).

and this might explain how the existing traditional print model is at least partially resistant to some of the "centrifugal forces of computerization."[21]

Unquestionably, the private publishing companies that created many of the existing traditional legal research and information frameworks never envisioned the far-reaching impact of the modern Internet. However, the leading private legal publishing companies have historically acknowledged the importance of technology as a useful tool in the legal research process. For instance, West Publishing created the Westlaw computer-assisted legal database in 1975. As a way to keep pace with the digitalization of legal information, private legal publishing companies, including Westlaw and LexisNexis, have created comprehensive online, fee-based commercial legal databases. These for-profit legal databases still command a majority of the market share involving legal research in the United States.

The Open Access Legal Movement: The "New" Model of Legal Information Access

While computer-assisted legal research (CALR) has been available to the U.S. legal community since the mid-1970s, it was the creation and public availability of the Internet beginning in the 1990s, which facilitated web-based access to legal information and fundamentally changed the way we conduct and retrieve legal information. According to the American Bar Association's (ABA) most recent *2013 Legal Technology Survey Report,* a staggering 96 percent of U.S. attorneys surveyed indicated that they conduct the vast majority of their legal research online.[22] More interestingly, 92 percent of the attorneys surveyed revealed that they often begin their legal research using free, open access online legal resources.[23] Based on the ABA's *2013 Legal Technology Survey Report,* Table 1 indicates the free, online resources used most frequently by attorneys for their own legal research. Table 2 shows the three most popular fee-based online legal database services attorneys indicated that they used most for legal research. As internet access increased significantly in the early 2000s, a growing number of online, lower-cost legal database alternatives to the existing expensive, commercial legal information databases, namely LexisNexis and Westlaw, have been developed. Some of the more

---

[21] *Id.* at 363.

[22] AM. BAR ASS'N, 2013 LEGAL TECHNOLOGY SURVEY REPORT (2013).

[23] *Id.*

popular, low-cost online legal databases include *Casemaker*,[24] *Fastcase*,[25] *Loislaw*,[26] and *VersusLaw*.[27]

Table 1: Free Open Access Legal Resources Used Most By Attorneys

Free, Open Access Legal Resource	Percentage
Google	36%
State Bar Association offering	25%
Federal or State Government legal websites	14%
Cornell Law School's Legal Information Institute (LII)	10%
Findlaw	9%

Table 2: Fee-Based Online Legal Sources Used Most by Attorneys

Fee-Based Online Legal Resource	Percentage
WestlawNext	28.10%
WestLaw	25.70%
Lexis	24.10%

This increasingly popular movement to digitize legal information ranging from primary legal documents, including legal cases, to secondary sources, such as legal scholarship, unquestionably represents a massive undertaking.[28]   Despite the workload associated with digitizing massive amounts of legal information, there are significant advantages of online digital legal information compared to traditional print legal materials. A particularly attractive feature associated with online digital information, especially legal information, is the potential for dramatically increased access. For example, the ability to transform information that has been traditionally limited exclusively to print-based distribution to online, open access legal information makes this information accessible to a wider and more diverse audience. This is a compelling reason for digitalizing legal information to an online, open access format.

A second compelling advantage of online digital legal information compared to the traditional print model of legal information is substantially lower production-related costs.[29] Quite simply, online digital

---

[24] CASEMAKER, http://www.casemaker.us/ (last visited January 4, 2014).

[25] FASTCASE, http://wwwfastcase.com/ (last visited January 4, 2014).

[26] LOISLAW, http://www.loislaw.com/ (last visited January 4, 2014).

[27] VERSUSLAW, http://www.versuslaw.com/ (last visited January 4, 2014).

[28] *See* Katie Hafner, *History, Digitized (and Abridged)*, N.Y. TIMES, Mar. 11, 2007, at 9 (estimates indicate that it will take over two thousand years to digitize the nearly nine billion traditional print records it currently has in its collection).

[29] Jessica D. Litman, *Open Access Publishing and the Future of Legal Scholarship: The Economics of Open Access Law Publishing*, 10 LEWIS & CLARK L. REV. 779 (2006).

information is much more affordable to store compared to traditional print legal materials. Within the U.S. legal community, for example, traditional print law journals published by law schools represent a publishing venue that would especially benefit economically by changing from a traditional print model to a completely online, open access method of distributing its legal information and related commentaries. Since the majority of print-based legal scholarship relies on only a few commercial publishers, most legal journals are largely dependent on unpaid law students to perform the selection and copy editing of legal commentaries and scholarship. Additionally, the printing costs associated with producing most of today's law reviews are subsidized by individual law schools with subscription and royalty revenues being insufficient to cover publication-related costs.[30]

In addition to enhanced access to legal information and significantly lower production-related costs, another benefit of online, open access legal information is its potential to raise legal awareness and knowledge through increased legal literacy. Central to the open access movement's philosophy is that the dissemination of important information should be available digitally, online, at no expense to the user, and free from most copyright and licensing restrictions. Price barriers, such as subscriptions, licensing fees, and pay-per view fees and most permission barriers, such as copyright and licensing restrictions often associated with traditional print materials, are often eliminated in an online, open access publishing model. One of the more commonly accepted definitions of the modern open access movement is the "free availability on the public Internet, permitting any users to read, download, copy, distribute, print, search, or link to the full texts of these articles, crawl them for indexing, pass them as data to software, or use them for any lawful purpose, without financial, legal, or technical barriers other than those inseparable from gaining access to the Internet itself."[31]

In his influential 2006 book, *The Access Principle: The Case for Open Access for Research and Scholarship*, author John Willinsky contends that the primary goal of the open access movement is greatly improved access to important information, including legal information, that should be readily available to the public at no cost on the Internet.[32] One of the modern leaders of the open access movement in the U.S. is Carl Malamud,

---

[30] *Id.*

[31] 2002 BUDAPEST OPEN ACCESS INITIATIVE, http://www.budapestopenaccessinitiative.org/read (last visited December 12, 2013).

[32] JOHN WILLINSKY, THE ACCESS PRINCIPLE: THE CASE FOR OPEN ACCESS FOR RESEARCH AND SCHOLARSHIP (2005).

who founded *Public.Resource.Org*, a nonprofit organization, whose primary goal is the placement of governmental information free and online to the public.[33]   As explicitly stated in the organization's *Articles of Incorporation*, "the specific purpose of this corporation [*Public.Resource.Org*] is to create, architect, design, implement, operate and maintain public works projects on the Internet for educational, charitable, and scientific purposes to the benefit of the general public and the public interest."[34]

Following the current trend to digitize traditional print records, influential companies, including Google, are emerging as leaders in the online, open access movement.   The creation of *Google Scholar*, for example, has greatly improved the ability of anyone using the Internet to conduct free, online searches of legal information through a comprehensive, regularly updated, and relatively user friendly searchable online legal database of legal cases separated and searchable by both court jurisdiction as well as topic.[35]

The Open Access Movement's Influence on Primary Legal Materials

While the U.S. legal community has been generally characterized as slow in both its adoption and integration of technology, considerable progress has been made in placing certain primary legal materials online, including federal and state-level laws, state statutes and regulations.   For example, the Education Commission of the States (ECS) has a fairly comprehensive online site detailing each state's statutes and administrative codes.[36]

Despite its current ban on the videotaping of live oral arguments and the live audio streaming of its proceedings on the Internet, the U.S.

---

[33] Carl Malamud is one of the leading open access proponents in the world and created the open access website, Public.Resource.Org.

[34] *See* PUBLIC.RESOURCE.ORG BYLAWS, https://public.resource.org/about/index.html (last visited October 30, 2013).

[35] GOOGLE SCHOLAR, http://scholar.google.com (last visited January 3, 2014). As evidence of Google Scholar's ability to perform comprehensive online searches of legal information, online users can access United States Supreme Court cases dating back to 1791 as well as U.S. federal district, appellate, tax, and bankruptcy courts beginning 1923. At the state level, Google Scholar's online, legal database currently includes all U.S. state appellate cases dating back to 1950. In addition to primary legal information, namely cases, Google Scholar provides access to a growing number of secondary legal sources, including law journals and law reviews.

[36] *See States and Territories: Statutes and Administrative Codes*, EDUC. COMM'N OF THE STATES (ECS), http://www.ecs.org/html/statesTerritories/50state_Leg_info.asp (last visited January 8, 2014).

Supreme Court is historically considered an early technology adopter in the movement to provide free, online access of its cases.[37] As early as 1990, for example, the U.S. Supreme Court, in collaboration with the *Hermes Project* at Case Western Reserve University School of Law, made all Supreme Court legal decisions freely available on the Internet.[38] Unfortunately, however, the website was considered very difficult to navigate and many users lacked the skills to effectively navigate the online site.[39] As a result, the *Hermes Project* ultimately failed before Internet access dramatically increased worldwide.

Shortly after the creation of the *Hermes Project*, two law professors, Peter W. Martin and Thomas R. Bruce created Cornell University's *Legal Information Institute* (LII) in 1992 with the ultimate goal of making both primary and secondary legal materials freely available to the general public.[40] Compared to the earlier *Hermes Project*, Cornell University Law School's LII website is considerably more user-friendly and is constantly updated to include more legal materials. In 1995, the U.S. Library of Congress created the open access website, *THOMAS*, which was created to provide the public free online access to proposed legislation by Congress.[41] The passage by Congress of the E-Government Act of 2002[42] encourages U.S. federal courts to maintain online, open access of its legal opinions at no expense to the public. Overall, the open access movement

---

[37] *See* Jack M. Balkin, *Online Legal Scholarship: The Medium and the Message*, 116 YALE L.J. POCKET PART 20 (2006), *available at* http://www/thepocketpart.org/2006/09/balkin.html.

[38] In 1990, the U.S. Supreme Court collaborated with the Hermes Project at Case Western Reserve University's School of Law in a concerted effort to make all U.S. Supreme Court legal opinions available online at no cost.

[39] One of the primary reasons given for the failure of the Hermes Project was that most of the public were not very skilled at using the Internet, which was only available to the public beginning in the early 1990s.

[40] LEGAL INFORMATION INSTITUTE, http://www.law.cornell.edu/lii.html (last visited December 24, 2013). Cornell University Law School's Legal Information Institute (LII) is a not-for-profit organization that subscribes to the principles of the open access movement and publishes free, online legal information as well as exploring new technologies to assist others in better understanding the law. The LII website is maintained at Cornell University Law School and includes a multidisciplinary group of legal scholars, computer scientists, government agencies, and other interested groups that promote online, open access to the law.

[41] THOMAS, http://www.thomas.gov/ (last visited on December 26, 2013). For a more detailed discussion of the creation of the U.S. Library of Congress' THOMAS website, *see* Steve Gelsi, *Jefferson's Legacy*, FORBES (SEPT. 17, 1997), *available at* http://www.forbes.com/1997/09/17/feat_side3.html.

[42] E-Government Act, 44 U.S.C. § 101 (2002).

involving primary legal materials continues to be quite successful and anticipates considerable expansion in the near future.

The Open Access Movement's Influence on Secondary Legal Materials

In addition to primary sources of law, mainly legislation and caselaw, secondary legal sources, including books, treatises, law reviews, and journals, are all considered influential sources of legal information. Since the nineteenth century, for instance, articles published in U.S. legal journals, such as law reviews have been the leading source of legal scholarship. While the number of open access sites for primary legal materials continues to grow exponentially, the number of open access legal journals is surprisingly low.[43] For example, there are about 655 student-edited legal journals published at ABA-approved law schools with a total number of approximately 993 published legal journals published by commercial publishers, state bar associations, or other legal publishing venues.[44] Of these 993 legal journals, only 134 (*See Appendix A*) of these legal journals are currently available in an online, open access format at no cost.[45]

From purely an economic perspective, the vast majority of traditional print versions of student-edited law journals do not generate much revenue and are often heavily subsidized.[46] Jessica Litman, a law professor at the University of Michigan contends that U.S. law schools continually lose money through the production of traditional print law reviews and related legal journals. Given the current economic climate coupled with decreasing law school student enrollments, it is worth asking: Why would U.S. law schools continue to invest in the publication of traditional print legal journals with a loss of revenue?

There is little debate that the transition to a fully online, open access secondary legal information publication infrastructure, including legal commentaries and scholarship would not only reduce publication costs but also improve the overall accessibility of legal information to the general public.[47] Unfortunately, there is a continuing and major tension in the

---

[43] Richard A. Danner, *Open Access to Legal Scholarship: Dropping the Barriers to Discourse and Dialogue*, 7 J. INT'L. COMP. L. & TECH. 65 (2012).

[44] *Law Journals: Submissions and Rankings 2006-2013*, WASH. & LEE UNIV. SCH. OF LAW, http://lawlib.wlu.edu/lj/index.aspx (last visited January 8, 2014).

[45] LAW REVIEW COMMONS, http://lawreviewcommons.com/ (last visited December 28, 2013).

[46] *See* Litman, *supra* note 29.

[47] Nicholas Bramble, *Preparing Academic Scholarship for an Open Access World,* 20 HARV. J.L. & TECH. 209 (2006).

legal publishing world between academic scholars and for-profit publishers. While scholars and researchers often seek the widest distribution and impact of their work, for-profit publishers, on the other hand, often seek the highest profits.[48]

There are, however, growing opportunities for today's legal scholars to publish their research in an online, open access format. For instance, the relatively recent creation of two popular online, open access repositories, the Social Science Research Network's (SSRN) Legal Scholarship Network[49] and the Berkeley Electronic Press Legal Repository[50] allow today's U.S. legal scholars the opportunity to post online draft versions of their scholarly research either before it has been officially accepted by a legal journal or as a working draft paper.

Among members of today's U.S. law school community, an increasing number of law school faculty members are advocating to have their legal research and scholarship available in an online, open access format. For the vast majority of legal scholars in the U.S., the main publishing venue is a law review affiliated with one of the nation's ABA accredited law schools. The new technologies associated with electronically-based publishing have gradually perpetuated a paradigm shift away from traditional print law review journals to legal journals that are now supported by a fully online, open access format.[51]

Nearly a decade ago, several prestigious law schools, including Harvard and Yale Law Schools began digitally archiving their entire traditional print collections of legal scholarship, including their entire law review editions, into an open access format available to the general public.[52] One of the leaders of the modern open access legal movement has been Duke University Law School. In 2005, for instance, the *Duke Law Scholarship Repository* created electronic, open access to all of Duke University Law School faculty's scholarship dating back to over a half century.[53] More significantly, in 2009, Duke University Law School

---

[48] *See* Kevin P. Brady & Justin M. Bathon, *Education Law in the Digital Age: The Growing Impact of the Open Access Legal Movement*, 277 EDUC. L. REP. 589 (2012).

[49] *See Legal Scholarship Network*, SOC. SCI. RESEARCH NETWORK (SSRN), http://www.ssrn.com/en/index.cfm/lsn/ (last visited Dec. 28, 2013).

[50] *See* BERKELEY ELECTRONIC PRESS, http://www.bepress.com (last visited December 28, 2013).

[51] Carol A. Parker, *Institutional Repositories and the Principle of Open Access: Changing the Way We Think About Legal Scholarship*, 37 N.M. L. REV. 431 (2007).

[52] *See* DIGITAL ACCESS TO SCHOLARSHIP AT HARVARD (DASH), http://dash.harvard.edu/ (last visited December 17, 2013) and YALE LAW SCHOOL'S LEGAL SCHOLARSHIP REPOSITORY, http://digitalcommons.law.yale.edu (last visited January 3, 2014).

[53] *See* DUKE LAW SCHOOL FACULTY SCHOLARSHIP DIGITAL REPOSITORY,

published, *The Durham Statement on Open Access to Legal Scholarship* (*See: Appendix B*), a statement advocating the open access of legal information collectively created by a group of 12 law library directors from some of the nation's leading law schools.[54] The primary goal of the *Durham Statement* was to actively encourage U.S. law schools to cease print publishing of their law reviews and journals and to rely exclusively on an open access digital format that is both accessible and free of charge to anyone that wants to read them.

Blogging and Social Media: The Emergence of New Online Legal Research and Scholarship Communities

According to results from the ABAs recent 2013 *Legal Technology Survey Report,* blogging among U.S. attorneys is gaining momentum.[55] Approximately 27 percent of U.S. lawyers and law firms now have blogs.[56] Increasingly, blogs are being used by today's legal scholars to facilitate online discussions. While online blog-based legal discussions rarely match the level of intensity or length of law review articles, there is evidence that some of today's blogs are influential, are cited in some judicial decisions, and are playing an increased role in generating important legal discussions, including advocacy for open access.[57] Another shortened version of blogging, referred to as "microblogging" is becoming increasingly popular within the legal community through online social media sites, such as *Twitter*. For instance, the popular social media site, *Twitter* limits users to online postings of no more than 140 characters, which is approximately half of one sentence. Some legally-based *Twitter* sites include sources, such as *@SCOTUSOpinions*, which provides the latest U.S. Supreme Court opinions or *@OpenGov* (the Whitehouse Open Government Initiative), and *@LawLibCongress* (the Law Library of Congress). It is clear that the traditional legal research and scholarship

---

http://scholarship.law.duke.edu (last visited December 13, 2013).

[54] THE DURHAM STATEMENT OF OPEN ACCESS TO LEGAL SCHOLARSHIP, http://cyber.law.harvard.edu/publications/durhamstatement (last visited December 18, 2013). *See* Appendix B for the full Durham Statement on Open Access to Legal Scholarship.

[55] AM. BAR. ASS'N, *supra* note 22. Blogging refers to a discussion or informational site published online on the Internet consisting of discrete entries, or "posts" by individuals on a particular blog in which the entries are usually displayed in reverse chronological order.

[56] *Id.*

[57] Lee F. Peoples, *The Citation of Blogs in Judicial Opinions*, 13 TUL. J. TECH. & INTELL. PROP. 39, 79 (2010).

landscape is rapidly changing and a more diverse audience is being exposed to lively and important online legal discussion and debate.

The Open Access Movement: Impact on the Education Law and Policy Community

Given the universal nature and importance of education in our society, legal information involving educational law and policy issues should be shared through an online, open access system to support increased educational law and policy advocacy and literacy.[58]   For example, there is evidence that legal literacy and understanding among today's public school employees, especially teachers is currently alarmingly low.[59] Fortunately, a growing number of online, open access resources are available on the Internet to encourage others, especially educators and parents, to better understand legal developments in educational law and policy.

Open Access Materials in Educational Law and Policy: Primary Legal Sources

Primary legal sources, including laws, statutes, regulations, and case law involving educational law and policy are plentiful. In addition to general online legal databases, such as *Google Scholar*, there are a growing number of online open access sites catering specifically to educational law and policy concerns. For instance, the National School Board Association's (NSBA) *Legal Clips* provides online summaries of recent educational law cases and news stories at no cost that can be accessed through a weekly email newsletter.[60]   Another example of an online open access resource specifically targeting educators is Education Week's *School Law Blog*, an online resource providing concise and timely analysis and commentary on important educational law and policy cases and issues.[61]   At the more localized level, a rapidly growing number of today's college and university regulations, and school district compliance policy manuals are available online to the public at no cost.

---

[58] *Id.*

[59] David Schimmel & Matthew Militello, *Legal Literacy for Teachers: A Neglected Responsibility*, 77 HARV. EDUC. REV. 257 (2007).

[60] *Legal Clips*, NAT'L SCH. BDS. ASS'N, http://legalclips.nsba.org/ (last visited December 27, 2013).

[61] Mark Walsh, *The School Law Blog*, EDUCATION WEEK, http://blogs.edweek.org/edweek/school_law/ (last visited December 27, 2013).

Open Access Materials in Educational Law and Policy: Secondary Legal Sources

Given the current availability of online, open access materials to those in the educational law and policy community, the real deficit and limitations in online, open access materials is found in the area of secondary legal information, namely online access to educational law and policy research and scholarship.[62] For instance, none of the existing four leading legal journals specializing in educational law and policy issues, including the *Brigham Young University Education and Law Journal*,[63] *Journal of College and University Law*,[64] *Journal of Law and Education*,[65] or West's *Education Law Reporter*[66] have online, open access to the articles published in these journals. Since these four legal journals are fee-based, online commercial legal databases, attorneys or researchers interested in educational law and policy issues must either individually subscribe to these journals or have a professional affiliation with an institution, such as a college/university or law firm, that has an existing paid subscription.

Educational Law and Policy Blogs: A Limited Online Community Presence

While still limited in number, there is a growing cadre of quality blogs addressing educational law and policy issues. Four leading educational

---

[62] Kevin P. Brady & Justin M. Bathon, *Education Law in the Digital Age: The Growing Impact of the Open Access Legal Movement*, 277 EDUC. L. REP. 589 (2012).

[63] Created in 1992, the *Brigham Young University Education and Law Journal,* was developed to provide important information and generate scholarship discussion surrounding educational issues and concerns. No online access to the journal is provided unless you have a paid subscription or have access to one of the leading fee-based, commercial legal databases, such as WestLaw or LexisNexis.

[64] The *Journal of College and University Law* is published jointly by the National Association of College and University Attorneys and the Notre Dame Law School. Since its creation in 1973, the journal has had a high national circulation but it is only available through a paid individual or institutional subscription.

[65] The *Journal of Law and Education* is edited at both the University of South Carolina Law School and the University of Louisville School of Law. This journal is only available on the fee-based, commercial legal databases, including WestLaw and LexisNexis.

[66] West's *Education Law Reporter* is directly published by West's fee-based commercial legal database system and in addition to legal commentary and scholarship covers selected federal and state-level educational law cases.

law and policy blogs, include *The Edjurist,*[67] *Education Law Review,*[68] *Education Law Prof. Blog,*[69] and *Education Law Insights: Legal Insights for School Leaders.*[70] Interestingly, there are a growing number of quality blogs developed specifically to address legal issues related to students with special needs and disabilities. Two particular special education law related blogs are the *Special Education Law Blog*[71] and *Wrightslaw.*[72]

It is clear that the educational law and policy community have limited digital, open access to secondary legal information, especially in terms of quality online journals specializing in educational law and policy issues and concerns. Is also seems that supplemental and open access online resources, including blogs and social networking sites provide the right technologies to provide accurate and timely educational law and policy news as well as enhance legal discussions and informative debate.

Conclusion

As we celebrate the inaugural issue of the *Education Law & Policy Review* (ELPR), an online, peer-reviewed open access journal, it is clear that the addition of this particular journal addresses a current void in the educational law and policy community, namely the existence of a high quality educational law and policy journal accessible at no cost to anyone interested in the myriad of law and policy issues impacting education ranging from elementary to postsecondary levels. At a minimum, there are three conditions that are improved by having comprehensive and open online access to educational law and policy materials. They include:

---

[67] THE EDJURIST, http://www.edjurist.com/ (last visited on December 19, 2013). Note that one of the authors of this article, Justin Bathon is the founder of this blog.
[68] EDUCATION LAW REVIEW, http://www.educationlawreview.com (last visited December 12, 2013). This blog is primarily authored by Kent Talbert, the former General Council to the U.S. Department of Education.
[69] EDUCATION LAW PROF BLOG, http://lawprofessors.typepad.com/education_law/ (last visited January 12, 2014). This recently created blog is co-authored by law school professors Derek W. Black at the University of South Carolina Law School and LaJuana Davis at the Samford University Cumberland School of Law.
[70] EDUCATION LAW INSIGHTS, http://edlawinsights.com/ (last visited January 12, 2014). This blog is maintained by the law firm, Franczyk Radelet P.C., one of the largest education law firms in the state of Illinois.
[71] SPECIAL EDUCATION LAW BLOG, http://blog.foxspecialedlaw.com/parent_advocacy/ (last visited December 19, 2013). This blog was created by education law attorney, Charles Fox, who has a son with a disability.
[72] THE WRIGHTSLAW WAY TO SPECIAL EDUCATION LAW AND ADVOCACY, http://www.wrightslaw.com/blog/ (last visited December 19, 2013).

1. *Improved Access:* At the core of the open access movement is improved access, especially to those individuals who have been traditionally unrepresented in the U.S. legal system. Since education has such a universal impact on our society, it is particularly important that educational law and policy issues have greater transparency through improved public access as a fundamental and core value.

2. *Improved Equity:* Since exposure to law and policy issues impacting education raging from the elementary through postsecondary level is so central to the public interest, the availability of free and comprehensive online educational law and policy materials will undoubtedly result in improved equity or fairness. Providing the public-at-large, regardless of factors, such as affiliation with certain institutions or monetary sources, with the same and unfiltered open access to legal information involving educational law and policy issues aligns well with the goals and aspirations of our democratic system, especially as it relates to education as a public good.

3. *Improved Legal Literacy:* There is evidence demonstrating the need for greater legal literacy among many education advocacy groups, including school administrators, teachers, and parents. One specific way of addressing legal illiteracy as it relates to educational law and policy issues is to have legal information readily and openly available to the public-at-large. Moreover, the recent emergence of growing online communities discussing educational law and policy issues has the potential to dramatically improve legal literacy and improve the educational advocacy of others based on the improvement of their educational law knowledge base.

In conclusion, the educational law and policy community is currently well positioned to take full and immediate advantage of the many and varied benefits associated with the open access legal movement. However, compared to other professional fields, even within the larger legal community, the *Education Law & Policy Review* represents necessary progress in providing quality legal research and scholarship to a diverse and growing educational law and policy community. The authors are confident that the publication of this open access journal, the *Education Law & Policy Review*, will act as a positive catalyst for other online open access publications outlets addressing educational law and policy issues and ultimately expand access, equity, and literacy for the at-large educational law and policy community.

APPENDIX A

CURRENT ALPHABETICAL LISTING OF OPEN ACCESS
U.S. LEGAL JOURNALS

Administrative Law Review
Alaska Law Review
American University Business Law Review
American University Criminal Law Brief
American University International Law Review
American University Law Review
American University National Security Law Brief
Annals of Health Law
Annual Survey of International & Comparative Law
Annual Survey of Massachusetts Law
Arbitration Brief
Berkeley Journal of African-American Law & Policy
Berkeley Journal of Criminal Law
Berkeley Journal of Entertainment and Sports Law
Berkeley Journal of International Law
Bond Law Review
Bond University Student Law Review
Boston College Environmental Affairs Law Review
Boston College International and Comparative Law Review
Boston College Journal of Law & Social Justice
Boston College Law Review
California Law Review
Cal Law Trends and Developments
Campbell Law Review
Capital Defense Journal
Cleveland State Law Review
Duke Environmental Law & Policy Forum
Duke Forum for Law & Social Change
Duke Journal of Comparative & International Law

Duke Journal of Constitutional Law & Public Policy
Duke Journal of Gender Law & Policy
Duke Law Journal
Duke Law & Technology Review
Federal Communications Law Journal
Florida Law Review
Fordham Environmental Law Review
Fordham Intellectual Property, Media and Entertainment Law Journal
Fordham International Law Journal
Fordham Journal of Corporate & Financial Law
Fordham Law Review
Fordham Urban Law Journal
Georgia State University Law Review
Golden Gate University Environmental Law Journal
Golden Gate University Law Review
Hamline Law Review
Hofstra Labor and Employment Law Journal
Human Rights Brief
Indiana Journal of Global Legal Studies
Indiana Journal of Law and Social Equality
Indiana Law Journal
Intellectual Property Brief
IP Theory
Jeffrey S. Moorad Sports Law Journal
Journal of Business & Technology Law
Journal of Civil Law Studies
Journal of Criminal Law and Criminology
Journal of Dispute Resolution
Journal of Gender, Social Policy & the Law
Journal of International Business and Law
Journal of Law and Health
Journal of Law and Practice

Journal of the National Association of Administrative Law Judiciary
Labor & Employment Law Forum
Legislation and Policy Brief
Lincoln Memorial University Law Review
Louisiana Law Review
Loyola of Los Angeles Entertainment Law Review
Loyola of Los Angeles International and Comparative Law Review
Loyola of Los Angeles Law Review
LSU Journal of Energy Law and Resources
Marquette Elder's Advisor
Marquette Intellectual Property Law Review
Marquette Law Review
Marquette Sports Law Review
Maryland Journal of International Law
Maryland Law Review
Michigan State International Law Review
Missouri Law Review
Montana Law Review
Nebraska Law Review
Nevada Law Journal
Northwestern Journal of International Law & Business
Northwestern Journal of Law & Social Policy
Northwestern Journal of Technology and Intellectual Property
Pace Environmental Law Review
Pace Environmental Law Review Online Companion
Pace International Law Review
Pace I.P., Sports & Entertainment Law Forum
Pace Law Review
Penn State Journal of Law & International Affairs
Pepperdine Law Review
Public Land and Resources Law Review
Santa Clara Computer & High Technology Law Journal

Santa Clara Journal of International Law
Santa Clara Law Review
Seattle University Law Review
Seton Hall Circuit Review
Seton Hall Journal of Sports and Entertainment Law
Seton Hall Law Review
South Carolina Journal of International Law and Business
Southern Illinois University Law Journal
St. John's Law Review
Sustainable Development Law & Policy
Tennessee Journal of Race, Gender, & Social Justice
The Modern American
Touro Law Review
Transactions: The Tennessee Journal of Business Law
Transitional Justice Review
Tulsa Law Review
University of Cincinnati Law Review
University of St. Thomas Law Journal
UNLV Gaming Law Journal
Urban Law Annual ; Journal of Urban and Contemporary Law
Valparaiso University Law Review
Villanova Environmental Law Journal
Villanova Journal of Law and Investment Management
Villanova Law Review
Washington and Lee Journal of Civil Rights and Social Justice
Washington and Lee Journal of Energy, Climate, and the Environment
Washington and Lee Law Review
Washington University Global Studies Law Review
Washington University Journal of Law & Policy
Washington University Jurisprudence Review
Washington University Law Review
Western New England Law Review

William and Mary Law Review
William and Mary Review of Virginia Law
William & Mary Bill of Rights Journal
William & Mary Business Law Review
William & Mary Environmental Law and Policy Review
William & Mary Journal of Women and the Law
William Mitchell Law Review
Yale Journal of Health Policy, Law, and Ethics
Yale Journal of Law & the Humanities

Source: Law Review Commons: The Largest Collection of Free and Open Law Review Scholarship
(http:lawreviewcommons.com/peer_review.list.html).

APPENDIX B

THE DURHAM STATEMENT OF OPEN ACCESS TO LEGAL SCHOLARSHIP
February 11, 2009

Objective: The undersigned believe that it will benefit legal education and improve the dissemination of legal scholarly information if law schools commit to making the legal scholarship they publish available in stable, open, digital formats in place of print. To accomplish this end, law schools should commit to making agreed-upon stable, open, digital formats, rather than print, the preferable formats for legal scholarship. If stable, open, digital formats are available, law schools should stop publishing law journals in print and law libraries should stop acquiring print law journals. We believe that, in addition to their other benefits, these changes are particularly timely in light of the financial challenges currently facing many law schools.

Rationale: Researchers – whether students, faculty, or practitioners – now access legal information of all sorts through digital formats much more frequently than in printed formats. Print copies of law journals and other forms of legal scholarship are slower to arrive than the online digital versions and lack the flexibility needed by 21st century scholars. Yet, most law libraries perceive a continuing need also to acquire legal scholarship in print formats for citation and archiving. (Some libraries are canceling print editions if commercial digital versions are available; others continue to acquire print copies but throw them away after a period of time.)

It is increasingly uneconomical to keep two systems afloat simultaneously. The presumption of need for redundant printed journals adds costs to library budgets, takes up physical space in libraries pressed for space, and has a deleterious effect on the environment; if articles are uniformly available in stable digital formats, they can still be printed on demand. Some libraries may still choose to subscribe to certain journals in multiple formats if they are available. In general, however, we believe that, if law schools are willing to commit to stable and open digital storage for the journals they publish, there are no longer good reasons for individual libraries to rely on paper copies as the archival format. Agreed-upon stable, open, digital formats will ensure that legal scholarship will be preserved in the long-term.

In a time of extreme pressures on law school budgets, moving to all electronic publication of law journals will also eliminate the substantial costs borne by law schools for printing and mailing print editions of their school's journals, and the costs borne by their libraries to purchase, process and preserve print versions.

Additionally, and potentially most importantly, a move toward digital files as the preferred format for legal scholarship will increase access to legal information and knowledge not only to those inside the legal academy and in practice, but to scholars in other disciplines and to international audiences, many of whom do not now have access either to print journals or to commercial databases.

Call to Action: We therefore urge every U.S. law school to commit to ending print publication of its journals and to making definitive versions of journals and other scholarship produced at the school immediately available upon publication in stable, open, digital formats, rather than in print.

We also urge every law school to commit to keeping a repository of the scholarship published at the school in a stable, open, digital format. Some law schools may choose to use a shared regional online repository or to offer their own repositories as places for other law schools to archive the scholarship published at their school.

Repositories should rely upon open standards for the archiving of works, as well as on redundant formats, such as PDF copies. We also urge law schools and law libraries to agree to and use a standard set of metadata to catalog each article to ensure easy online public indexing of legal scholarship.

As a measure of redundancy, we also urge faculty members to reserve their copyrights to ensure that they too can make their own scholarship available in stable, open, digital formats. All law journals should rely upon the AALS model publishing agreement as a default and should respect author requests to retain copyrights in their scholarship.

Source: Berkman Center for Internet & Society: Durham Statement on Open Access to Legal Scholarship
(http://cyber.law.harvard.edu/publications/durhamstatement).

A Critique of the Federal Challenge to Financing Public Education along Racial Lines in *Lynch v. Alabama*: How the Plaintiffs, the Defendants, and the Federal District Court Erred in Examining the Funding of Public Education in Alabama

R. Craig Wood, Ph. D.[*]

Knight and Sims v. Alabama[1] and its progeny *Lynch v. Alabama*[2] are unique federal cases that have dominated the funding decisions for higher education as well as public elementary and secondary education for many years within the state of Alabama. The issues raised in these cases will most likely continue into the future, as evidenced by the attempt to mutate the issues raised in *Knight and Sims* into broader public policy applications for the financing of public elementary and secondary schools within the state of Alabama in *Lynch v. Alabama*. These substantial public policy issues, as raised in these two cases, had the potential to affect the Alabama Legislature, virtually all taxpayers in the state, and all of higher education as well as elementary and secondary public education throughout the state of Alabama. *Knight and Sims v. Alabama* (hereinafter *KnightSims*) originally began in 1986 as an attempt to desegregate a highly unequal system of higher education in the state of Alabama,[3] but continues to influence the broader debate over public education funding in Alabama.

---

[*] R. Craig Wood is a Professor of Educational Administration and Policy at the University of Florida in Gainesville, Florida. Note that an earlier version of this paper was presented at the International Conference on Interpreting the South African Constitution in Educational Contexts, Inter University Centre for Education Law, Education Leadership, and Education Policy, Centre for Education Law and Policy, Johannesburg, South Africa, July 2012.

[1] Knight v. Alabama (*Knight VI*), 458 F. Supp. 2d 1273 (N.D. Ala. 2004), *aff'd* 476 F.3d 1219 (11th Cir. 2007), *cert. denied*, 127 S. Ct. 3014 (2007).

[2] Lynch ex rel. Lynch v. Alabama, 568 F. Supp. 2d 1329 (N.D. Ala. 2008).

[3] *See also* United States v. Alabama, 628 F. Supp. 1137 (1985). It should be noted that this lengthy opinion was largely void of finance data as proposed within this paper. The opinion was largely historical, descriptive, and an overview of the differences among the various universities of the state of Alabama.

The Issues of *KnightSims*

The original concept as presented in *KnightSims* was that the segregated system of higher education in the state of Alabama resulted in inferior racially identifiable institutions of higher education.[4] The dual system of higher education based on race, particularly in the Deep South, was racially discriminatory, economically inefficient, and often a convoluted manner of educating the general population with duplicative programs that begged a variety of economic and legal public policy issues. The history of *KnightSims* represents ten years of litigation, and two trials.[5]

In 1987, *Knight II* issued a lengthy and detailed opinion finding liability on the part of the state of Alabama.[6] In 1995, the Eleventh Circuit reviewed and issued a remedial decree ordering numerous changes to the public higher educational system in the state of Alabama. The court also maintained jurisdiction in the matter.[7] The court stated that it intended to return control of the higher education system to the state in 2005.[8]

One of the major issues addressed within this paper is the concept of the financial basis and the applicability of this racially dual system of higher education and how this concept mutated into a United States Constitutional claim regarding the financing of public elementary and secondary education within the state of Alabama. In fact, as a specific result of *KnightSims*, plaintiffs attempted to move the logic and application within this higher education desegregation case into the realm

---

[4] The history of racial integration in public elementary and secondary schools is long and complex. In the educational context, *Brown v. Board of Education*, 374, U.S. 483 (1954), is the most critical. For those cases examining racial integration within an educational context *see, e.g.:* McLaurin v. Okla. State Regents, 339 U.S. 637 (1950); Sweatt v. Painter, 339 U.S. 629 (1950); Missouri ex rel. Gaines v. Canada, 305 U.S. 337 (1938); Gong Lum v. Rice, 275 U.S. 78 (1927); Carter v. Sch. Bd., 182 F.2d 531 (4th Cir. 1950); Davis v. Cnty. Sch. Bd., 103 F. Supp. 337 (E.D. Va. 1952); Butler v. Wilemon, 86 F. Supp. 397 (N.D. Tex. 1949); Pitts v. Bd. of Tr., 84 F. Supp. 975 (E.D. Ark. 1949); Freeman v. Cnty. Sch. Bd., 82 F. Supp. 167 (E.D. Va. 1948).

[5] *See* Knight v. Alabama (*Knight I*), 628 F. Supp. 1137 (N.D. Ala. 1985), *rev'd*, 828 F.2d 1532 (11th Cir. 1987) (*Knight II*), *cert. denied*, 487 U.S. 1210 (1988), *on remand*, 787 F. Supp. 1030 (N.D. Ala. 1991) (*Knight III*), *aff'd in part, rev'd in part, vacated in part*, 14 F.3d 1534 (11th Cir. 1994) (*Knight IV*), *on remand*, Knight v. Alabama (*Knight V*), 900 F. Supp. 272 (N.D. Ala. 1995), Knight v. Alabama (*Knight VI*), 458 F. Supp. 2d 1273, (N.D. Ala. 2004), *aff'd*, 476 F.3d 1219 (11th Cir. 2007) (*Knight VII*), *cert. denied*, 127 S. Ct. 3014 (2007).

[6] *Knight III*, 787 F. Supp. at 1030.

[7] *Knight V*, 900 F. Supp. at 272.

[8] *Id.* at 274.

of an equity and adequacy claim, under the U.S. Constitution, regarding the financing of public elementary and secondary education throughout the state of Alabama. Prior to the date of returning control to the state legislature under *KnightSims*, plaintiffs filed a motion asking that "an injunction ordering Alabama to fund adequately its system of *lower* [*i.e.*, K-12] education."[9]

Despite being focused on higher education, within *KnightSims,* the plaintiffs argued that specific sections of the Alabama Constitution prevented an equitable and adequate education in terms of public elementary and secondary education. The following six sections were specifically noted:

- Article XI, section 214, as amended, limits the rate of *ad valorem* taxation the Alabama legislature may place on taxable property;[10]
- Article XI, section 215, as amended, limits the rate of *ad valorem* taxation counties may place on taxable property;[11]
- Article XI, section 216, as amended, limits the rate of *ad valorem* taxation municipalities may place on taxable property;[12]
- Article XIV, section 269, as amended, limits the rate of *ad valorem* taxation counties may place on taxable property for the benefit of public education, and further requires approval of those property taxes by the voters in a referendum election;[13]

---

[9] *Knight VI*, 476 F.3d at 1223.

[10] Section 214 states that "[t]he legislature shall not have the power to levy in any one year a greater rate of taxation than sixty-five one-hundredths of one per centum on the value of the taxable property within this state." ALA. CONST. of 1901 art. XI, § 214.

[11] Section 215 states, in pertinent part, that "[n]o county in this state shall be authorized to levy a greater rate of taxation in any one year on the value of the taxable property therein than one-half of one per centum." ALA. CONST. of 1901 art. XI, § 215.

[12] Section 216 states, in pertinent part, that "[n]o city, town, village, or other municipal corporation, other than as provided in this article, shall levy or collect a higher rate of taxation in any one year on the property situated therein than one-half on per centum of the value of such property as assessed for state taxation during the preceding year." ALA. CONST. of 1901 art. XI § 216.

[13] The text of this provision reads as follows: "The several counties in this state shall have the power to levy and collect a special tax not exceeding ten cents on each one hundred dollars of taxable property in such counties, for the support of public schools; provided, that the rate of such tax, the time it is to continue, and the purpose thereof, shall have been first submitted to a vote of the qualified electors of the county, and voted for by

- Amendment 325 changed the language of Article XI, § 217 of Alabama's 1901 Constitution, establishing *three* classes of property for purposes of *ad valorem* taxation, lowering assessment ratios, requiring voter approval of all property tax increases, and establishing a cap (or "lid") on total *ad valorem* taxes;[14] and

- Amendment 373, further changed the language of Article XI, § 217, as previously revised by Amendment 325, establishing four classifications of property subject to taxation, furthering lower assessment ratios, establishing the so-called "current use' method of property assessment, and establishing lower caps (or "lids") on total *ad valorem* taxes.[15]

In *KnightSims,* the district court concluded "the current *ad valorem* tax structure is a vestige of discrimination inasmuch as the constitutional provisions governing the taxation of property are traceable to, rooted in, and have their [sic] antecedents in an original segregative, discriminatory policy."[16] The court further stated "the current tax structure in Alabama cripples the effectiveness of state and local governments in Alabama to raise funds adequate to support higher education"[17] but concluded that:

> The relationship between the funding of higher education and f[u]nding of K-12 is marginal insofar as ad valorem property tax is concerned. Put differently, the effect of the state's inability to raise revenue due to the challenged constitutional provisions is simply too attenuated to form a causal connection between the tax policy and any segregative effect on school choice.[18]

---

three-fifths of those voting at such election; but the rate of such special tax shall not increase the rate of taxation, state and county combined, in any one year, to more than one dollar and twenty-five cents on each one hundred dollars of taxable property." ALA CONST. of 1901 art. XIV, § 269.

[14] Amendment 325 established three classes of property: Class I–All property of utilities used in the business of such utilities, with an assessment ratio of 30 per centum; Class II–All property not otherwise classified, with an assessment ratio of 24 per centum; and Class III–All agricultural, forest and residential property, with an assessment ration of 15 per centum. ALA. CONST. of 1901 amend. 325.

[15] ALA. CONST. of 1901 amend. 373. For ease of reorganization, the author has renumbered these issues.

[16] Knight v. Alabama (*Knight VI*), 458 F. Supp. 2d 1273, 1311 (N.D. Ala. 2004).

[17] *Id.*

[18] *Id.* at 1312 (emphasis added).

On appeal, the Eleventh Circuit agreed with the district court that the "plaintiffs' present claim is fundamentally about reforming Alabama's K-12 school funding system, and not about desegregating its colleges and universities."[19] While ruling against this specific claim in *KnightSims*, the decision indicated that such a constitutional complaint might be warranted in a separate action in the future. Thus, *Lynch* was the direct progeny of *KnightSims*.

Lynch v. Alabama and the Funding of Public Education

In *Lynch v. Alabama,*[20] the plaintiffs argued generally that the system of taxing property for purposes of funding public education was unconstitutional in that it was a vestige of racial discrimination from the past.[21] In 2008, this attempt resulted in *Lynch v. Alabama,*[22] in which the plaintiffs, a group of African-American and White students, challenged the validity of the State of Alabama's property tax system. Specifically, the plaintiffs challenged the state constitutional limitations on property taxes, *i.e.*, the main source of funding for public elementary and secondary education.

Lynch must be understood within the context of earlier education finance litigation within Alabama. *Lynch* is a reflection of a series of cases and issues in which the plaintiffs were not successful for a variety of reasons. In contemporary times, the most significant challenges to Alabama's public school funding system occurred in *Alabama Coalition for Equity, Inc. v. Hunt* in 1990[23] and *Harper v. Hunt* in 1991.[24] These two cases were consolidated resulting in the 1993 *Opinion of the Justices*.[25]

A trial court had ruled in favor of the plaintiffs, declaring that the system of public education violated the state constitutional mandate. The court ruled that the system was inequitable and inadequate and it retained

---

[19] Knight v. Alabama (*Knight VII*), 476 F.3d 1219, 1223 (11th Cir. 2007) (emphasis added).

[20] Lynch ex. rel. Lynch v. Alabama, 568 F. Supp. 2d 1329 (N.D. Ala. 2008).

[21] *See supra* notes 10 through 15; Complaint at 2, Lynch ex rel. v. Alabama, 568 F. Supp. 2d 1329 (N.D. Ala. 2008) (No. 5:08cv00450) 2008 WL 7242459, at *2 (citing *Knight VI*, 58 F. Supp. 2d at 1311).

[22] 568 F. Supp. 2d 1329 (N.D. Ala. 2008).

[23] Ala. Coal. for Equity, Inc. v. Hunt, No. CV-90-883-R, 1993 WL 204083 (Ala. Cir. Apr. 1, 1993).

[24] No. CV-91-0117-R (Ala. Cir. Jan. 19, 1991).

[25] 624 So. 2d 107 (Ala. 1993).

jurisdiction to fashion a remedy.[26] Later, the Alabama Supreme Court issued an opinion *sua sponte*, declaring that the trial court's remedial orders could not stand given the separation of powers doctrine.[27] The Alabama Supreme Court then dismissed all of the cases and left the resolution of the issues to the state legislature.[28]

Specifically, in *Lynch*, the plaintiffs argued that as a class action, the children of the state were "injured by the racially discriminatory property tax restrictions in the Alabama Constitution, which impede their ability and the ability of their elected representatives to raise state and local revenues adequately to fund the public services they need, including public education."[29]

Unique to state constitutional challenges to state education finance distribution formulas, this complaint essentially argued the state education finance distribution formula violated the United States Constitution due to the Alabama state constitutional limitations regarding ad valorem taxes. Interestingly, the plaintiffs faced a dilemma--they could not argue that the language of the state constitution was in and of itself a violation of the U.S. Constitution, based purely on state constitutional grounds as did virtually all other challenges.[30] Nor could the plaintiffs argue that the

---

[26] Following this ruling, the Alabama Supreme Court ruled that in *Opinion of the Justices*, 624 So. 2d 107 (Ala. 1993) that the Legislature would have to follow the ruling; in *Pinto v. Alabama Coalition*, 662 So. 2d 894 (Ala. 1995), the Court ruled that the trial court erred in denying certain interveners in the remedy phase of the trial. Subsequently the Judge withdrew from further proceedings. *See also* Ex parte James, 713 So. 2d 869 (Ala. 1997).

[27] Ex Parte James, 836 So. 2d 813 (Ala. 2002). *Sua sponte*, Latin for "of his or her own will," generally refers to a judge's order made without a request by any party to the case.

[28] *Id.*

[29] Lynch ex. rel. Lynch, 568 F. Supp. 2d 1329, 1335 (N.D. Ala. 2008).

[30] *See generally*, R. Craig Wood, *Constitutional Challenges to State Education Finance Distribution Formulas: Moving from Equity to Adequacy*, 23 ST. LOUIS U. PUB. L. REV. 531 (2004). The relevant education finance cases as sorted by state are: **Alabama**: James v. Alabama, 836 So.2d 813 (Ala. 2002); Op. of the Justices, 624 So.2d 107 (Ala. 1993). **Alaska**: Matanuska-Susitna v. State, 931 P.2d 391 (Alaska 1997). **Arizona**: Roosevelt v. Bishop, 877 P.2d 806 (Ariz. 1994); Shofstall v. Hollins, 515 P.2d 590 (Ariz. 1973). **Arkansas**: Lake View v. Huckabee, 91 S.W.3d 472 (Ark. 2002) Dupree v. Alma Sch. Dist., 651 S.W.2d 90 (Ark. 1983). **California**: Serrano v. Priest, 557 P.2d 929 (Cal. 1976); Serrano v. Priest, 487 P.2d 1241 (Cal. 1971). **Colorado**: Lobato v. State, 304 P.3d 1132 (Colo. 2013); Lobato v. Colorado, 218 P.3d 358 (Colo. 2009); Lujan v. Colo. State Bd. of Educ., 649 P.2d 1005 (Colo. 1982). **Connecticut**: Conn. Coal. for Justice in Educ. Funding, Inc. v. Rell, 990 A.2d 206 (Conn. 2010); Horton v. Meskill, 376 A.2d 359 (Conn. 1977). **Florida**: Schroeder v. Palm Beach Cnty. Sch. Bd., 10 So.3d 1134 (Fla. Dist. Ct. App. 2009); Coal. for Adequacy and Fairness in Sch. Funding v. Chiles, 680 So.2d 400 (Fla. 1996). **Georgia**: McDaniel v. Thomas, 285 S.E.2d 156 (Ga. 1981). **Idaho**: Idaho Sch. for Equal Educ. Opportunity v. Evans, 850 P.2d 724 (Idaho 1993);

Thompson v. Engelking, 537 P.2d 635 (Idaho 1975). **Indiana**: Bonner ex rel. Bonner v. Daniels, 907 N.E. 2d 516 (Ind. 2009). **Illinois**: Committee v. Edgar, 672 N.E.2d 1178 (Ill. 1996); Blase v. Illinois, 302 N.E.2d 46 (Ill.1973). **Kansas**: Gannon v. Kansas No. 10-c-1569 (D.Kan. Jan. 11 2013); Montoy v. Kansas, 102 P.3d 1160 (Kan. 2005), *supplemented*, 112 P.3d 923 (Kan. 2005), *republished with concurring opinion*, 120 P.3d 306 (Kan. 2005); Unified Sch. Dist. v. Kansas, 885 P.2d 1170 (Kan. 1994). **Kentucky**: Rose v. Council for Better Educ., 790 S.W.2d 186 (Ky. 1989). **Louisiana**: La. Ass'n of Educators v. Edwards, 521 So. 2d 390 (La. 1988); La. Fed'n of Teachers v. State, 118 So. 3d 1033 (La. 2013). **Maine**: Sch. Admin. Dist. v. Comm'r, 659 A.2d 854 (Me. 1995). **Maryland**: Hornbeck v. Somerset, 458 A.2d 758 (Md. 1983). **Massachusetts**: Hancock v. Comm'r of Educ., 822 N.E.2d 1134 (Mass. 2005); McDuffy v. Sec'y of the Exec. Office of Educ., 615 N.E.2d 516 (Mass. 1993). **Michigan**: Milliken v. Green, 212 N.W.2d 711 (Mich. 1973). **Minnesota**: Skeen v. Minnesota, 505 N.W.2d 299 (Minn. 1993). **Missouri**: Comm'n for Educ. Equality v. Missouri, 294 S.W.3d 477 (Mo. 2009); Comm'n for Educ. Quality v. Missouri, 878 S.W.2d 446 (Mo. 1994). **Montana**: Columbia Falls Elementary Sch. Dist. No. 6 v. Montana, 109 P.3d 257 (Mont. 2005); Helena v. Montana, 769 P.2d 684 (Mont. 1989); Montana ex rel. Woodahl v. Straub, 520 P.2d 776 (Mont. 1974). **Nebraska**: Neb. Coal. for Educ. Equity and Adequacy v. Heinman, 731 N.W.2d 164 (Neb. 2007); Gould v. Orr, 506 N.W.2d 349 (Neb. 1993). **New Hampshire**: Londonderry Sch. Dist. SAU #12 v. New Hampshire, 958 A.2d 930 (N.H. 2008); Claremont Sch. Dist. v. Governor, 703 A.2d 1353 (N.H. 1993); Claremont Sch. Dist. v. Governor, 635 A.2d 1375 (N.H. 1993). **New Jersey**: Abbott v. Burke, 971 A.2d 989 (N.J. 2009); Abbott v. Burke, 693 A.2d 417 (N.J. 1997); Abbott v. Burke, 575 A.2d 359 (N.J. 1990); Robinson v. Cahill, 303 A.2d 273 (N.J. 1973). **New York**: Campaign for Fiscal Equity v. State, 801 N.E.2d 326 (N.Y. 2003); Reform Educ. Fin. Inequities Today v. Cuomo, 606 N.Y.S. 2d 44 (N.Y. App. 1994); Bd. of Educ., Levittown v. Nyquist, 439 N.E.2d 359 (N.Y. 1982). **North Carolina**: Hoke Cnty. Bd. of Educ v. State, 731 S.E.2d 691 (N.C. Ct. App. 2012); Hoke Cnty. Bd. of Educ. v. North Carolina, 599 S.E.2d 365 (N.C. 2004); Leandro v. N.C. State Bd. of Educ., 468 S.E.2d 543 (N.C. App. 1996), *rev'd* 488 S.E.3d 249 (N.C. 1997); Britt v. N.C. State Bd. of Educ., 357 S.E.2d 432, (N.C. App.) *aff'd mem.*, 361 S.E.2d 71 (N.C. 1987). **North Dakota**: Bismarck Pub. Sch. Dist. v. North Dakota, 511 N.W.2d 247 (N.D. 1994). **Ohio**: Ohio ex rel. Ohio v. Lewis, 789 N.E.2d 195 (Ohio 2003); DeRolph v. Ohio, 780 N.E.2d 529 (Ohio 2002); DeRolph v. Ohio, 677 N.E.2d 733 (Ohio 1997); Bd. of Educ. of the City Sch. Dist. of the City of Cincinnati v. Walter, 390 N.E.2d 813 (Ohio 1979). **Oklahoma**: Okla. Educ. Ass'n v. Okla., 158 P.3d 1058 (Okla. 2007); Fair Sch. Fin. Council v. Oklahoma, 746 P.2d 1135 (Okla. 1987). **Oregon**: Pendleton v. Oregon, 185 P.3d 471, (2008); Withers v. Oregon, 891 P.2d 675 (Or. App. 1995); Coal. for Equitable Sch. Funding v. Oregon, 811 P.2d 116 (Or. 1991); Olsen v. Oregon, 554 P.2d 139 (Or. 1976). **Pennsylvania**: Marrero v. Pennsylvania, 739 A.2d 110 (1999); Danson v. Casey, 399 A.2d 360 (Pa. 1979). **Rhode Island**: City of Pawtucket v. Sundlun, 662 A.2d 40 (R.I. 1995). **South Carolina**: Abbeville Cnty. Sch. Dist. v. South Carolina, No. 2007-065159 (S.C. 2012). Abbeville Cnty. Sch. Dist. v. South Carolina, 515 S.E.2d 535 (S.C. 1999); Richland Cnty. v. Campbell, 364 S.E.2d 470 (S.C. 1988). **South Dakota**: Olson v. Guindon, 771 N.W.2d 318 (S.D. 2009). **Tennessee**: Tenn. Small Sch. Sys. v. McWherter, 91 S.W.3d 232 (Tenn. 2002); Tenn. Small Sch. Sys. v. McWherter, 894 S.W.2d 734 (Tenn. 1995); Tenn. Small Sch. Sys. v. McWherter, 851 S.W. 2d 139 (Tenn. 1993). **Texas**: Tex. Taxpayer & Student Fairness Coal. v. Scott, No. D-1-GN-11-

property tax statutes were in conflict with the state constitution because the statutes perfectly reflected the state constitutional proscriptive language. Thus, the plaintiffs challenged the funding scheme based on the Civil Rights Act of 1964[31] and the Equal Protection Clause of the Fourteenth Amendment[32] to the United States Constitution. They specifically sought "a prohibitory injunction against their [sic] future enforcement."[33]

The plaintiffs acknowledged that property taxes would increase throughout the state if such an injunction were granted.[34] Of significant note was the public policy discussion by the plaintiffs, the defendants, and the court regarding the economic impact of raising taxes in a precipitous manner for the purposes of funding public education. In theory, the application of the constitution cannot be influenced by either positive or negative economic consequences. Yet, the state argued that the overwhelming results would make it unenforceable and unreasonable when applied to the question before the court. This point illustrates the nature of education finance litigation, *i.e.*, the juxtaposition of economic, social, and political interpretations of the applicability of a constitutional principal.

003130 (Tex.D.C. 2013); Neeley v. West Orange-Cove Consol. Indep. Sch. Dist., 176 S.W.3d 746 (Tex.2005); Edgewood Indep. Sch. Dist. v. Kirby, 804 S.W.2d 491 (Tex. 1991); Edgewood Indep. Sch. Dist. v. Kirby, 777 S.W.2d 391 (Tex. 1989). **Vermont**: Brigham v. Vermont, 692 A.2d 384 (Vt. 1997). **Virginia**: Scott v. Virginia, 443 S.E.2d 138 (Va. 1994). **Washington**: McCleary v. Washington, 173 Wash. 2d 477 (Wash. 2012) (en banc); Fed. Way Sch. Dist. v. Washington, 219 P.3d 941 (Wash. 2009); Sch. Dist. Alliance for Adequate Funding of Special Educ. v. Washington, 202 P.3d 990, (Wash. App. 2009); Seattle Sch. Dist. v. Washington, 585 P.2d 71 (Wash. 1978); Northshore Sch. Dist. No. 417 v. Kinnear, 530 P.2d 178 (Wash. 1974). **West Virginia**: Bd. of Educ. of the Cnty. of Kanawha v. W.Va. Bd. of Educ., 639 S.E. 2d 893 (W. Va. 2006); W.Va. ex rel. Bd. of Educ. v. Bailey, 453 S.E.2d 368 (W. Va. 1994); Pauley v. Kelly, 255 S.E.2d 859 (W. Va. 1979). **Wisconsin**: Vincent v. Voight, 614 N.W.2d 388 (Wis. 2000); Kuker v. Grover, 436 N.W.2d 568 (Wis. 1989). **Wyoming**: Campbell Cnty. v. Wyoming, 181 P.3d 43 (Wyo. 2008); Wyoming v. Campbell Cnty. Sch. Dist., 32 P.3d 325 (Wyo. 2001); Wyoming v. Campbell Cnty. Sch. Dist., 19 P.3d 518 (Wyo.2001); Campbell Cnty. Sch. Dist. v. State, 907 P.2d 1238 (Wyo. 1995); Washakie Cnty. Sch. Dist. v. Herschler, 606 P.2d 310 (Wyo. 1980); Sweetwater Cnty. Planning Comm'n for Org. of Sch. Dist. v. Hinkle, 491 P.2d 1234 (Wyo.1971).

[31] 42 U.S.C. § 1981.

[32] U.S. Const. art. XIV

[33] Lynch ex. rel. Lynch v. Alabama, 568 F. Supp. 2d 1329, 1335 (N.D. Ala. 2008).

[34] *Id.* at 1335 (citing Doc. No. 31, Plaintiffs Brief in Opposition to Defendants. Motion to Dismiss, at 9011. According to the defendants, residential property taxes could increase as much as 1,000 percent).

The plaintiffs did note that the remedy to their complaint would be for the court to allow the state legislature "'an opportunity' to adopt an appropriate, and constitutionally sound, alternative property tax scheme."[35] The plaintiffs did not ask the court to oversee the remedy or to retain jurisdiction if their complaint was successful.

In a lengthy discussion regarding the issues of standing, the court noted: "Reduced to jurisprudential buzzwords, this constitutional formula requires: (1) 'an injury in fact'; (2) 'causation'; and (3) 'redressability.'"[36] The court examined each of these issues at length and examined the questions in a thorough manner. It concluded that in the instant case the state of Alabama intended to present a "*factual* attack," and a defense that "challenges the existence of subject matter jurisdiction using material extrinsic from the pleadings, such as affidavits or testimony."[37]

The court stated that the plaintiff is "required to submit facts through some evidentiary method and has the burden of proving by a preponderance of the evidence that the trial court does have subject matter jurisdiction."[38] The court went on to state:

> Because the evidence that plaintiffs need to submit to establish standing is identical to the evidence needed to substantiate their claim of a cognizable Fourteenth Amendment violation, this paradigm would require them to *prove their case* at the beginning of the lawsuit, without the benefit of any discovery, and without the usual presumption, applicable on Federal Rule of Civil Procedure 12(b)(6) motions and at summary judgment, that all well pleaded allegations and/or disputed facts are construed in the light must favorable to the nonmovant. This is obviously not a workable formulation.[39]

---

[35] *Id.* at 1335. ("Prejudice against discrete and insular minorities may be a special condition, which tends seriously to curtail the operation of those political processes ordinarily to be relied upon to protect minorities, and which may call for a correspondingly more searching judicial inquiry."). *See* United States v. Carolene Prods. Co., 304 U.S. 144, 155 n.4 (1938); *see also* Graham v. Richardson, 403 U.S. 365 (1971); Loving v. Virginia, 388 U.S. 1 (1967); Oyama v. California, 332 U.S. 633 (1948).

[36] *Lynch,* 568 F. Supp. 2d at 1337 (citations omitted).

[37] *Id.* at 1339 (citing Stalley v. Orlando Reg'l Health Care Sys., Inc., 524 F.3d 1229 (11th Cir. 2008)).

[38] *Id.* at 1339-40 (citing Paterson v. Weinberger, 644 F.2d at 523 (5th Cir. 1981)).

[39] *Id.* at 1340 (citations omitted).

The court continued to examine the issues of standing at length, reaching the overall conclusion that it could only accept jurisdiction and address any objections as attacks on the merits of the case. Thus, the court determined that the questions concerned the material nature of the claim. The "sheer number of pages devoted to plaintiffs' theory of discrimination" suggested to the *Knight VI* court that the claim was "both material and substantial."[40] The court went on to summarize the plaintiffs' allegations as follows:

> The black plaintiffs in this action allege that they were singled out for unequal treatment because of their race: in other words, they allege that the drafters of the subject constitutional provisions made a series of conscious decisions to limit their ability to compete for government dollars on an equal footing with their white counterparts (and, thereby, hampered the black plaintiffs' attempts to dismantle structural barriers to change) based on animosity toward their race. The complaint alleges that the inclusion of certain racially discriminatory provisions in the Alabama Constitution has, perhaps unexpectedly, also resulted in the denial of equal access to educational benefits and other public services to whites, especially those who reside in poor, majority-black school districts. These are troubling allegations of deep-rooted, invidious discrimination, not entirely unlike those that gave rise to the Supreme Court's watershed decision in the case of *Brown v. Board of Education.*[41]

Given this reasoning, the court did not dismiss the plaintiffs' complaint based on standing.[42] Wood has specifically examined this point as early as 2004, noting:

> [I]f the Court's apparent mandate in *Brown* were to be satisfied fully, educational opportunity would have strong application to fiscal resources as uneven revenues are at the root of most other forms of inequality. Although it had not been a simple matter to force condemnation of racial inequality, at least there had been a

---

[40] *Id.* at 1341.
[41] *Id.* (citations omitted).
[42] *Id.*

long record of discrimination lawsuits against which concepts and theories could be empirically tested.[43]

Additionally, the state of Alabama argued that the Tax Injunction Act of 1937[44] prevented any claim by the plaintiffs in this regard. The court rejected this argument citing *Hibbs v. Winn.*[45] The court noted that *Hibbs* clearly stated that Congress had focused its intention on taxpayers who wished to avoid paying their taxes. The Supreme Court was of the view that in examining the legislative history, Congress did not display any intent to prevent "federal-court interference with *all* aspects of state tax administration."[46] The Court distinguished its actions over the years in those cases where the granting of federal relief "would have operated to reduce the flow of state tax revenue."[47]

The Supreme Court noted that other federal courts had construed the Act "to restrain state taxpayers from instituting federal actions to contest their liability for state taxes, but not to stop third parties from pursing constitutional challenges to tax benefits in a federal forum."[48] The court rejected the defendants' claim that *Hill v. Kemp* was controlling. Specifically, the District Court opined that the Tenth Circuit in *Hill* misinterpreted *Hibbs* in that third party suits are significant and could not be limited only to the context of tax credits and benefits.[49]

As a defense the state of Alabama raised the doctrine of "comity."[50] The defendants argued that the doctrine of comity barred the plaintiffs' claim. The court rejected this argument, viewing this concept as nothing

---

[43] Wood, *supra* note 30, at 536. *See also* R Craig Wood and Bruce D. Baker, *An Examination and Analysis of the Equity and Adequacy Concepts of Constitutional Challenges to State Education Finance Distribution Formulas*, 27 U. ARK. LITTLE ROCK L. REV. 125, 130 (2004).

[44] 28 U.S.C. § 1341.

[45] 542 U.S. 88 (2004).

[46] Lynch ex. rel. Lynch v. Alabama, 568 F. Supp. 2d 1329, 1342 (N.D. Ala. 2008) (citing *Hibbs*, 542 U.S. at 105).

[47] California v. Grace Brethren Church, 457 U.S. 393 (1982); Arkansas v. Farm Credit Serv., 520 U.S. 821 (1997); Nat'l Private Truck Council v. Oklahoma Tax Comm'n, 515 U.S. 582 (1996); Fair Assessment in Real Estate Ass'n v. McNary, 454 U.S. 100 (1981); Roswell v. LaSalle Nat'l Bank, 450 U.S. 503 (1981).

[48] *Hibbs*, 542 U.S. at 108-109 (citing In re Jackson Cnty., 834 F.2d 150, (8th Cir. 1987); Dunn v. Carey, 808 F.2d. 555 (7th Cir. 1986); Wells v. Malloy, 510 F.2d 74, (2d Cir. 1975); *cf*, Hill v. Kemp, 478 F.3d 1236 (10th Cir. 2007).

[49] *Lynch*, 568 F. Supp. 2d at 1344.

[50] Comity is defined as "[t]he doctrine holding that a federal court must refrain from hearing a constitutional challenge to state action if federal adjudication would be considered an improper intrusion into the state's right to enforce its own laws in its own courts." BLACK'S LAW DICT., 284 (8th ed. 2004).

more than an encapsulation of policy, not a source of judicial power.[51] Thus, the District Court ordered the defendants to respond to the plaintiffs' motion for summary judgment.[52]

The Conceptual Framework of *Lynch v. Alabama*

The U.S. District Court heard the case in 2011. The unpublished opinion[53] was issued November of 2011. As of the time of this examination, it had not been published. The opinion numbered 844 pages and reflected an exhaustive court record. The actual court hearing was approximately three weeks. The court heard testimony from thirty-six witnesses and admitted more than seven hundred exhibits, received nine expert witness reports, received ten affidavits and declarations, and received briefs in excess of one thousand pages.

Lynch was a federal challenge to the manner of funding public elementary and secondary education within the state of Alabama, resting on the concept that the public schools of Alabama are fundamentally financed along racial lines. However, rather than challenging the Alabama statutes that control property assessment and funding as unconstitutional, the plaintiffs chose to challenge certain specified sections of the state constitution itself. They argued that the language of the state constitution was racially motivated resulting in damage to African-American children, and hence certain portions of the Alabama Constitution violated the United States Constitution.

The thrust of the plaintiffs' contention is exceedingly difficult to argue because when assessed values are artificially controlled by the state constitution, then all children, both African-American and White, are affected throughout the state, diminishing the racial motivation argument. The plaintiffs should have made the argument that the manner in which the assessment ratios were inconsistent with the retail values across the state prevented African-American children from receiving an equitable and adequate public education. The manner of determining the retail value is one of a statutory nature, not one of a constitutional nature. The retail value, or the true market value, is what a property would actually be worth in a retail transaction. There are numerous mechanical means to make adjustments of assessed value to retail value for purposes of financing public elementary and secondary education. For example, state

---

[51] *Lynch*, 568 F. Supp. 2d at 1347.

[52] *Id.* at 1348.

[53] CV No. 08-S-450-NE, (N.D. Ala. 2011), *available at* http://knightsims.com/pdf/11_10_25/Doc_294_opinion_on_merits_10-21-11.pdf.

statutes can create a process by which a valid statistical sample of all property actually sold within a school district is taken; the state would then determine the ratio between the assessed value and the actual market transaction price. From this valid sample, an "adjusted assessed valuation" would be created by which state aid and local property taxes would be based. Hence, artificially low assessed valuations would be brought in line with actual value for purposes of state aid and local taxation. The plaintiffs' arguments should be on the inconsistency of the relationship and how largely it disadvantages African-American school districts.

This lack of relationship between assessed values and retail values presents a basis to argue that education for African-American children in Alabama is inadequate and that it is unconstitutional at the federal level. Thus, the case would present a rather straightforward issue of measuring the language of the state constitution, the statutes that make the education finance distribution formula operate, and the test scores reflecting achievement of African-American children throughout the state.

In this scenario, the state would be forced to defend itself by asserting that the system was adequate, constitutional, and reflective of the values of the people via the state legislature. The state would further argue that the federal court should not have jurisdiction because no federal issues were involved. At this point, the plaintiffs would argue that the Alabama public schools were overwhelmingly African-American and the entire financial manner of funding public elementary and secondary schools leaves African-American children, *i.e.*, a suspect class, harmed and thus the issues belong in federal court. It must also be noted that to date, no claim has been made in federal court regarding adequacy of education. All such claims have been made in state courts under controlling state constitutional language.[54]

As the plaintiffs presented their case, they argued that the assessment limitations, as found within the state constitution, were racially motivated in harming minority children. Thus, the long and painful history of racial segregation, its motivations, and its results were presented at trial. Since the argument rests almost exclusively on the alleged fact that African-American children were harmed, this forced Alabama to make a unique and somewhat strange defense.

This defense, however, may prove to be ultimately successful for the state of Alabama. That is, it is virtually impossible to show that African-American children were harmed and White children were not harmed.

---

[54] *See* R. CRAIG WOOD, EDUCATIONAL FINANCE LAW: CONSTITUTIONAL CHALLENGES TO STATE AID PLANS-AN ANALYSIS OF STRATEGIES (3rd ed., 2007).

The relative harm may be difficult to measure as well. That is, the defendants would argue that if harm were to exist, it existed for all children, since the state does not have African-American school districts and White school districts.[55] If the plaintiffs could demonstrate that wealth neutrality was correlated with race their argument would be enhanced. Hence, if this claim were to demonstrate harm, it would be harmful to all. Adding to this claim, is the reality that society within a given state is not based on a simple diversity of African-American and White population. In reality, it is reflective of a highly complex and diverse population, going far beyond simply White or African-American or even simply that of race.

Most public school districts throughout the United States reflect diverse populations of children with a multitude of demographic backgrounds and many learning issues, *i.e.*, homelessness, migrant parents, special education needs, language and cultural barriers, as well as race and poverty.[56] Simply to argue race may prove to be difficult due to these realities and may be self-defeating in such an action.

The *Lynch* Opinion

Lynch is essentially a sequel to *KnightSims*. The 844-page court opinion[57] begins with a quote from the Declaration of Independence. Then in its opening overview, the court notes that both the *KnightSims* and *Lynch* cases "[i]mplicate the Nation's original sin, slavery, and its post-emancipation manifestations: segregation and oppression of African-Americans in virtually all aspects of their lives, but especially in educational opportunities."[58] The opinion recites the long history of slavery in the United States, the issues of the Civil War, and racial segregation cases throughout the history of the nation. The court spent considerable time examining the issues of race, slavery, and

---

[55] For more discussion of racial discrimination in public education *see, e.g.,* James Ryan, *Race Discrimination in Education: A Legal Perspective*, 105 TEACHERS COLL. RECORD 1087 (2003).

[56] Christy Lleras, *Race, Racial Concentration, and the Dynamics of Educational Inequality Across Urban and Suburban Schools*, 45 AM. EDUC. RES. J. 886 (2008); *see also* Kori J. Stroub & Meredith P. Richards, *From Resegregation to Reintegration: Trends in the Racial/Ethnic Segregation of Metropolitan Public Schools, 1993-2009*, 50 AM. EDUC. RES. J. 497 (2013).

[57] Additionally, this opinion included a lengthy table of contents.

[58] Lynch ex rel. Lynch v. Alabama, CV No. 08-S-450-NE at 1-2 (N.D. Ala. 2011), *available at* http://knightsims.com/pdf/11_10_25/Doc_294_opinion_on_merits_10-21-11.pdf.

discrimination in the Southern states, and particularly in the State of Alabama.[59]

The court specified that the case was, as the plaintiffs' claimed, about taxation--specifically, the State of Alabama's *ad valorem* property tax system.[60] This is perhaps a natural conclusion given the way the plaintiffs' complaint was presented. However, the court's view reflects the weaknesses of the claim as presented. In reality, it is a complaint concerning the revenue streams to fund public elementary and secondary education for all children, *i.e.*, a claim as to whether the system of financing public education produces a violation of the U.S. Constitution, being racially discriminatory because it results in an inequitable and inadequate system that harms African-American children throughout a given state.

The plaintiffs specifically argued that the state system of taxing property "is a vestige of discrimination inasmuch as the [State] constitutional provisions governing the taxation of property are traceable to, rooted in, and have their antecedents in an original segregative discriminatory policy."[61] The plaintiffs also claimed they were affected by "a set of Alabama constitutional provisions rooted in historic racially discriminatory policies and practices that directly create multiple barriers

---

[59] *Id.* at 5.

[60] *Id.* at 15. The court quoted H.H. Haden, *Equality–The Cornerstone of Democracy*, 21 ALA. LAW 269, 270-71 (1960) (emphasis found in *Lynch*), noting that *ad valorem* property taxes are: "[T]he oldest type tax that we know anything about. As far as history shows, there was no tax used earlier than the ad valorem property tax. I suppose that when the very first group organized into a unit of society and decided to have one police force to protect the property of all rather than to operate as they had in the past with each man protecting by force his own property, that the first question to arise was how the cost of this one police force would be met. I suppose that the obvious answer to this question was that the man with the most property would bear the greater portion of the cost, and the man with least property would bear the least portion of the cost. *This seems to be such an obvious and fair answer to this problem that it is amazing that today we have large groups of individuals denying openly that this would be a fair manner in which to divide the cost of government. This is the basic premise upon which the* ad valorem *property tax is built.* The words 'ad valorem' mean in Latin 'by value.' Ad valorem 'by value' property tax is the only kind of property tax we can have under the Alabama Constitution. In some states you can have a per specie property tax, but not in Alabama." The difficulty of the Haden analysis is the undeniable fact that present day *ad valorem* taxes pay for a variety of local services from streets, highways, bridges, hospitals, fire and police protection, public elementary and secondary education, and in some instances public utility companies. Thus, the example suffers from the fact that individuals, despite the value, or lack of value, of their property consume services and benefits independent of their property wealth.

[61] *Id.* at 18 (quoting Knight v. Alabama, 458 F. Supp. 2d 1273, 1311 (N.D. Ala. 2004)).

to the ability of black citizens to obtain school revenues through ad valorem taxes."[62] The challenged provisions of the Alabama Constitution are discussed above.[63]

The *Lynch* opinion spent considerable time examining the various elements of the Alabama property tax system. For example, the court noted that Amendment 373:

> [I]mposed variable caps (or "lids") on the *total* amount of *ad valorem* taxes that can be levied on a particular parcel of taxable property within one year by *all* taxing authorities: state, county, municipalities, *and* school districts *combined*. These absolute dollar limits are based upon the *appraised value* (estimated fair and reasonable market value) of the property–*not* its *assessed value*–and the sum of *all* property taxes levied by *all* taxing authorities may not exceed in any one year: 2% (0.02) of the fair market value of Class I property; 1.5% (0.015) of the fair market value of Class II property; 1% (0.01) of the fair market value of Class III property; and 1.25% (0.0125) of the fair market value of Class IV property. Thus, the computation of the absolute dollar limits on the aggregate amount of all *ad valorem* property taxes is made *before* applying the *assessment* ratio applicable to the class in which the property is grouped.[64]

In this selected passage, the court succinctly summarizes the constitutional requirements. The issue for the plaintiffs is demonstrating how these constitutional requirements harm African-American children. While there is clearly a lack of a relationship between the assessed valuations and the ability to raise local moneys for schools, the plaintiffs consistently fail to examine the relative harm to African-American children. The burden was on the plaintiffs to demonstrate the relative harm to African-American children due to these specific clauses found within the state constitution.

---

[62] *Id.* (quoting Doc. No. 31 (Plaintiffs' Brief in Opposition to Defendants' Motion to Dismiss, at 16).

[63] *See* ALA. CONST., *supra*, notes 12-16.

[64] Lynch ex rel. Lynch v. Alabama, CV No. 08-S-450-NE at 24-25 (N.D. Ala. 2011) (citations omitted), *available at* http://knightsims.com/pdf/11_10_25/Doc_294_opinion_on_merits_10-21-11.pdf.

Local Revenue Streams

Lynch is interesting because of its comparative implications. Virtually every state legislature controls, in some manner, the limitations on *ad valorem* taxes, particularly for public elementary and secondary education. Virtually every education finance distribution formula has mechanisms found within it that limit, or apply a range, to local boards of education and/or counties from levying property taxes in some manner. State statutes control some combination of the levy, the tax rate, and the manner that property is assessed. Why this is unique and harming only African-American students is not found within the plaintiffs' arguments. And yet, both the plaintiffs, and the court, seemed to find this limitation of assessed values to be of major importance. That is, testimony was presented that virtually every Alabama legislature has tended to protect agricultural interests. However, it was argued that Alabama differed significantly from other states in that Alabama applied this tax limitation concept statewide thus harming the more rural and specifically African-American demographic communities of the state.

For purposes of funding public education, state legislatures must have a uniform practice of assessing and classifying local property wealth in order to have an education finance distribution formula that operates in an efficient and equitable manner. Within the realm of financing public elementary and secondary education, it has always been an issue that some school districts are poorer than others. Virtually all state legislative education finance distribution formulas are designed to distribute more state moneys to those school districts that have less assessed valuations. The issue is not one of unfair assessments. Assuming the assessments ratios are reasonably uniform; it is an issue that the overall education finance distribution formula does not compensate to the extent that African-American children are harmed, in an inequitable and inadequate public school system, and thereby federal issues might be raised under the concept of disparate impact.[65]

At this point, the plaintiffs argued that they were injured by the Alabama system of property taxes because the constitutional language "impede[s] their ability and the ability of other elected representatives to raise state and local revenues adequately to fund the public services they need, including public education."[66] Again, the plaintiffs' arguments, as

---

[65] For an overview of the definitions and interpretations of racial discrimination over the years *see* Reva B. Siegel, *From Colorblindness to Antibalkanization: An Emerging Ground of Decision in Race Equality Cases*, 120 YALE L.J., 1278 (2011).

[66] Lynch ex rel. Lynch v. Alabama, CV No. 08-S-450-NE at 32 (N.D. Ala. 2011),

well as the state's response to them, are puzzling. The threshold issue is whether the counties and school districts throughout the state were at the maximum tax limitations as proscribed by the constitution and statutes. The court record seemed to indicate that the vast majority of counties and districts were not at the maximum limits.   The plaintiffs have to empirically demonstrate that the various counties and school districts were overwhelmingly at the maximum tax limitations and unable to deliver educational services within those revenue limits. It seems as if the parties did not conceptually understand how a public education finance distribution formula is designed and what it is supposed to accomplish as a public policy. That is, if every school district and/or county were allowed to levy and/or assess property taxes in any manner it chose to raise local revenues to a level it thought necessary to provide educational services to the local population the results would be inequitable. If the state did not equalize these revenues and expenditures, the state legislature could not fund its portion or taxpayers would face very unequal burdens of taxation.

Low Property Tax Revenues

The court observed that throughout the case the plaintiffs argued that "the effect of low property tax revenues has had a crippling effect on poor, majority black school districts."[67] The plaintiffs do not appear to grasp the education finance research concepts--the issue is not one of low property taxes, but one of alleged insufficient revenues to make up for these alleged deficiencies and how the state education finance formula has specifically harmed children along racial lines.

There is no evidence that school districts in the state of Alabama with fewer African-American students are advantaged in terms of revenues. The plaintiffs had the burden of demonstrating that access to total revenue existed along racial lines.   That is, if the overall education finance distribution formula were working properly, there should be no significant differences in revenue, or expenditure patterns, on a per-pupil basis across the state. Essentially, this is the issue that both parties and the court seem to have ignored throughout the process. The plaintiffs had to statistically demonstrate that African-American students were harmed at a greater rate due to the overall deficiencies of the available revenue streams, while predominately African-American school districts were at the maximum tax revenue capabilities.

---

available at http://knightsims.com/pdf/11_10_25/Doc_294_opinion_on_merits_10-21-11.pdf.

[67] *Id.* at 34 (citations omitted).

At this point, probative education finance distributive formula issues should have been raised and yet were never addressed in the court record. Assuming that the plaintiffs' claims are meritorious and there is an exceedingly low assessed valuation in predominately African-American populated school districts, how do the residents of these school districts benefit from raising their school district/county taxes? How does this remedy benefit the communities that supposedly reflect the poorest of society within a given state? The issue is one of state aid, and whether the overall education finance distribution formula measures the local ability to fund public education in order to provide an equitable and adequate education for all the children of the state. Thus, even if the plaintiffs' were to prevail, one has to question the remedy, *i.e.*, raising taxes on the very poorest of society. To argue that property values, whether assessed or retail, have no relation to actual wealth of the residents of a given school district could only be remedied by a state-wide property tax mechanism for the support of elementary and secondary education. A statewide legislative property tax mechanism would take into account any degree of absentee landlords as argued by the plaintiffs. Even if the plaintiffs' position were correct, the remedy sought was deeply flawed.

The Socio-Economic Status of Financing Public Education and the Remedy

There is no question within the education finance research literature that socio-economic status (SES) is the main predictor of success in schools. Thus, one wonders why the plaintiffs did not try to measure SES, and then argue the lack of achievement of low SES students throughout the state. The education finance research regarding SES, school expenditures, achievement, and how the formula affects different school districts is strangely absent in both parties' discussions. In this manner, SES becomes a proxy for race. The plaintiffs would actually measure SES, but constantly label it as a race, so as to demonstrate a disparate impact as these data across the state of Alabama may actually support this approach.

Plaintiffs clearly stated "the relevant question is not the distribution of school revenues among school systems in Alabama, but 'whether the six challenged constitutional provisions cause a substantial diminution of the amount of local school revenues available to residents and students in Sumter, Lawrence, and other similarly impacted counties and school systems.'"[68] This is another example of the plaintiffs' failure to challenge the overall education finance distribution formula. Plaintiffs' arguments were confined to two specified counties throughout the trial. Assuming the court was to rule on the plaintiffs' behalf, would the remedy simply be applied to the specified counties? Thus, it is assumed that this would result in the filing in numerous courts, as each jurisdiction would have to be judged as to be "similarly situated" as they were in *Lynch*. Since this would be a rather laborious process, no education finance distribution formula could operate with each local school district or county having a totally different manner of assessing valuations. If the local levy were to increase, in theory, barring any adjustment mechanism, state aid would decrease under a normally operating education finance distribution formula.

The plaintiffs argued that the *"[l]ack of adequate school revenues, especially at the local level, is the injury caused by the racial discrimination."*[69] Later, the plaintiffs' complaint stated that the state constitutional provisions were intended "to benefit white landowners and to make it more difficult to raise local school revenues for black students, particularly for those black students in the targeted Black Belt school systems."[70] Interestingly, the plaintiffs do not demonstrate, by way of empirical evidence, that only African-American students were affected by this claim. In fact, the plaintiffs do not demonstrate that any students are harmed by this claim. Ignoring this lack of any statistical proof and assuming the claims to be true, then the state constitutional limitations apply to all counties and school districts, and by definition, all students are affected and thus the entire state system would have to be determined to be inadequate as opposed to just an inadequate system for African-American students in two selected counties. The plaintiffs' claim should have centered on the fact African-American students, by way of the total revenue stream, suffered in the form of disparate impact within this educational system.

The defendants' arguments in opposition are summed by the court as follows:

---

[68] *Id.* at 37 (citations omitted).

[69] *Id.* at 40.

[70] *Id.* at 41 (citing Doc. No 280 Plaintiffs' Response to Defendants' Post-Trial Brief, at 78). The court spent considerable time examining the term, "Black Belt," and the historical aspects of the formation of the state, *see id.* at 45-60. The term "Black Belt" refers generally to the rich agricultural land within a section of the state in which the selected counties existed. On occasion, it is utilized to refer to this same general area but in reference to the area as largely African-American in population.

For the sake of introduction, however, and in only the most general of terms, the primary arguments defendants advance are that this court does not have jurisdiction, that plaintiffs have failed to prove that the challenged provisions were enacted with a discriminatory intent, that plaintiffs have failed to prove any discriminatory effect of the challenged provisions, and that plaintiffs have failed to prove a violation of Title VI.[71]

Lynch differs significantly from every education finance constitutional challenge to this point in time. Unlike many constitutional challenges to a state education finance distribution formula, *Lynch* presented a long and detailed discussion of the history of the state from the earliest days to more contemporary times.[72]

The court examined the issue of standing and subsequently ruled on behalf of the plaintiffs, adopting the reasoning that if the plaintiffs had to show actual causation then the merits of the case would have to be demonstrated before the actual trial, stating:

> It is true that "standing in no way depends on the merits of the plaintiff's [sic] contention that particular conduct is illegal." Nevertheless, standing, as previously noted, "often turns on the *nature* and *source* of the claim asserted." Essentially, the standing question in such cases is whether the constitutional or statutory provision on which the claim rests properly can be understood as granting persons in the plaintiff's [sic] position a right to judicial relief.[73]

The court upheld its own memorandum opinion regarding the applicability of the Tax Injunction Act of 1937. The court again rejected the defendants' interpretation of *Hibbs*.[74] Additionally, the court maintained its previous position in its memorandum opinion regarding comity.[75] Thus, the court ruled against the defendants on all of its three objections.

---

[71] *Id.* at 43.

[72] *See id.* at 45-95, in which the court examines the terms, "Black Belt" (45-82); "Big Mules" (82-86); "Carpetbaggers" (86-87); "Scalawags" (87-88); "Radical Republicans" (88); "Conservative Democrats" and "Bourbons" (89-91); "Black Codes" (91); "Redeemers" (91-93); and "Jim Crow Laws" (93-95).

[73] *Id.* at 96 (citations omitted).

[74] *Id.* at 111-12.

[75] *Id.* at 115.

The court also rejected the defendants' claim that Eleventh Amendment Immunity protected the state and its officers.[76] The court determined that *Fitts*[77] and *Young*[78] did not prevent this particular claim. The plaintiffs were asking for a declaration that the provisions of the constitution were unconstitutional and for a future injunction prohibiting the enforcement.[79]

The court took considerable effort to understand the revenue and expenditure variables within the education finance distribution formula. The court relied heavily on a number of Alabama education finance experts in this regard. The Alabama Legislature uses a form of a basic foundation system in which the state funds at a decreasing rate as local wealth increases. The court noted this in the following passage:

> The amount of revenue thus distributed by the State to local school systems on a *per capita* (per student) basis, as determined by the ADM, is *inversely proportional* to the amount of revenue the school system is able to raise in local sources for each pupil. *For example*, the Homewood school system, which raised $8,407.08 in local tax revenue for each student in 2009, received State Foundation funds in the amount of $3,833.16 per pupil, while the Linden school system, which raised only $2,291.98 per pupil in local tax revenues during the same year, received $8,263.34 per student from the State. Even though the total amount of local and State revenue received by Homewood ($12,240.24 per student) still exceeded the aggregate funding of the Linden school system ($10,555.32 per pupil) by $1,684.92, the disparity between the amount of revenue available for the education of public school students in the wealthy Birmingham suburb of Homewood *vis-a-vis* the less wealthy town of Linden was ameliorated by the Foundation Program.[80]

The court's example is problematic. Assuming the information is entirely correct, one does not quite know what it indicates. If the figures

---

[76] U.S. CONST. amend. XI ("The Judicial Power of the United States shall not be construed to extend to any suit in law or equity, commenced or prosecuted against one of the United States by Citizens of another State, or by citizens or Subjects of any Foreign State").

[77] Fitts v. McGhee, 172 U.S. 516 (1899).

[78] Ex Parte Young, 209 U.S. 123 (1908).

[79] Lynch ex rel. Lynch v. Alabama, CV No. 08-S-450-NE at 123-137 (N.D. Ala. 2011), *available at* http://knightsims.com/pdf/11_10_25/Doc_294_opinion_on_merits_10-21-11.pdf.

[80] *Id.* at 152-153 (citations omitted).

represent the overall spending pattern of the state, it is indeed problematic for the defendants. On the other hand, is the example a reflection of statistical outliers? These data appear to simply reflect the range. Thus, it is not particularly robust or informative as to the issues before the court. If the figures reflect serving students with special needs then the figure may, or may not, be acceptable. If, on the other hand, it is merely a figure without accounting for the needs of students, it is problematic for the defendants as well as the plaintiffs. If this illustration is representative, then one wonders why the plaintiffs did not pursue an equity and adequacy suit based on race. If the figure were not representative, why is it that the defendants did not illustrate the overall equity and adequacy of the state formula? Strangely absent is an examination of the equity and adequacy of the system and how this harms African-American students in a disparate manner. Given the nature of this almost anecdotal information presented to the court, one cannot empirically reach any conclusions. This single example cannot provide empirical evidence to indicate whether a state education finance formula is, or is not, in compliance with any constitutional standard.

The Conceptual Question of *Lynch*

Regardless of these questions, one conceptual issue remains unanswered within *Lynch*. Assuming that this illustration is indicative of the entire system of financing schools in the state, or even in the selected counties, how is it that raising *ad valorem* taxes in the poorest counties of the state, while state aid is still flowing to other school districts in the same state-wide pattern, will assist the plaintiffs fiscally, and more importantly, African-American children within the 'Black Belt' of the state?

Again, *Lynch* is an enigma in that none of the parties seemed to understand the measures and mechanisms of education finance research and how to actually demonstrate the effects of an education finance distribution formula. The court took note of numerous ways and mechanisms under the constitution and statutes by which Alabama counties could increase the present property tax levies while both parties stipulated that neither Sumter nor Lawrence Counties had levied all of the generally-authorized tax rates.[81]

The state of Alabama has had difficulty, from an economic and political perspective, regarding the issue of establishing the concept and

---

[81] *Id.* at 167. Interestingly, under the various mechanisms neither county had approved, via a referendum, the increase of property tax rates.

practice of aligning the appraised value to the retail value.[82] In any education finance distribution formula, wherein local wealth is a variable, the assessed valuations and retail prices should be closely aligned throughout the state in order for the formula to be equitable and adequate. Assuming the two figures are not closely aligned, which is often the case, the relationship between the two figures should be, at a minimum, consistent throughout the state. Absent this close relationship, or consistency, a legislature has to create adjustments/indexes for each school district so as to create a proxy for local wealth, in order for state fiscal aid to reach each school district, as it is intended and designed to fiscally assist the poorest school districts of the state. In some instances, state legislatures also have indexes that reflect "adjusted assessed valuations" taking into account over or under assessments of property as to the actual retail value of property for purposes of funding public education. As another variation, some state legislatures have tax rates that only apply to certain funds, *e.g.*, the general fund and not short-term capital outlay or maintenance of facilities.

Race and Complex Populations

Lynch examined an education finance distribution formula along racial lines. The reality is that poor individuals are both African-American and White throughout a given state. Depending upon the uniqueness of the state, they may be mostly rural, mostly urban, or some combination thereof. The plaintiffs failed to recognize the concept of complex populations that may have strengthened their arguments. However, in some ways, such an acknowledgment of complex populations concurrently diminishes their argument to the extent that it is more than simply an African-American versus White dichotomy, as they tended to present. Yet, the defendants do not utilize this fact either. The issue is one of the plaintiffs statistically demonstrating a disproportional impact. The court summed up several of these issues in the following passage:

> In the course of this action, there has been some disagreement and confusion regarding the meaning of what the Supreme Court has variously termed "racially disproportionate impact," "disproportionate effects along racial lines," racially "disparate impact," or racially "discriminatory effect." As plaintiffs correctly point out, this element of an equal protection claim does not entail

---

[82] *Id.* at 259-330 (discusses this history at length).

proof that *more blacks* than whites were adversely affected by the contested law, because such a requirement of proof would undermine the central minority-protective rationale for the Equal Protection Clause by setting an often-insurmountable evidentiary hurdle. Rather than requiring proof that *more blacks* than whites are adversely affected, the discriminatory effects requirement in a race-classification case under the Equal Protection Clause contemplates proof that *blacks are more affected* than are whites. In other words, racially motivated legislation violates the constitution only when it "affect[s] blacks differently than whites," or better stated, when the law disadvantages "*a greater proportion* of one race than of another."[83]

One of the major difficulties of the plaintiffs' case is its very nature of arguing that the various people over the course of history in Alabama were motivated in a particular way. In reality, the preponderance of the plaintiffs' contention is largely based on this historical legacy. In fact, this focus actually takes away from the core of the potentially successful data proofs that might have made for successful probative arguments. Regarding the historical legacy, the court quoted *United States v. O'Brien*:[84]

Inquiries into congressional motives or purposes are a hazardous matter. When the issue is simply the interpretation of legislation, the Court will look to statements by legislators for guidance as to the purpose of the legislature, because the benefit to sound decision-making in this circumstances is thought sufficient to risk the possibility of misreading Congress' purpose. It is entirely a different matter when we are asked to void a statute that is, under well-settled criteria, constitutional on its face, on the basis of what fewer than a handful of Congressmen said about it. *What motivates one legislator to make a speech about a statute is not necessarily what motivates scores of others to enact it, and the stakes are sufficiently high for us to eschew guesswork.*[85]

Lynch noted that the U.S. Supreme Court clarified "that there must exist a strong, direct, causal relationship between the racially-discriminatory intent motivating a facially-neutral statute, *and,* its

---

[83] *Id.* at 406-407 (citations omitted).
[84] United States v. O'Brien, 391 U.S. 367 (1968).
[85] *Id.* at 413, (quoting *O'Brien*, 391 U.S. at 383-384).

disproportionate effects upon the targeted population."[86] The court went on to note that the Supreme Court has stated that such an action is unconstitutional "under the Equal Protection Clause *only if that impact can be traced to a discriminatory purpose.*"[87] *Lynch* specifically rejected the plaintiffs' concept that "it is not necessary to show that modern-day legislators were aware of the history of discrimination."[88]

Demographic Data and Funding Education

Lynch reviewed the educational system of the state at length.[89] Of the 67 counties, 11 counties had a majority-African-American population. Of the 131 school systems, 36 of the districts reflected majority-African-American student enrollments.[90] In 2009, 16 of the state's 131 school systems were located in the "Black Belt."[91] Data reflected that ten districts had more than 90 percent African-American enrollment.[92]

Evidence showed that African-American residents had a significantly lower median household income per capita than White residents throughout the state. In 2006, it was estimated that approximately 30 percent of African-American residents lived below the poverty line while only approximately 12 percent of Whites did so.[93] For the 2007-08 school year, free and reduced price lunch counts reflected that every majority African-American school system exceeded the statewide mean.[94] Data reflected that within the "Black Belt," per-capita income for African-American citizens was $8,847 and White citizens reflected an amount of $18,189.[95]

As noted by the court, the distribution of "Class III" property *i.e.*, residential agricultural, timber, and historic properties, is assessed at the lowest ratio for the four classifications, (*i.e.*, 10 percent of the appraised value). Additionally, Class III property owners may elect to have the

---

[86] *Id.* at 419 (citing Freeman v. Pitts, 593 U.S. 467, 506 (1992) (emphasis in *Lynch*)).

[87] *Id.* (quoting Personnel Admin. of Mass. v. Feeney, 442 U.S 256, 272 (1979) (emphasis in *Lynch*)).

[88] Lynch ex rel. Lynch v. Alabama, CV No. 08-S-450-NE at 428 (N.D. Ala. 2011), *available at* http://knightsims.com/pdf/11_10_25/Doc_294_opinion_on_merits_10-21-11.pdf (citing Feeney, 442 U.S. at 274).

[89] An abundance of data was County based and analyzed in that more than one school district may exist within a County.

[90] *Id.* at 693.

[91] *Id.* at 694.

[92] *Id.* at 694.

[93] *Id.* at 695.

[94] *Id.* at 696.

[95] *Id.* at 696.

value for other proper determined as to its appraised or "current use."[96] However, the issue is not how the state appraises property. The issue is how the state education finance distribution formula accounts for such appraisals for the purposes of state aid. That is, if the formula were flawed, it lends itself to an equity and adequacy challenge to the overall education finance distribution formula as to how it affects African-American students.

The plaintiffs provided data indicating that White citizens within the "Black Belt" largely owned such property.[97] Again, data were presented based on counties and, in some instances, based on school districts. In all education finance distribution formula challenges, data are reflective of availability. However, it must be understood that when these data cannot be identified specifically by school district, many observations are weakened as to the applicability of how public schools are financed.

Data Analysis

The defendants' and plaintiffs' data analysis was quite limited in this Constitutional challenge. The plaintiffs argued the system was inequitable and yet only presented data limited to the mean,[98] the median,[99] correlation coefficients,[100] and the weighted averages. Neither the plaintiffs nor the defendants presented data regarding the range,[101] the restricted range,[102] the federal range ratio,[103] the variance,[104] the standard deviation,[105] or the coefficient of variation.[106] Perhaps these data would

---

[96] *Id.* at 698.

[97] *Id.* at 701.

[98] $\sum X_i \div N$, where $\sum$ is the sum of all districts; X_i is the value of a given variable in district I, and N is the number of districts.

[99] There is no one acceptable formula for computing the median, due to the nature of data examined. In education finance research, depending upon the type of data being examined, it is often the 50th percentile.

[100] Correlation coefficients generally measure the strength of a relationship between two variables. There are several different formulas depending upon the types of variables being measured. It does not explain why a relationship may or may not exist.

[101] Highest X_i – Lowest X_i, where: X_i is the variable considered in district i.

[102] X_i at 95th percentile – Xi at 5th percentile, where x_i is the variable considered in district i.

[103] Restricted Range $\div X_i$ at 5th percentile, where X_i is the revenue per pupil in district i.

[104] $\sum P_i (X_p – X_i)^2 \div \sum P_i$, where $\sum$ is the sum of pupils in all districts; P_i is the number of students in district I; X_p is the mean of some tested variable for all pupils, and X_i is the same variable in district i.

[105] $\sqrt{\sum P_i (X_p – X_i)^2} \div \sum P_i$, where the standard deviation is simply the square toot of the variance.

have enhanced the plaintiffs' arguments or the defendants' rebuttal more than simple observations regarding the mean and median. Even more revealing for the court's examination would have been an examination of the concept of wealth neutrality and tax yield as evidenced particularly by the McLoone Index[107] and the Gini Coefficient.[108]

These are examples of education finance research equity measures that will vary from state to state depending upon the availability of data and the nature of the education finance distribution formula. Additionally, resource accessibility can be measured in a number of ways including the plaintiffs' districts versus all districts and examining match pairs in terms of expenditures and access to revenues to meet state instructional mandates.

An illustration of the use of these concepts along racial lines would be the application of the McLoone Index. One could apply the McLoone Index with and without predominately African-American school districts to examine whether the mean differences reflected statistically significant difference between the two measures. Then, assuming a significant statistical difference, a t-test would be conducted to see if this were a function of random occurrence. Assuming the results did not indicate a random occurrence, the researchers could investigate what caused this difference. This example would have provided probative value for the court's consideration.

The plaintiffs' case was essentially flawed. By selecting certain school districts that anecdotally represented their claims, the plaintiffs lost any robustness in terms of education finance research design. If mostly African-American schools were indeed poor, then, in fact, race becomes a proxy for poverty. If the plaintiffs' contentions particularly applied along racial lines, the plaintiffs could perhaps demonstrate that African-American students were disproportionately affected by the Alabama education finance distribution formula. It is possible that these equity measures would indicate that the formula is perhaps not equalized, or adequate to meet state mandated standards, and that African-American students disproportionately do less well on these measures.[109] Thus, the

---

[106] $\sqrt{[\Sigma P_i (X_p - X_i)^2 \div \Sigma P_{i]} \div X_p}$, where X_p is the mean of some variable for all districts.

[107] $\Sigma(1...j) P_i X_i \div M_p \Sigma(1...j)P_i$, where j are below the median; Σ is the sum of pupils in all districts 1 to j; P_i is the number of pupils in district i; X_i is the expenditure per pupil in district i; and M_p is the median expenditure per pupil for all students.

[108] $\Sigma_i \Sigma_j P_i P_j (X_i - X_j) \div 2(\Sigma_i P_i)^2 X_p$, where Σ is the sum for all pupils in districts i and j; P_i is the number of pupils in district i; P_j is the number of pupils in district j; X_i is the expenditure per pupil in district i; X_j is the expenditure per pupil in district j; and X_p is the mean expenditure per pupil for all districts.

[109] *See, e.g.,* Nicola A. Alexander, *Race, Poverty, and the Student Curriculum:*

case would be, from an education finance research perspective, argued based on demonstrated facts and empirical evidence as opposed to merely statements of impressions. Conversely, the defendants, utilizing the same measures, could potentially refute these anecdotal attacks as lacking robustness and validity in any education finance research sense.

As discussed, this 844 plus page opinion, is absent the basic education finance measures of equity and fails to actually measure education finance adequacy[110] particularly as it operates along racial lines. Plaintiffs fail to demonstrate a sound substantive education finance research foundation upon which a Constitutional claim might be made.[111]

Thus, the data presented in *Lynch* were largely descriptive. While certainly informative, one cannot prove or disprove any substantive issue of finance and race regarding the funding of public elementary and secondary education within the state of Alabama. Again, it must be stressed, even if the system of collecting revenue were extremely flawed, the issue is not one of revenue, but one of how the education finance distribution formula accounts for this flaw and finances public education throughout the state and of disproportionate damage to African-American children.

In terms of adequacy, the plaintiffs demonstrated that each mill within the "Black Belt" yielded less money as compared to the select comparison groups of school districts. The issue is one of how the education finance distribution formula accounts for the differences making total revenues reasonably equal. The plaintiffs, as well as the defendants, could have conducted a robust adequacy study so as to inform the court as to the exact revenue and expenditure needs to meet any Alabama statutory standards regarding quality education.[112] Thus, copious arguments by both sides appear to be rather uninformative and lacking in probative value.

Implications for Standards Policy, 39 AM. EDUC. RES. J. 675, 693 (2002).

[110] Typically, the education finance research literature assumes that the plaintiffs conduct adequacy studies in order to show the shortcomings of the education finance distribution formula. However, it should be understood that such studies may be able to support a state legislature's position, *see, e.g.,* R. Craig Wood, et al., *Determining the Cost of Providing an Adequate Education in the State of Montana,* (2005), *available at* http://woodrolleand associates.com/; *see* R. Craig Wood, et al., *State of Rhode Island Education Adequacy Study: Final Report* (2007), *available at* http://woodrolleand associates.com/.

[111] This point is discussed at length regarding state constitutional issues in, R. Craig Wood, *Justiciability, Adequacy, Advocacy, and the 'American Dream,'* 98 KY. L.J., 739 (2009).

[112] *Id.* Wood discusses the issue of measurement of educational adequacy at length.

There are several ways to actually measure adequacy in public elementary and secondary education for the court's consideration.[113] State legislatures, as well as the parties in constitutional education finance distribution formula challenges have utilized these measures. Essentially, the following models are found within the public elementary and secondary education finance research literature. They are:

- Professional Judgment Model;
- Statistical Analysis Models;
- Evidence-Based Model; and
- Successful Schools Model.

The Professional Judgment Model is utilized in a variety of ways by various researchers. The most valid methodology of Professional Judgment is to conduct statewide surveys of building principals to statistically judge the professional opinion of this entire population. Thus, the Professional Judgment Model can develop numerous focus groups with "expert educators" to attempt to estimate the various financial adequacy levels for various prototype schools. The research protocols should be designed to withstand legal challenge in terms of validity. It has been the most widely utilized model used in attempts to establish the expenditures necessary to provide an adequate education. In many instances, the protocols have been modest and the results have been less than robust. Wood and Rolle specifically observed "that when expert educators attempt to determine the level of fiscal adequacy, it also becomes the major limitation of the method."[114] Specifically, these education finance researchers note that educators who will be receiving the services may be biased and overstate the requirements. The Professional Judgment Model would utilize the surveys of principals for examining prototype schools. These hypothetical prototype schools are based on state specific financial data and requirements. Different expert panels are constructed to represent various types of schools and districts ranging from largely poor districts to those districts that are high performing on statewide achievement tests.

---

[113] This discussion of adequacy is largely taken from, R. Craig Wood and R. Anthony Rolle, *Improving 'Adequacy' Concepts in Education Finance; A Heuristic Examination of the Professional Judgment Research Protocol*, 35 EDUC. CONSIDERATIONS 51 (2007). For a more detailed discussion of the various models including the strengths and weaknesses of each *see* Wood & Baker, *supra* note 43.

[114] *Improving 'Adequacy', supra* note 113, at 52.

Statistical Analysis Models create regression equations utilizing multiple variables to create a curve of best fit.[115] Briefly, stated, Statistical Analysis Models generally are used to:

- Estimate the quantities and qualities of educational resources associated with higher or improved educational outcomes (an education production function), and
- Estimate the costs associated with achieving a specific set of outcomes in different school districts serving different student populations (an education cost function).

The Evidence-Based Model is constructed around the concept of multiple educational strategies that are thought to be the most successful in maintaining and improving school performance. This model's protocol attempts to integrate a variety of proven effective strategies, *e.g.* class size reductions.

The Successful Schools Model is a process of examining the expenditures of schools deemed successful based on state assessments already in place. This model uses student outcome data regarding measures such as attendance, dropout rates, and test scores to identify a set of schools or school districts in a state that meets chosen accountability standards. Then to determine levels of expenditures, an average or some percentile of the expenditures of those schools or school district is generally considered adequate.[116]

The purpose of this brief discussion is to provide an overview of different strategies for measuring educational adequacy exhibited in the education finance research literature. Again, it must be noted that state legislatures, as well as litigant groups, have utilized some, or all, of these measures. Yet, the plaintiffs in *Lynch* argued that the manner and mechanism of raising revenues, at least in the identified school districts, is inadequate and is constitutionally invalid because it is based on race. However, nowhere in the record do the plaintiffs actually measure and demonstrate a level of inadequacy for the court to examine. Demonstrating the alleged level of inadequacy throughout the state by engaging in these models would have enhanced the plaintiffs' case. Had the plaintiffs engaged in all four of these models, they may have produced a range of expenditures that operationalized their statements in their complaint.

---

[115] *Id.*
[116] *Id.* at 53.

On the other hand, had the defendants engaged in these models, they might have been able to demonstrate that whatever inadequacies that might have been present were not along racial lines, were not a condition of the manner of raising local revenues, and were perhaps a function of local decision making by local school districts. Regardless, simply to argue inadequacy, absent actual education finance revenue and expenditure data or achievement data weakens both arguments and does not allow the court a sound basis to judge such claims on empirical grounds.

Tax Revenue

The opinion explained tax revenue and tax capacity as follows:

> Tax revenue is a measure of the actual amount of revenue generated by *ad valorem* property taxes in a particular tax jurisdiction. For purposes of this analysis, tax revenue is measured by school tax revenue at the county level and thus, accounts for all property taxes a county raised for schools. The measure is analyzed both per-capita and per-student. Tax revenue is a very different measuring tool from tax capacity, in that revenue is a measure of actual results, whereas capacity is a measure of potential. A measurement of tax revenue reflects the "extent to which [a jurisdiction's] capacity is *actually* being accessed by the counties and the school systems." Two variables impact the amount of tax revenue by a taxing jurisdiction: capacity and the millage rate imposed.[117]

This being the case, one has to question why the plaintiffs did not bring a claim against the counties and/or the school districts within the "Black Belt." The state would have argued that the Legislature, via the state education finance distribution formula, did not cause this problem. This is, in fact, a local issue regarding local officials who may have failed to meet the Constitutional mandates within their jurisdictions.

The court examined per pupil expenditures. Four categories of expenditures in terms of percentages above the mean and median were conducted for the analysis:

---

[117] Lynch ex rel. Lynch v. Alabama, CV No. 08-S-450-NE at 722 (N.D. Ala. 2011), *available at* http://knightsims.com/pdf/11_10_25/Doc_294_opinion_on_merits_10-21-11.pdf.

16 "Black Belt" School Systems;
40 Rural, Non-"Black Belt" County School Systems;
15 Urban County School Systems; and
60 City School Systems.

This analysis reveals that the "Black Belt" school systems fared better than all other school system types, except for the sixty city school districts, in terms of per-pupil expenditures. A comparison of the mean per student and local expenditures essentially showed the same results.[118]   Any examination of simple means, whether above or below, does not explain to the court, how the education finance distribution formula is constitutionally flawed or how minority children are harmed as a result.

The Usage of State Definitions of Achievement Standards and Expectations

An illustration of the total lack of education finance measurement in *Lynch* may be found in *Columbia Falls Elementary School District No. 6 v. Montana.*[119] Assuming the plaintiffs could have based race arguments along the following lines, as set forth in *Columbia Falls,* they could have operationalized their complaint along the racial composition of the school districts throughout the state.   Adjusting the specific standards, the following issues could have possibly been raised for the predominately African-American school districts in the poorest sections of the state:

1. Definition of a quality or adequate education for the entire state.
2. The number of school districts budgeting at the maximum authority.
3. Problems with accreditation standards in predominately African-American school districts.
4. Problems attracting and retaining teachers in predominately African-American school districts.
5. Elimination of educational programs in predominately African-American school districts.
6. Deterioration of educational facilities in predominately African-American school districts.

---

[118] *Id.* at 728-729.
[119] Columbia Falls Elem Sch. Dist. No. 6 v. State, No. BDV-2002-528, 2004 WL 844055 (D. Mont. 2004).

7. Increasing competition over general fund dollars between special education and general education funds in predominately African-American school districts.

8. Whether the funding provided by the state relates to the needs of providing a quality education in predominately African-American school districts.

9. Failure to have a study to determine the costs of providing a quality education for at-risk students who are predominately African-American.

10. Ability to provide a quality education to African-American students in predominately African-American school districts.

11. Implementation of the state education finance formula that disadvantages predominately African-Americans in predominately African-American school districts.

12. Provisions for at risk students who are disproportionately African-American in predominately African-American school districts.[120]

Had the plaintiffs utilized *Columbia Falls* type issues, they may have been able to demonstrate that the funding formula was disproportionately inequitable and inadequate for African-American students who go to school in predominately African-American school districts. Simply describing the medians and means for groups of school districts does not demonstrate inequity or inadequacy.

Plaintiff Scenarios

"What if" scenarios were conducted by plaintiffs' expert witness. In this methodology, various projections were made regarding what would happen if these properties were assessed with the state constitutional restrictions lifted. This was done in various ways. The court rejected the scenarios based on increased percentages and stated that per capita measures were a better indicator.[121]

---

[120] See the standards as articulated in Columbia Falls Elem Sch. Dist. No. 6 v. State, No. BDV-2002-528, 2004 WL 844055, at *3-4 (D. Mont. 2004). The standards as shown within this article are ones of a generalizable nature that would be demonstrated so as to prove, or disprove, by the parties the specific harm along racial lines within the predominately African-American school districts of the state. The author has modified the standards for purposes of illustration to the instant case.

[121] Lynch ex rel. Lynch v. Alabama, CV No. 08-S-450-NE at 741 (N.D. Ala. 2011), *available at* http://knightsims.com/pdf/11_10_25/Doc_294_opinion_on_merits_10-21-11.pdf.

As discussed, this approach assumed that if the constitutional provisions were lifted, then the local levy would increase in these selected school districts. If the local levy were to increase, the state aid would decrease in any normal foundation state aid distribution formula. The plaintiffs' view only seems logical if one assumes that state aid will, in fact, not decrease; but actually increase, which is the antithesis of a foundational formula. Specifically, the complaint only seems logical if absentee landlords pay the increased levy and the state aid remains constant, or does not decrease.[122] Even if state aid remains the same, it is only a matter of time before the state legislature would adjust the basis of the state aid distribution and decrease the amount in that the local school district would now be considered wealthier with greater ability to pay for public elementary and secondary education.

Uniform Assessment Rates

Next, the court examined the concept of uniform assessment ratios for all properties across the state. The concept of uniform assessment is a sound public policy component within any state education finance distribution formula. As previously discussed, adjustments must be incorporated within the formula in order to overcome this inherent and fundamental flaw for the education finance distribution formula to work as intended. Notwithstanding this observation, the fact of the matter is that the court correctly observed "applying a uniform assessment ratio to all properties would improve the condition of the Black Belt counties, but would not remove the current inequality among the remaining county groups, in terms of school tax revenues."[123] Obviously, those school districts with greater disparities between actual assessments and the retail value of property would benefit from any adjustments relative to other school districts if it were assumed that state aid would remain constant. However, as discussed herein, in a well-designed formula, the state aid would actually decrease, unless offset by vertical adjustments, recognizing special needs populations and other economic factors.

Based on plaintiffs' expert work, the court concluded:

---

[122] It must be noted that in "Reward for Effort" education finance distribution formulas the very poorest school districts tend never to be able to compete with the wealthiest because the school districts do not have the fundamental taxing ability of the wealthiest school districts.

[123] *Id.* at 734.

Statewide, the what-if analysis does not show a benefit to blacks as opposed to whites due to a change to a uniform assessment ratio *and* the abolition of the "current use" appraisal methodologies. Significantly, the four counties with almost half of Alabama's black population (49%) would see a *decrease* in their per-capita school tax base from 120.37% of the statewide mean before the change to 102.95% of the statewide mean after the change. The correlation coefficient for the percentage of a county's population that is black and the county's per-capita school tax revenue is currently statistically-insignificant at -0.07, and it would remain statistically insignificant at 0.00 after the hypothetical change.[124]

This observation reflects the limitations of correlation coefficients in the application to how public elementary and secondary education is financed. It is simply not a robust statistic that is informative as to what causes any relationship for a court's review.

The court determined that virtually every aspect of the 1901 Alabama Constitutional Convention was motivated by racially discriminatory intent. The court noted:

> The pervasive theme of the Convention's records is, unquestionably, that of adopting provisions to strip the franchise from virtually all black citizens--and, in the bargain, great numbers of those poor-white yeoman agrarians who had formed the economic and political base of the Populist revolt during the last decade of the nineteenth century. Even so, the records also clearly and convincingly establish that another objective of nearly equal importance to a large majority of the delegates was that of reaffirming those provisions of the 1875 Constitution suppressing the millage rates of *ad valorem* property taxes that could be devoted to the support of black education at public expense . . . Even so, plaintiffs do not challenge the 1901 Constitution it its entirety, nor the legitimacy of its ratification. Instead, the gravamen of their complaint focuses on the taxation provisions added to the basic document by amendments ratified more than seven decades after the alleged "ratification" of the 1901 charter.[125]

---

[124] *Id.* at 746-747.
[125] *Id.* at 750-751.

The court noted that it was bound to consider the actual motivation of the amendments:

> In other words, it must be shown that those amendments were drafted by their sponsors, adopted by the State Legislature, and ratified by the citizens *because of* their racially adverse effects. Further, that racially-discriminatory intent must have been a "substantial," or "motivating," factor in each step of the process. The racist, white supremacist intent of the delegates to the 1901 Constitutional Convention, most of whom were two generations in the grave by the decade between 1972 and 1982, cannot be imputed to be the persons who drafted, adopted, and ratified amendments 325 and 373 and the 1982 implementation statutes.[126] Stated differently, the precedent that controls this court's decision is a case of this nature creates a secular theology devoid of the doctrine of original sin.[127]

Thus, *Lynch* stressed that the plaintiffs had the burden of demonstrating that such a racially disproportionate effect had to exist within the present day.[128]

The court extensively analyzed the challenged provisions. The court reached the conclusion that the 1901 Constitutional provisions were enacted with racially discriminatory intent. However, the court found no evidence that the two amendments adopted in the 1970s were done so for racial reasons. In fact, the motivation was a reaction to protect property owners from higher taxes.

Obviously, the amendments at issue applied to the entire state. Yet, the plaintiffs consistently analyzed the constitutional provisions as applied to

---

[126] *Id.* at 751-752 (citing McLesky v. Kemp, 481 U.S. 279, 298 n. 20 ("[W]e cannot accept official actions taken long ago as evidence of current intent"); Johnson v. Governor of Fla., 405 F.3d 1214, 1219, 1225-26 (11th Cir. 2005) (en banc), *cert denied sub nom*; Johnson v. Bush, 546 U.S. 1015 (2005) (holding that, even assuming "racial discrimination may have motivated certain . . . provisions in Florida's 1968 constitution," a similar provision passed in 1968, without evidence of racially discriminatory motivation at that time, was unconstitutional).

[127] *Id.* at 752 (citing City of Mobile v. Bolden, 446 U.S. 55, 74 (1980) ("[P]ast discrimination cannot, in the manner of original sin, condemn government action that is not itself unlawful.") (Stewart J., plurality opinion) (superseded by statute in non-relevant part). *In dicta*, note 1863, "This cannon of constitutional jurisprudence is to be distinguished from the New Testament theology undergirding the most common offense in contemporary federal criminal law, conspiracy: *i.e., "Whenever two or more are gathered in Satan's name, therein lies a conspiracy."*

[128] *Id.* at 416.

the selected counties. The court correctly noted that the "Black Belt" counties were *different from* rather than representative of the state.[129] This point illustrates the issue that the plaintiffs did not understand how a challenge to the education finance distribution formula should be approached either conceptually or as to the analysis of educational finance data. Based on the education finance statistical analysis presented by the parties, a statewide analysis does not demonstrate that African-American citizens are impacted more than White citizens by the challenged provisions.[130] Specifically, the court noted:

> The *ad valorem* tax yield per-mill per-student is the most effective measure of the effects of the challenged provisions on local education funding, because its per-student measure ties it directly to the students among whom local education funds must be divided. Its yield per-mill measure cause it to show only the effects of statewide provisions on local tax revenues, and leaves out the effects of the particular millage rate chosen by a particular jurisdiction.[131]

In this type of constitutional claim, the plaintiffs have to statistically demonstrate a relationship between local wealth and expenditure patterns with low achievements of African-American students in a disproportionate manner. An education finance distribution formula should be wealth neutral, *i.e.*, local wealth should not have a statistical relationship to expenditures. The plaintiffs' conundrum is that the local tax rate is, to a high degree, reflective of local officials and their decisions. The issue is one of attempting to establish how this is a flaw of the education finance distribution formula or even the state constitution. Nonetheless, this demonstrates a lack of understanding of sound education finance research in order to operationalize the claim. The plaintiffs argued that in selected, low-wealth, predominately African-American communities, the seriously flawed property tax assessment system was racially motivated. A better strategy would have been that extreme poverty was not addressed within the education finance distribution formula, and that African-American students throughout the state were disproportionately harmed as a result of this inequitable and inadequate system of funding public education by virtue of being unable to meet state mandated student achievement standards.

---

[129] *Id.* at 778, (emphasis in *Lynch*).
[130] *Id.* at 779.
[131] *Id.* at 772-773.

In summation, the court stated that despite racist origins and the "massive resistance" after *Brown* the constitutional provisions challenged retained a relationship to the legitimate government interest in promoting education. The court stated:

> Plaintiffs have proven a disparity in funding among the State's public school systems, but not a disparity along racial lines. Faced with similar facts in *San Antonio Independent School District v. Rodriquez*,[132] the Supreme Court ruled that such a variation in funding is rationally related to the legitimate government interest in "permit[ting] and encourag[ing] a large measure of participation in and control of each district's schools at the local level." In sum, each of the challenged provisions, individually, is rationally related to a conceivable, legitimate governmental interest. Additionally, Alabama's school funding system, on the whole, bears a strong resemblance to that considered in *Rodriguez*. For these reasons, the court has no choice but to rule that the challenged provisions survive rational basis review and are, therefore, constitutional.[133]

The issues as determined by the U.S. Supreme Court in *Rodriguez*[134] were problematic for the plaintiffs. In fact, they seemed to use the terms almost interchangeably throughout their arguments. An examination of *Lynch* reveals a pattern by the plaintiffs of following the design of *Rodriquez* with the selection of certain "Black Belt" school districts. Thus, it appears that the plaintiffs did not fully understand how to design their complaint to show greater harm to African-American students throughout the state. This is a critical distinction as the plaintiffs, present data reflecting poverty throughout the instant case. Plaintiffs' own data reflect the intersection of race and poverty. Forcing strict judicial scrutiny is a difficult task. Plaintiffs in *Rodriquez,* as well as in *Lynch,* made the same argument, albeit unwittingly, that the injured class should be comprised of all students living in the selected poor school districts. By definition, the plaintiffs in *Lynch* argue against themselves. Based on

---

[132] San Antonio Indep. Sch. Dist. v. Rodriguez, 411 U.S. 1 (1972).
[133] Lynch ex rel. Lynch v. Alabama, CV No. 08-S-450-NE at 784-785 (N.D. Ala. 2011), *available at* http://knightsims.com/pdf/11_10_25/Doc_294_opinion_on_merits_10-21-11.pdf (citing R*odriquez*, 411 U.S at 49).
[134] *Rodriguez*, 411 U.S. 1. *See also* Plyer v. Doe, 457 U.S. 202 (1982); Kadrmas v. Dickinson Publ. Sch., 487 U.S. 450 (1988) for further federal court interpretations regarding public elementary and secondary education.

Rodriguez, the court once again, viewed "wealth discrimination as being limited to absolute deprivation rather than relative differences."[135]

Next, the court ruled regarding the plaintiffs' Title VI claim.[136] Having previously concluded that the plaintiffs failed to prevail on their Fourteenth Amendment claims, the court rejected these claims as well.[137] The court went on in its summation to state:

> Like it or not, Supreme Court precedent compels a conclusion that the property tax scheme embedded in Alabama's 1901 Constitution and subsequent amendments does not offend the Fourteenth Amendment's Equal Protection Clause. The inability of plaintiffs to prove both that the challenged constitutional provisions are the product of a racially-discriminatory intent, and that the provisions produce a racially-disproportionate effect, mandates the application of a 'rational basis' standard of judicial review . . . None of this is meant to say, however, that the court is satisfied as to either the *quality* or *equality* of public education in this State. Alabama continues to be plagued by an inadequately-funded public school system--one that hinders the upward mobility of her citizens, black and white alike, especially in rural counties . . . State powerbrokers perceive little benefit from investing in a quality *statewide* public school system, because the children of their most influential constituents are generally enrolled in exclusive suburban school systems, with large *local* tax bases, or in private schools. Many of those private schools sprouted following court-mandated integration. As demonstrated in this opinion, however, "white flight" to the suburbs or private schools has not *disproportionately* harmed blacks. Instead, it also punishes many white students who remain in the public school systems. The children of the rural poor, whether black or white, are left to struggle as best as they can in underfunded, dilapidated schools. Their resulting lack of an adequate education not only deprives

---

[135] Wood, *supra* note 30, at 539 (citing *Rodriquez* 411 U.S. at 20-22 (noting Griffin v. Illinois, 351 U.S. 12 (1956) (on transcripts) and Douglas v. California, 372 U.S. 353 (1963) (on hiring counsel)).

[136] 42 U.S.C. § 2000d, et seq. ("No person in the United States shall, on the ground of race, color, or national origin, be excluded from participation in, be denied the benefits of, or be subjected to discrimination under any program or activity receiving Federal financial assistance."

[137] Lynch ex rel. Lynch v. Alabama, CV No. 08-S-450-NE at 794 (N.D. Ala. 2011), *available at* http://knightsims.com/pdf/11_10_25/Doc_294_opinion_on_merits_10-21-11.pdf

those students of a fair opportunity to prepare themselves to compete in a global economy, but also deprives the State of fully-participating, well-educated adult citizens.[138]

On October 21, 2011, the U.S. District Court issued its opinion. The trial began on March 21 and ended April 10, 2011. After quoting the Declaration of Independence and Bob Dylan the court ruled on behalf of the defendants.[139] The court then issued a further opinion stating:

> After considering all the evidence and the arguments of counsel, the court concludes that plaintiffs have failed to meet their burden of demonstrating, by a preponderance of the evidence, that defendants have violated either the Equal Protection Clause of the Fourteen Amendment to the United States Constitution, or Title VI of the Civil Rights Act of 1964. Therefore . . . it is entered in favor of defendants on all claims.[140]

Plaintiffs' Appeal

As a result of this ruling, the plaintiffs appealed in a ninety-page brief. The appeal has several claims. Essentially, the appeal asked if the district court findings of fact regarding the intentional discrimination violated the Equal Protection Clause and Title VI. Further, the plaintiffs argued that the court erred in concluding that the plaintiffs failed to prove a constitutionally significant adverse impact on any suspect class.[141]

Specifically, the plaintiffs argued that the district court misapplied the controlling case law with its findings of fact when the court concluded that there was no racially discriminatory intent in the enactment of the two amendments in question.[142] Additionally, the plaintiffs argued on appeal that the district court erred in that it "applied the pattern-and-practice standard of *Rodriguez* to assess continuing adverse effects instead of the focused casual effects standard of *Hunter v. Underwood*."[143]

---

[138] *Id.* at 792-793.

[139] Lynch ex rel. Lynch v. Alabama, CV No. 08-S-450-NE at 1-2 (N.D. Ala. 2011) (citations omitted), *available at* http://www.knightsims.com/pdf/11_10_25/Doc_293_final_judgment.pdf..

[140] *Id.* at 1-2.

[141] Brief of Appellants India Lynch et al. at 2, Lynch ex rel. Lynch v. Alabama, No. 11-15464-BB (11th Cir. Dec. 20, 2011), *available at* http://www.knightsims.com/pdf/11_12_28/Lynch_appellants_brief_final.pdf.

[142] *Id.* at 48.

[143] *Id.* at 71; Hunter v. Underwood, 471 U.S. 222 (1985).

The plaintiffs argued that *Rodriquez* was not controlling because the plaintiffs did not question the entire state system of distributing funds by the specific issue of raising revenue in selected counties along racial lines. The difficulty of this logic is perplexing. Again, even in the appeal, the plaintiffs ignored the consequences to the overall education finance distribution formula. That is, if revenues were somehow raised in the selected counties, at some point, it would be offset by less state aid. Further, it is unclear how the formula is to operate with each county/school district setting an unlimited tax rate. If each county/school district were to set its own tax rate, the results would be that the wealthier counties/school districts could tax and be rewarded and the poorer counties/school districts would have difficulty in setting a tax rate that was comparable. Hence, the formula would have systemic operational difficulties.

According to the plaintiffs, the third major error was that the District Court erred in its conclusion that, standing alone, Sections 214-215-216, and 269 have no continuing adverse racial impact.[144]

The fourth complaint was the application of *Fordice* as "amendments 325 and 373 were enacted with the purpose and have the effect of perpetuating *de jure* segregation in the Black Belt."[145] This complaint is somewhat perplexing in that previous evidence showed these school districts to be overwhelmingly African-American, thus the issue of establishing *de jure* segregation is confusing.[146]

The defendants' brief of fifty-two pages agreed that the issues were straightforward.[147] The defendants stated that the state's property tax system has nothing to do with race and applied across the state to all counties and school districts. The state pointed out that each of the constitutional sections called for millage caps along with mechanisms to

---

[144] *Id.* at 77.

[145] *Id.* at 82.

[146] Interestingly, Brief of Amicus Curiae Alabama State University Board of Trustees, et al. at 4, Lynch ex rel. Lynch v. Alabama, No. 11-15464-BB (11th Cir. Dec. 30, 2011), *available at* http://www.knightsims.com/pdf/12_02_24/Amicus_brief_final_12-30-11.pdf, raises the point that the testimony of the local school superintendents seemed to be ignored by the District Court. Each school superintendent testified that nearly all the students in the districts were educationally at risk. However the *Amicus Curiae* brief did not speak to how the lack of local property revenue caused this fact or how if this revenue were increased how this condition would be curtailed.

[147] Appellee's/Cross-Appellants' Principal Brief, Lynch ex rel. Lynch v. Alabama, No. 11-15464-BB (11th Cir. Feb. 22, 2011), *available at* http://www.knightsims.com/pdf/12_02_24/Appellees-cross_appellants_brief_filed_02-22-12.pdf.

increase the millage rates.[148] The defendants claimed that many of the plaintiffs' arguments had been previously rejected in *Knight v. Alabama.*[149]

Additionally, the defendants argued that if the plaintiffs were to prevail, the tax system would be placed in disarray. Further, the state argued the plaintiffs had failed to establish that there "was a racially discriminatory effect."[150] Specifically, the defendants argued:

> The District Court conducted an exhaustive analysis of local jurisdictions' property tax "capacity" and concluded that "[f]or all measures of impact, black students or citizens statewide were equal to, above, or insignificantly below white students and citizens in terms of tax revenue and school funding." The plaintiffs do not dispute this finding. Before this court, they instead focus on a group of counties in the Alabama Black Belt which scored worse on a few measures of tax capacity than some other groupings of counties. But focusing on the plaintiffs' hand-selected group of counties is wholly at odds with the plaintiffs' litigating position below, not to mention sound principles of Equal Protection analysis.[151]

The Alabama Farmers Federation entered an *Amici Curiae* brief on behalf of the defendants. The *Amici Curiae* brief stated:

> Plaintiffs admit they are attempting to force a restructuring of the state's *ad valorem* property tax system so as to make the system produce more revenue for public schools, maintaining that their case is primarily one concerning "adequacy" of education funding and not the equality of it. But Plaintiffs presented no evidence to indicate that a favorable decision in federal court striking down the challenged constitutional provisions would in fact actually redress this alleged injury . . . On the merits, Plaintiffs cannot support their claims. Through a "guilt by association" argument, Plaintiffs effectively maintain that if the proponents of tax legislation can be found to have possessed personal racially discriminatory views on one subject, such as franchise, the legislative handiwork of those

---

[148] *Id.* at 4.
[149] *Id.* at 13.
[150] *Id.*
[151] *Id.* (citations omitted)

persons on other subjects, whether in regard to taxes or otherwise, must be similarly tainted.[152]

The defendants disputed each of the plaintiffs' claims and concluded that after its exhaustive analysis, the District Court's judgment revealed that the tax provisions in support of public education do not discriminate on the basis of race.[153]

The plaintiffs' response stated:

> The district court mistakenly thought the state constitutional provisions that were intended to restrict local school revenues going to the targeted black students in the Black Belt would not violate the Equal Protection Clause unless there was proof that the restrictions injured African-American students more than they injured white students statewide and injured African-American students in the Black belt counties more than they injured students in other rural counties . . . But the districts court's mistaken reliance on *Rodriguez* led it to demand proof that counties and school boards outside the Black Belt were less injured or were not equally inured by these provisions. The district court erroneously adopted the State's contention, repeated here on appeal, that the *Lynch* plaintiffs have suffered no particularized injury, because "the challenged provisions do not impose 'different injuries' on black students as compared to white students," and "they are affected no differently from any other child in Alabama's rural districts.'[154]

In summation, the plaintiffs argued that the District Court erred in its reliance on *Rodriguez,* and the historical issues created by the constitutional provisions regarding the property tax mechanisms, and that affected African-American students within the "Black Belt" section of Alabama.

---

[152] Brief for Alabama Farmers Federation and Alabama Forestry Foundation as Amici Curiae at 7-8, Lynch ex rel. Lynch v. Alabama, No. 11-15464-BB (11th Cir. Feb. 29, 2012), *available at* http://www.knightsims.com/pdf/12_03_23/AFF_Amicus_Brief.pdf.
[153] *Id.* at 49.
[154] Response and Reply Brief of Appellants/Cross-Appellees India Lynch et al. at 43, Lynch ex rel. Lynch v. Alabama, No. 11-15464-BB (11th Cir. Mar. 22, 2012) (citations omitted), *available at* http://www.knightsims.com/pdf/12_03_23/Lynch_reply_brief_filed_03-22-12.pdf. Lynch v. Alabama, , Nos. 11-15464-BB & 11-15789 at 43.

Appeal to the Eleventh Circuit

The United States Court of Appeals, Eleventh Circuit, heard oral arguments in December of 2012.[155] The Eleventh Circuit issued its opinion on January 10, 2014.[156] The Court of Appeals affirmed in part, and remanded with instructions to dismiss without prejudice in part for lack of standing. The Court of Appeals examined the issues in three parts. The court examined the issues of standing for the various claims, the Tax Injunction Act, the principles of comity and the merits of the claims. The court noted the complexity of the issues as well as the 800 pages plus decision of the district court. In ruling that the plaintiffs had standing, the Court of Appeals concluded "that impediments to public education funding arising from racially discriminatory state laws can constitute particularized and concrete injury for purposes of standing."[157] The court noted that "[a] more difficult question is whether this alleged injury is redressable through the relief sought."[158] The plaintiffs were asking for injunctive relief and thus burdened to demonstrate they would likely be able to resolve their inability to adequately raise revenue for public education.[159] The court determined that the remedy sought would not redress the asserted injury, "which at bottom is the inability of the plaintiffs and their elected officials to raise state and local revenue for public education."[160] On appeal the state had abandoned the position that taxes would increase and argued that local officials would have no ability to raise taxes to support public education. Again, as discussed herein, the actual formula and how local assessments factor in the amount of state aid was not examined nor presented to the court. Each side could have projected the actual costs to the state and local school districts, at various points, as opposed to speculating as to the impact of the changes. Additionally, the court noted that the specific school districts in question were not at the maximum tax millage and thus the elimination of millage caps would "not likely redress the plaintiffs' injury."[161] Thus, plaintiffs lacked standing to challenge the millage cap provisions.

---

[155] Lynch ex rel. v. Alabama, No. 11-15464-BB (11th Cir. 2012).

[156] I.L. v. Alabama, 739 F.3d 1273 (11th Cir. 2014).

[157] *Id.* at 1278-1279, (citing Petrella v. Brownback, 697 F.3d 1285 (10th Cir. 2012); Heckler v. Mathews, 465 U.S. 728 (1984); Common Cause/Ga. v. Billups, 554 F.3d 1340 (11th Cir. 2009); *cf.* United States v. Hays, 515 U.S. 737 (1995); Allen v. Wright, 468 U.S. 737 (1984)).

[158] *Id.*, at 1279.

[159] *Id.*

[160] *Id.* at 1280.

[161] *Id.* at 1281.

The state of Alabama argued that the Tax Injunction Act prevented the district court from ruling on this specific question.[162]   The Court of Appeals guided by *Hibbs*[163] agreed with the district court that the Act did not bar such a review. The Court of Appeals stated:

> This appeal presents us with our first opportunity to apply *Hibbs* in a published decision.   The district court concluded, based on *Hibbs*, that the Tax Injunction Act did not divest it of jurisdiction because "[t]he undisputed, direct effect of the requested injunction would be to increase property tax revenue."   In reaching this conclusion, the district court relied in part on Alabama's own concession that the requested injunction would lead to significant increases in property taxes, potentially as high as 1,000%.   On appeal, the State has changed its jurisdictional tune, and now argues that "prohibiting enforcement of [its] property-valuation scheme . . . could take a . . . detrimental toll on public revenue collections" because "tax officials in all jurisdictions may well be powerless to issue property valuations," and "without valid property valuations, they would be powerless to collect any property tax at all."   Alabama's newly-minted factual maybes, however, do not require reversal of the district court's jurisdictional ruling as to the Tax Injunction Act.[164]

The court went on to observe "[t]he State's new position that tax revenues *might* decrease is not based on any record evidence."[165]   This discussion by the Court of Appeals underlines the nature and methodology of both the plaintiffs and defendant throughout the issue, *i.e.*, the lack of an education finance methodological approach to proving or disproving the claims. The court went on to state that the Tax Injunction Act does not bar the plaintiffs' challenges. Relying on *Hibbs*, the court stated:

> As the Supreme Court explained in *Levin*, "*Hibbs* held that the TIA d[oes] not preclude a federal challenge by a third part who object[s] to a tax credit received by others, but in no way object[s]

---

[162] *Id.* at 1283. 28 U.S.C. § 1341, states: "The district courts shall not enjoin, suspend or restrain the assessment, levy or collection of any tax under State law where a plain, speedy and efficient remedy may be had in the courts of each state."
[163] Hibbs v. Winn, 542 U.S. 88 (2004).
[164] *Id.* at 1283-1284 (citations omitted).
[165] *Id.* at 1284.

to her own liability under any revenue-raising tax provisions." That is precisely the case here.[166]

The state of Alabama had asserted the doctrine of comity as a threshold defense.[167] The Court of Appeals stated the following in rejecting this defense:

> We need not express any view on Alabama's comity argument. During oral argument, counsel for the State told us the following: "[E]ven if the court is persuaded by comity, we would especially ask [you], in light of the expense the State has gone to, to reach the merits and affirm." Upon further questioning by the panel, counsel indicated that Alabama preferred not to prevail on comity grounds alone because such a ruling would presumably invite (or at least permit) state-court litigation of the same issues. We construe these statements by counsel as a request by Alabama to abandon its comity argument on appeal. Because comity is not jurisdictional in nature, the State is free to withdraw the comity argument, and we grant its request to do so.[168]

At this point, the Court of Appeals turned to the only remaining issue, that of the manner of property tax classifications. The Court of Appeals noted that the district court had acknowledged Alabama's long history of racial discrimination and the district court acknowledged Alabama's "racist past . . . cast long shadows."[169] However, these property tax classifications were financially, not racially, motivated by public reactions to increase property tax assessments.

In summation, the Court of Appeals stated:

> Here, because the requested remedy would not redress the alleged injury, the plaintiffs lack standing to challenge the constitutional millage cap provisions despite the district court's finding that they were enacted with discriminatory intent. The plaintiffs' challenges to these provisions are therefore dismissed without prejudice. The plaintiffs' challenges to the State's property classifications system . . . are not similarly barred, yet these claims fail because we cannot say that the district court clearly erred in finding that

---

[166] *Id.* at 1285.
[167] *Id.* at 1285.
[168] *Id.* at 1285 (citations omitted).
[169] *Id.* at 1275.

this system was not the product of invidious discriminatory intent. Although the evidence presented could have supported a finding of discriminatory intent, sufficient evidence also rendered permissible the district court's finding that these Amendments were financially, and not discriminatorily, motivated. Under clear-error review, we are not free to second-guess the district court's choice between two permissible views of the evidence. Accordingly, we affirm in part as to the claims related to Amendments 325 and 373 to Section 217, and vacate and remand in part with instructions to dismiss, without prejudice, the claims related to Sections 214, 215, and 216 of Articles XI and Section 269 of Article XIV.[170]

The Court of Appeals noted this overall observation of the highly complicated and far-reaching issue of funding public education:

In deciding this difficult appeal, we are cognizant of Alabama's deep and troubled history of racial discrimination, and given the evidence at trial, we share in the district court's concern regarding Alabama's public education system: Alabama continues to be plagued by an inadequately funded public school system–one that hinders the upward mobility of her citizens, black and white alike, especially in rural counties . . . [As a result,] [t]he children of the rural poor, whether black or white, are left to struggle as best as they can in underfunded, dilapidated schools. Courts, however, are not always able to provide relief, no matter how noble the cause.[171]

Conclusion

Lynch presents a long and difficult course of action for all the parties regarding the funding of education in the state of Alabama. The issues reflect the political, social, and economic tensions of a present day society that is reflective of decisions made many years ago within a relatively poor state. The issues of *KnightSims* resulted in its attempted application to gain greater revenues for the financing of public elementary and secondary education within the state.

The future of *Lynch* is obviously uncertain. It could end on this appeal or it could conceivably make its way to the United States Supreme Court. As discussed within this paper, the plaintiffs have yet to empirically demonstrate that the Alabama education finance distribution formula is

---

[170] *Id.* at 1288.
[171] *Id.* (citing Defendant's Exhibit 296-1 at 797-98).

inequitable or inadequate and that it disproportionately harms African-American children throughout the state of Alabama.

This article does not offer an opinion regarding the current system of financing public elementary and secondary education in the state of Alabama. Specifically, this article does not offer an empirical opinion as to whether the system of financing public education within the state of Alabama is equitable and/or adequate or whether African-American children are harmed by the state education finance distribution formula. However, this article does reflect that the specific issues raised by the plaintiffs in *Lynch* are problematic, as well as the understanding of the defendants and the court. It is conceivable, as discussed within this analysis, that cases based on a set of circumstances, within a given state, could present a successful challenge if done so as discussed herein. Just as conceivable state defendants could mount a successful defense, as discussed herein, in the same manner. Until such challenges to a state education finance distribution formula are based on empirical research and education finance research literature, the cases will continue to be largely based on discussions that offer little assistance to the courts in determining the actual effects of such education finance distribution formulas on selected segments of society.

Teacher Evaluation: Principal Perceptions of the Barriers to Dismissal
Research, Policy, and Practice

Vincent J. Connelly, Ed. D.
Todd A. DeMitchell, Ed. D.
Douglas Gagnon, ABD (Ph. D.)[*]

The U.S. Supreme Court in 1952 asserted "that school authorities have the right and the duty to screen the officials, teachers, and employees as to their fitness to maintain the integrity of schools as a part of ordered society cannot be doubted."[1] Some 60 years later we are revisiting that duty with a renewed zeal for accountability in the classroom. Susan Moore Johnson summed up the importance of this duty when she asserted, "Who teaches matters."[2] Teachers stand at the crossroads of education. It is chiefly through their efforts that the goals of education are achieved or thwarted. If teachers matter, then the policies and practices that structure their recruitment, selection, and retention matter.[3] However, as critical as the

---

[*] Vincent J. Connelly is an Associate Professor in the Education Department at the University of New Hampshire; Todd A. DeMitchell is a Professor in the Education Department & the Justice Studies Program at the University of New Hampshire; and Douglas Gagnon is a Research Assistant in the Carsey Institute at the University of New Hampshire.

[1] Adler v. Bd. of Educ., 342 U.S. 485, 493 (1952).

[2] SUSAN MOORE JOHNSON, TEACHERS AT WORK: ACHIEVING SUCCESS IN OUR SCHOOLS xii (1990). *See also*, Elizabeth A. City, *Leadership in Challenging Times*, 70 EDUC. LEADERSHIP 11 (2013) ("People are the most precious resource in a school.") *id.*

[3] Issuance and control of educator certificates by state departments of education are an important part of the policies that structure employment as a public school educator. Conduct, as an example of character, prior to being issued a credential is one important gateway to teaching. For example, in Landers v. Arkansas Dept. of Educ., 374 S.W.3d 795, 796 (Ark. App. 2010), a teacher applicant was denied a teaching credential for having pled nolo contender for theft of property, a Class B felony. State law designated 33 disqualifying criminal offenses, one of which is theft of property, *id.* Even though the teacher's record was expunged, the State Department of Education could properly use the expunged felony conviction in deciding whether to issue a teacher certificate. Furthermore, a state board of education can suspend or revoke a teaching credential. The Ohio State Board of Education suspended the teaching certificate of Craig Robinson, a highly respected, 21-year veteran high school science teacher, for conduct unbecoming a teacher (Robinson v. Ohio Dept. of Educ., 971 N.E.2d 977, 979 (Ohio App. 2 Dist.

classroom teacher is to the core mission of the school, minimal attention up to now "has been given to the subset of teachers whose performance is marginal or incompetent."[4]

This research is divided into four parts. Part one focuses on the importance of the classroom teacher to student outcomes. In part two the emphasis on teacher evaluation will be explored. Part three reviews the role and perceptions of principals on the evaluation of teacher performance using data from the 2007-2008 administration of the *Public School Principal Questionnaire of the Schools and Staffing Survey* (National Center on Education Statistics, 2010). This nationally representative survey is administered by the National Center for Educational Statistics (NCES). Approximately 7,500 principals responded to the survey. In part four conclusions will be drawn for future practice and policy making.

Importance of the Classroom Teacher

Teachers occupy the pivotal position in the school. They provide instruction, structure learning activities, and assess the work of students. All other activities at the school are primarily designed to support, augment, and extend the primacy of the essential teacher-student instructional interaction. Consequently, "quality teaching plays a major, if not the most important, role in shaping students' academic performance."[5] Therefore, what teachers do in their classrooms is central to the effectiveness of the state's system of public education as well as in private education. Current research consistently finds that the quality of the teacher is one of the most important determinants of a student's academic success.[6] For example, Hanuschek states: "First, teachers are very

---

2012)). Robinson received and viewed during his planning an email containing four pictures, one of which showed the front view of a totally nude female. He shared the pictures with a teacher later in the day during class time with students present, although they did not see the pictures, *id*, at 980. The one-year suspension of his credential was upheld. *See also* Rush v. Bd. of Educ. of Crete-Monee, 245 Ill. Dec. 202, 203 (Ill. App. 3 Dist. 2000) (teaching certificate of a teacher of small engines classes was suspended for allowing students to trade detention for shocks from a small engine).

[4] Pamela D. Tucker, *Lake Wobegon: Where All Teachers Are Competent (Or, Have We Come to Terms with the Problem of Incompetent Teachers?)*, 11 J. PERS. EVAL. EDUC. 103 (1997).

[5] Jian Wang, Emily Lin, Elizabeth Spalding, Cari L. Klecka, & Sanra J. Odell, *Quality Teaching and Teacher Education: A Kaleidoscope of Notions*, 62 J. TCHR. EDUC. 331 (2011).

[6] *See* PATRICIA H. HINCHEY, NAT'L EDUC. POL'Y CTR., GETTING TEACHER ASSESSMENT RIGHT: WHAT POLICYMAKERS CAN LEARN FROM RESEARCHERS (2010).

important; no other measured aspect of schools is nearly as important in determining student achievement."[7]   And Rice concludes: "Teacher quality matters.   In fact, it is the most important school-related factor influencing student achievement."[8]   Consequently, the decision of whom to place in front of students in a classroom, how to assist that teacher to reach higher levels of excellence, when and how to identify deficiencies, and when to dismiss are critical decisions.

A classroom educator's decisions are directed at assisting and guiding their students to meet and exceed the learning outcomes--educational, social, and personal--established by the School Board.   In their study of effective and ineffective classroom practices, educational researchers Strong, Ward, and Grant found that the dimensions of teacher effectiveness included instructional delivery, student assessment, establishing a suitable learning environment, and the possession of personal characters such as fairness, respect,[9] and enthusiasm.[10]   The teacher stands at the crossroads of a student's education.   Therefore, excellence in schools is directly related to the performance of teachers acting in concert and individually.

Teacher Evaluation and the Principal

Principals and Evaluation

Principals are responsible for the school.   They manage resources, guide and develop programs, coordinate internal and external activities, communicate with constituencies, lead teachers and staff, and are held accountable for the smooth, effective functioning of all activities.   They are instructional leaders and often the school law leaders of the school.[11] Their responsibilities involve the sometimes conflicting roles of

---

[7] ERIC HANUSHEK, NAT'L CTR. FOR ANALYSIS OF LONGITUDINAL DATA IN EDUC. RESEARCH, THE ECONOMIC VALUE OF HIGHER TEACHER QUALITY 3 (2010).

[8] JENNIFER K. RICE, TEACHER QUALITY: UNDERSTANDING THE EFFECTIVENESS OF TEACHER ATTRIBUTES (2003), *available at* http://www.epi.org/publications/entry/books_teacher_quality_execsum_intro/#ExecSum.

[9] *See* Timpani v. Lakeside Sch. Dist., 386 S.W.3d 588, 597 (Ark. App. 2011) (terminating, in part, a tenured teacher for her remarks to the superintendent and principal that were "rude, disrespectful, and argumentative.").

[10] James H. Strong, Thomas J. Ward, & Leslie W. Grant, *What Makes Good Teachers Good? A Cross-Case Analysis of the Connection Between Teacher Effectiveness and Student Achievement*, 62 J. TCHR. EDUC. 339, 340-342 (2011).

[11] For an excellent discussion of principals as school law leaders, *see* DAVID M. SCHIMMEL, SUZANNE E. ECKES & MATTHEW C. MILITELLO, PRINCIPALS TEACHING THE LAW: 10 LEGAL LESSONS YOUR TEACHERS MUST KNOW (2010).

supporting and evaluating teachers.   DiPaola and Hoy note that "[a]lthough principals may be supportive and helpful to teachers, they also have the burden of making organizational decisions about competence."[12] As discussed above, their evaluation of the competence of teachers is critical because the role of teachers in the delivery of instruction and the establishment of the learning climate for students are the core activities and responsibilities of the school.

Jacob and Lefgren characterize the data that principals receive regarding a teacher's performance as "noisy signals." These signals, or data, included formal and informal observations, reports from parents, and student achievement scores.[13]   A principal's level of success in teacher supervision and evaluation depends in part on the level of sophistication with which data is collected and interpreted, his or her investment in time and energy in gathering the information, and his or her beliefs about the efficacy of a particular teacher.[14]   The researchers studied the effectiveness of principals in distinguishing high and low performing teachers.   They conclude "[p]rincipals are generally effective at identifying the very best and worst teachers. On average, however, they are not able to distinguish teachers in the middle of the achievement distribution."[15]

The evaluation of teachers calls for transparent, rigorous, and fair systems. The Joint Committee on Standards for Educational Evaluation[16] developed four standards (Propriety, Utility, Feasibility, and Accuracy)[17] that should guide evaluations. A review of teacher evaluation systems in California conducted by Stanford University stated that an "overarching principle" for evaluation must be "the improvement of teaching and

---

[12] MICHAEL F. DIPAOLA & WAYNE K. HOY, PRINCIPALS IMPROVING INSTRUCTION: SUPERVISION, EVALUATION, AND PROFESSIONAL DEVELOPMENT 24 (2008), stating "[t]he principal is responsible for the removal of incompetent, ineffective teachers from the profession." *Id.* at 165.

[13] Brain A. Jacob & Lars Lefgren, *Can Principals Identify Effective Teachers? Evidence on Subjective Evaluation in Education*, 26 J. LABOR ECON. 101, 105 (2008).

[14] *Id.*

[15] *Id.* at 129.

[16] JOINT COMMITTEE ON STANDARDS FOR EDUCATIONAL EVALUATION, THE PERSONNEL EVALUATION STANDARDS (1988), *available at* http://www.jcsee.org/personnel-evaluation-standards.

[17] *See* Daniel L. Stufflebeam & Diana Pullin, *Achieving Legal Viability in Personnel Evaluations*, 11 J. PERS. EVAL. EDUC. 215, 217 (1998) (Developing a draft standard on legal viability to be included in the Personnel Evaluation Standards: "Legal viability of an evaluation means that the evaluator can successfully address pertinent legal issues and avoid debilitating legal difficulties in the course of carrying out an ethical personnel evaluation and applying its results.").

promotion of better learning."[18]   Price argues, "Principals are central figures in schools whose actions directly shape their schools' climate."[19] Jacob states that principals primarily influence student performance by the faculty composition in their building through hiring and firing teachers.[20] Principal evaluations have long been the primary means by which teachers are supervised. Because principals are central to teacher evaluation, their role in the evaluation system is critical. Mayor Michael R. Bloomberg of New York City, discussing teacher evaluations on a radio talk show stated, "The principals' job is to decide who's good, who's bad.   It's their judgment, that's their job."[21]

"The most effective principals influence student performance through recruitment and retention of effective teachers," Jacob writes.[22] In his study of Chicago principals, he found that prior poor evaluations and frequent absences were two of the factors that were present in the dismissal of teachers.[23] The influence of prior evaluations on dismissal decisions is intuitive with empirical evidence from this study confirming the importance of evaluations. This also indicates that dismissal for incompetence is typically not a single evaluation event, but a pattern of behavior. Data gathering and analysis takes time to correctly identify the deficiency in order to provide a remediation plan. While teacher supervision and evaluation are important, they are just two of the challenges associated with leading a school that is generally larger than most businesses and often more complex. Demands on a principal often

---

[18] ACCOMPLISHED CALIFORNIA TEACHERS, NAT'L. BD.. RESOURCE CTR., A QUALITY TEACHER IN EVERY CLASSROOM: CREATING A TEACHER EVALUATION SYSTEM THAT WORKS FOR CALIFORNIA 13 (2010), *available at* http://nbrc.stanford.edu/act/reports/a-quality-teacher-in-every-classroom.html.

[19] Heather E. Price, *Principal—Teacher Interactions: How Affective Relationships Shape Principal and Teacher Attitudes*, 48 EDUC. ADMIN. Q. 39, 40 (2012). *See also* GREGORY F. BRANCH, ERIC A. HANUSHEK, & STEVEN G. RIVKIN, NAT'L CTR. FOR ANALYSIS OF LONGITUDINAL DATA IN EDUC. RES. (CALDER), ESTIMATING THE EFFECT OF LEADERS ON PUBLIC SECTOR PRODUCTIVITY: THE CASE OF SCHOOL PRINCIPALS 3 (Jan. 2012) (writing, "The leadership and decision-making provided by a school principal is proximate and tied directly to outcomes in her school, unlike that of a superintendent of a large district who operates more like a CEO in terms of providing broad policy guidance.").

[20] Brian A. Jacob, *Do Principals Fire the Worst Teachers?* 33 EDUC. EVAL. & POL'Y ANALYSIS 403, 406 (2011).

[21] Colin Campbell, *Bloomberg: Principals Should Remain in Full Control of Teacher Evaluations,* POLITICKER 1 (Jan. 6, 2012), *available at* http://www.politicker.com/2012/01/06/bloomberg-opposes-independent-commission-evaluating-teachers/.

[22] Jacob, *supra* note 20, at 404.

[23] *Id.* at 429.

exceed what the average line supervisor faces on a daily basis.[24]

Evaluation Systems: A Grade of "Needs Improvement"

The importance of the teacher to education and the need to place and keep quality teachers in the classroom is clear. As Rossow and Tate recognized: "Since the beginning of formal public education in America, teachers have been evaluated in some way or another by school authorities."[25] Given the high-stakes environment and evolving policy,[26] staffing classrooms with highly qualified teachers "is a critical national concern."[27] Consequently, the manner in which teachers are developed, evaluated, and dismissed is currently being re-examined. For example, a study of mid-career math teachers who had not been evaluated systematically in the Cincinnati Public Schools, found the teachers to be "more productive during the school year when they are evaluated, but even more productive in the years after evaluation."[28] Thus, this study strongly suggests that teacher productivity can be influenced by performance evaluation.[29]

---

[24] For example, "Very few managers in business and other professions are charged with supervising the work of so many employees, let alone taking charge of facilities, public relations, professional development, and miscellaneous tasks such as lunchroom supervision or chaperoning school dances (Accomplished California Teachers, *supra* note 18 at 3); Rick DuFour & Mike Mattos, *How Do Principals Really Improve Schools*, 70 EDUC. LEADERSHIP 34, 36 (2013) (recognizing the "crushing demands on the contemporary principal" which requires attention to at least 21 different demands principals must address.). *See also* Richard Vacca, Senior Fellow, Commonwealth Education Policy Institute, who asserts that the accountability movement may make principals more at risk than teachers (COMMONWEATH EDUC. POL'Y INST., *Principal Accountability and Student Achievement* (2012), *available at* http://www.cepi.vcu.edu/newsletter/2011-2012/2012-March-Principal-Accountability-Student-Academic-Achievement.html.).

[25] LAWRENCE F. ROSSOW & JAMES O. TATE, THE LAW OF TEACHER EVALUATION 1 (2d ed. 2003).

[26] *See* Regina Umpstead, Ben Pogodzinski, & Douglas Lund, *An Analysis of State Teacher Evaluation Laws Enacted in Response to the Federal Race to the Top Initiative*, 286 EDUC. LAW REP. 795 (2013) ("Recent reforms in the educational policy arena have sparked significant changes in public school teacher evaluation systems around the country.")

[27] Marco A. Munoz & Florence C. Chang, *The Elusive Relationship Between Teacher Characteristics and Student Academic Growth: A Longitudinal Multilevel Model for Change*, 20 J. PERS. EVAL. EDUC. 147 (2007).

[28] Eric S. Taylor & John H. Tyler, *The Effect of Evaluation on Teacher Performance*, 102 AM. ECON. REV. 3628 (2012).

[29] *Id.* at 3647. ("The estimates presented here provide evidence that subjective evaluation can spur growth in human capital that improves employee performance even after the evaluation period ends.") *Id.* at 3649.

However, a 2010 *Briefing Paper from the Economic Policy Institute* characterized schools as doing a "poor job of systematically developing and evaluating teachers."[30] The *New Teacher Project* considers the current system of teacher evaluation broken, calling it the "Widget Effect" in which all teachers are essentially the same--a collection of widgets.[31] A study by Pamela Tucker also suggests that teacher evaluation is flawed, finding that although five percent of tenured teachers are deemed incompetent by principals, only 2.65 percent of tenured teachers were documented as being incompetent.[32] Similarly, an eastern Pennsylvania study by Mata and Zirkel reported that 99 percent of school administrators gave teachers perfect ratings of 80 out of 80 points.[33] Edwin Bridges' seminal work on teacher dismissal identified three sets of interrelated problems that impact the evaluation of teachers:

> (1) the legal barriers to removing tenured teachers for incompetence in the classroom;
> (2) the technical problems in measuring teacher effectiveness; and
> (3) the human obstacles that are involved, including the willingness and the ability of supervisors to carry out their responsibilities for teacher evaluation, remediation, and dismissal.[34]

These studies raise the question of whether too often the principal's evaluation of teachers is an empty ritual, a ceremonial congratulations rather than a critical component in the delivery of a quality education to students. Evaluation as a basis for retention, improvement or dismissal is an important part of a school district's capacity to build human capital within its teaching ranks that may be given to little attention.

---

[30] EVA L. BAKER, ET AL., ECON. POL'Y INST., PROBLEMS WITH THE USE OF STUDENT SCORES TO EVALUATE TEACHERS 1 (AUG. 29, 2010).

[31] DANIEL WEISBERG, ET AL., THE NEW TCHRS. PROJ., THE WIDGET EFFECT: OUR NATIONAL FAILURE TO ACKNOWLEDGE AND ACT ON TEACHER EFFECTIVENESS (2d ed. 2009), *available at* http://widgeteffect.org/downloads/TheWidgetEffect.pdf.

[32] Tucker, *supra* note 4 at 103.

[33] Perry Zirkel, *Legal Boundaries for Performance Evaluation of Public Professional Personnel,* 172 EDUC. LAW REP. 1 (2003).

[34] EDWIN M. BRIDGES, MANAGING THE INCOMPETENT TEACHER 2 (2d ed. 1990), *available at* http://scholarsbank.uoregon.edu/jspui/bitstream/1794/3275/1/managing_the_incompetent.pdf.

But it must be underscored that the evaluation system must be fair, accurate, and conducted in good faith[35] if it is to be a positive and meaningful process that develops, improves, and maintains teaching skills and competencies.[36] Evaluation must be about more than dismissal and discipline. If it is only perceived as punitive and not a system infused with fairness built to identify, support, and build effectiveness, its true value of developing professionals may get lost in the turbulence of discipline and dismissal.[37]

A teacher evaluation system should be designed to first identify weaknesses, buttress strengths, and improve employee performance "so [teachers] can become successful and contribute to achieving the district's goals."[38] In deciding an issue over the inclusion of an unfavorable evaluation of an observation of a poetry lesson in a teacher's personnel file, the Supreme Court of South Dakota wrote: "The purpose of any evaluation is to monitor changes in performance and make improvements where necessary."[39] If the teacher does not improve and his or her teaching remains unsatisfactory, then school officials may determine that dismissal or contract nonrenewal is the outcome of the evaluation. An Ohio court of appeals held that their inquiry was limited to whether the school district offered "specific recommendations regarding any improvements needed."[40]

---

[35] See Joint Committee, supra note 16.

[36] See Mark Paige, Using VAM in High Stakes Employment Decisions, 94 PHI DELTA KAPPAN 29 (Nov. 2012) for a discussion about the use of Value-Added Modeling in teacher evaluations. Paige urges "extreme caution" when using VAM for employment decisions such as termination. He writes, "As discussed, in the cases of tenured teachers, the statistical validity issues surrounding VAM (e.g., the question is whether it can truly measure a teacher's effectiveness on student growth) could potentially frustrate a district's decision to terminate a tenured teacher." Id. at 31.

[37] See Craig D. Jerald, Ctr. for Am. Progress, Movin' it and Improvin' It! Using Both Education Strategies to Increase Teaching Effectiveness (2012), available at http://www.americanprogress.org/wp-content/uploads/issues/2012/01/pdf/movin_it_improvin_it.pdf (The first strategy, "movin' it," "treats a teacher's effectiveness as fixed at any given point in time, then uses selective recruitment, retention, and 'deselection' to attract and keep teachers with higher effectiveness while removing teachers with lower effectiveness evaluation results." The "improvin' it" strategy treats teacher effectiveness as a "mutable" trait or skill that can be improved.) Id. at 2.

[38] KELLY FRELS & JANET L. HORTON, A DOCUMENTATION SYSTEM FOR TEACHER IMPROVEMENT OR TERMINATION 1 (2007).

[39] Iverson v. Wall Bd. of Educ., 522 N.W.2d 188, 193 (S.D. 1994).

[40] McComb v. Gahanna-Jefferson City Sch. Dist. Bd. of Educ., 608 N.E.2d 767 (Ohio Ct. App. 1998).

As stated above, the school principal is central to teacher evaluation. This is the individual tasked with the responsibility of implementing the evaluation system. Consequently, the perceptions of principals on teacher evaluations are important to understanding the state of teacher evaluation. The next part explores the nationwide data set on principal perceptions of barriers to removing poor performing or incompetent teachers.

Research: Perceptions of Principals on the Barriers to Teacher Dismissal

This research is a secondary analysis of the data from the National Center for Education Statistics (NCES), the primary federal entity that collects and analyzes data related to education. NCES fulfills a Congressional mandate to collect, collate, analyze, and report statistics on the condition of American education. The *Schools and Staffing Survey* is one data collection undertaking of the NCES. The core component of this survey that is germane to this research is the *Principal Questionnaire*. The 2007-2008 School Year data was used for this study. Those questions related to the research questions were used in this study, as well as selected demographic information. In addition to reporting the data from the survey, the researchers conducted post hoc analyses when the data raised issues related to the research questions.

Demographics

The survey had 7,459 principal respondents. Of those respondents, 42.3 percent were female and 57.7 percent were male. The demographics on race showed that 87.4 percent of the respondents were White, 10.1 percent Black or African-American, 1.7 percent American Indian or Alaska Native, 1.1 percent Asian, and .6 percent Native Hawaiian or Other Pacific Islander. The mean age of the principals was 48.9 years with a median age of 50 years. Almost 86 percent (85.7%) of the principals had a master's degree or higher. The average experience of a principal was 7.72 years in the position with 12.5 years of teaching before becoming a principal.

Barriers to Dismissing Teachers

As noted above, there is ample evidence that few teachers are removed through the evaluation system of the employing school district. Because principals play a central role in teacher evaluations, their perception of the barriers that they face in dismissing incompetent teachers is important. Understanding the perceived barriers allows a supervisor of principals to assist the principal in addressing the perceived barriers. For example, in his classic work on incompetent teachers, Bridges noted that principals may rationalize their failure to address the incompetence of their teaching force.[41] It is surprising how many of these obstacles to evaluation are still being asserted over fifteen years later. Bridges offers some advice for countering such rationalizations or excuses as the following:

1. "It's too costly."
2. "You can never win."
3. "It's too time consuming."
4. "The morale of my staff would be destroyed."
5. "The next teacher will be even worse."[42]

As noted above, the cost of a dismissal proceeding is still cited as a concern. Estimates of the cost have included $250,000 to fire a teacher in New York City[43] and between five and six figures in Los Angeles to settle rather than litigate the dismissal.[44] There is no doubt that there is a cost associated with taking adverse employment action against any employee. However, the cost of acting must also be weighed against the cost of not acting in terms of money and values.

Referring to the rationalization that "you can never win," in an exhaustive analysis of court cases on dismissal, Zirkel concluded that when a dismissal is based on educator judgments of unsatisfactory behavior, courts "rarely" overturn the judgment of the professional educators.[45] However, when the teacher has largely received successful ratings, the teacher's case is of course much stronger.[46] A related issue is not observing teachers and concluding that she or he is unsatisfactory. For example, a Supreme Court in New York in 2011 wrote, "However, [the teacher] submitted evidence that the principal who made the determination to award the 2008-09 [unsatisfactory] rating did not observe [the

---

[41] Bridges, *supra* note 34.

[42] *Id.* at 59-62.

[43] Frank Eltman, *Firing Tenured Teachers Isn't Just Difficult, It Costs You*, USA TODAY (June 30, 2008), *available at* http://usatoday30.usatoday.com/news/education/2008-06-30-teacher-tenure-costs_N.htm.

[44] Beth Barret, *LAUSD's Dance of the Lemons*, LAWEEKLY (Feb. 11, 2010), *available at* http://www.laweekly.com/2010-02-11/news/lausd-s-dance-of-the-lemons/.

[45] Zirkel, *supra* note 33.

[46] *Id.* at 10-11.

teacher's] teaching during either of his final two years at the school."[47] Clearly, principals must meet their responsibilities by performing fair and accurate assessments of teaching.

Interestingly, the responding principals did not perceive termination decisions not being upheld as a barrier to pursing dismissal of an incompetent teacher: 80 percent are not deterred by court decisions that do not uphold the termination decisions of principals. However, Robin Chait, in a *Center for American Progress* report on ineffective teachers, asserts that decisions made by review boards are a barrier to removing ineffective teachers.[48] Chait concludes: "Districts and principals are likely to lose a significant proportion of their dismissal cases even when they invest the requisite time and money."[49] However, Zirkel's comprehensive analysis of court cases on dismissal found that upholding employer decisions are the norm and not the exception.[50] Permuth and Egley concur with Zirkel that the courts tend to look more favorably upon dismissal decisions when school districts provide a preponderance of evidence, which is developed, typically, through principal documentation.[51] Rossow and Tate offer some support for Zirkel's position commenting on dismissals for lack of classroom control, finding that "[i]n a majority of recent court cases, school districts have been successful against challenges from teachers."[52] The differences between Zirkel and Chait may be the locus of study of the termination decisions. Zirkel reviewed court cases, while Chait focused on the quasi-judicial decisions made by arbitrators and state required competence panels. Zirkel's research does support Chait's research on arbitration rulings, finding that a study of arbitration awards in Pennsylvania and Massachusetts favored teachers over administrators.[53]

---

[47] Kolmel v. City of N.Y., 930 N.Y.S.2d 573, 574 (A.D. 1 Dept. 2011).

[48] Robin Chait, CNTR. FOR AM PROGRESS, REMOVING CHRONICALLY INEFFECTIVE TEACHERS: BARRIERS AND OPPORTUNITIES (2010), *available at* http://www.scribd.com/doc/52784810/Removing-Chronically-Ineffective-Teachers.

[49] *Id.* at 11.

[50] Zirkel, *supra* note 33 at 10. However, *see* Principe v. New York City Dept. of Educ., 941 N.Y.S.2d 574, 576 (A.D. 1 Dept. 2012) (Overturning a hearing officer's decision, writing, "Thus, given all of the circumstances, including petitioner's spotless record as a teacher for five years and his promotion to dean two years prior to the incidents at issue, we find the penalty [termination] excessive and shocking to our sense of fairness.").

[51] Steve Permuth & Robert Egley, Permuth, S. & Egley R. (2002). *Letting Teachers Go – Legally*, PRINCIPAL LEAD. 22 (2002), *available at* http://www.principals.org/portals/0/content/47023.pdf ("it takes careful and dedicated hard work and documentation to remove a teacher who is detrimental to the well-being of the school."). *Id.* at 26.

[52] Rossow & Tate, *supra* note 25, at 21.

[53] Zirkel, *supra* note 33 at 5, n. 18. For a discussion of arbitration hearings and teacher

Various researchers discussed above have identified perceived barriers to effective and efficient dismissals. The responses to the *Principal Questionnaire* (listed below) add to our understanding of some of the issues that principals face in their schools.

Table 1: Participant responses to the following question: "In your opinion, are the following considered barriers to the dismissal of poor-performing or incompetent teachers in this school?"

Considered a Barrier	Yes	No
Tenure	70.8%	29.2%
Effort required for documentation	67%	33%
Teacher associations or unions	62.7%	37.3%
Length of time required for termination process	60.7%	39.3%
Personnel Policies	50.2%	49.8%
Tight timelines for completing documentation	35.8%	64.2%
Difficulty in obtaining suitable replacements	22.2%	77.8%
Termination decisions not upheld	19.6%	80.4%
Dismissal is too stressful and/or uncomfortable for you	14.6%	85.4%
Resistance from parents	4.7%	95.3%

dismissal involving technology, *see* Mark Paige & Todd A. DeMitchell, *Arbitration Litigation Concerning Teacher Discipline for Misuse of Technology: A Preliminary Assessment*, 296 EDUC. LAW REP. 22 (2013).

The principals perceive that tenure (with its due process requirements, the effort required to document a case for dismissal, teacher associations or unions, and the length of time required for termination) is the greatest barrier to dismissing poor-performing or incompetent teachers. Of the remaining survey choices, only personnel policies (50.2%) are close to this constellation of perceived obstacles. This may be due to the fact that personnel-related barriers, although undefined, may support the underlying due process of tenure, the contract negotiated with the local union, and their resulting advocacy for following the contract.

The top four barriers are interrelated. Tenure law holds that a teacher is entitled to procedural and substantive due process under the Fourteenth Amendment when liberty or the property of their position is significantly infringed on by the state.[54] Consequently, teachers are entitled to proper notice and a fair hearing. These steps require time to document and to assemble the case to prove incompetence; while competence is otherwise presumed. Dayton noted: "Dismissal proceedings succeed or fail based on the fundamental fairness of the process and the quality of the documentation."[55] Tenure, time, and effort through documentation are clearly linked.[56] Evaluation is an intensely personal activity that brings two educators face-to-face in a situation of potential conflict. Professors Permuth and Egley recommend that the principal separate his or her personal feelings from the situation but keep in mind that seeking a person's dismissal affects both parties.[57]

The teachers union, in regards to the perceived barriers, is the party that generally protects the employee to ensure that the process by which a teacher is judged is fair and comports with the established procedures, especially those procedures outlined in a collective bargaining agreement. Because the union is tasked with protecting the interests of its member teachers, it is not surprising that unions are considered barriers to

---

[54] *See* Perry v. Sindermann, 408 U.S. 593 (1972); Bd. of Regents of State Coll. v. Roth, 408 U.S. 564 (1974); Cleveland v. Bd. of Educ. v. Loudermill, 470 U.S. 532 (1985). For a checklist of due process requirements in employment decisions, *see* Michael Scriven, *Due Process in Adverse Personnel Action*, 11 J. PERS. EVAL. EDUC. 127 (1997) ("In both its ethical and practical aspects, due process deserves more serious attention than it is currently receiving in most training programs for school preservice and inservice administrators") *Id.*

[55] JOHN DAYTON, EDUCATION LAW: PRINCIPLES, POLICIES, AND PRACTICE 404 (2012).

[56] *See* Andrew Sullivan, *Firing Teachers with Due Process*, FORBES (March 4, 2011), *available at* http://www.forbes.com/sites/erikkain/2011/03/04/firing-teachers-with-due-process/. Sullivan provides a discussion and push back on the complaints about the cumbersomeness of due process.

[57] Permuth & Egley, *supra* note 51, at 25.

dismissal. Unions represent the interests of their members. DeMitchell noted: "[T]he union represents the employee's interests and rights regarding job security whether it involves discipline, layoffs, or dismissal."[58]

The union and collective bargaining, controversial features of American education in general,[59] have long been regarded by many as major obstacles to dismissing incompetent teachers, even though it is listed as the third barrier in this survey. Moe, a vocal critic of teachers unions, echoes the perception that unions are a barrier to the dismissal of ineffective teachers. He argues that despite "frenzied nonstop reforms" since *A Nation at Risk* in 1983 reform efforts have largely failed.[60] The failure of this "ineffective organization" of public schools is "largely due to the power of unions,"[61] he asserts. According to Moe, unions are not solely responsible for the nation's education problems, but they "are at the heart" of the problems.[62] Through collective bargaining, the unions shape the school's organization "from the top down."[63] Other commentators join Moe in arguing that unions are barriers not to just teacher evaluation, but to educational reform and to the governance of public education.[64] For example, DeMitchell and Carroll, in a study of superintendent and union officials' perceptions of reform and bargaining cite a superintendent from the southwestern portion of America, stated that bargaining collectively with the union "greatly constrained the implementation of a new evaluation system."[65] However, a suburban superintendent opined that bargaining on performance-based pay "[causes] both sides to truly and deeply discuss" the philosophy behind the reform.[66]

The issue of unions acting as a barrier to removing incompetent teachers is confounded by the perceptions of teachers on the role of their

---

[58] TODD A. DEMITCHELL, LABOR RELATIONS IN EDUCATION: POLICIES, POLITICS, AND PRACTICES 12 (2010) ("Unionism is predicated upon serving the needs of its members"). *Id.* 66.

[59] Joshua M. Cowen, *Teacher Unions and Teacher Compensation: New Evidence for the Impact of Bargaining*, 35 J. EDUC. FIN. 172 (2009).

[60] TERRY M. MOE, SPECIAL INTERESTS: TEACHER UNIONS AND AMERICA'S PUBLIC SCHOOLS (2011).

[61] *Id.* at 5.

[62] *Id.* at 6.

[63] *Id.*

[64] *See e.g.*, FREDERICK HESS & MARTIN WEST, A BETTER BARGAIN: OVERHAULING TEACHER COLLECTIVE BARGAINING (2006); PETER BRIMELOW, THE WORM IN THE APPLE: HOW TEACHER UNIONS ARE DESTROYING AMERICAN EDUCATION (2003).

[65] Todd A. DeMitchell & Thomas Carroll, *Educational Reform on the Bargaining Table: Impact, Security, and Tradeoffs*, 134 EDUC. LAW. REP. 675, 688 (1999).

[66] *Id.* at 687.

union. A study by DeMitchell and Cobb found that teachers responding to the prompt: "Unions support professionalism in the following ways" stated that unions protect professionalism by protecting teachers from being abused and from having their rights trampled.[67]   However, the second prompt, which stated: "Unions harm professionalism in the following ways," resulted in the same response: Protection. Protection of teachers was the highest thematic response for both prompts.[68]   This research highlighted the tangled relationship that teachers have with their unions when it comes to professionalism. The researchers wrote:

> Teachers feel a need to be protected as a precondition for professionalism, but that protection is not without a cost some teachers believe. That cost, some assert is exacted against the perception of professionalism. For those who hold the position of support there is a strong sense that unions stand up for teachers. To borrow a phrase from law enforcement, the union "gets" and "protects."[69]

To further complicate the relationship between teachers and their unions over professionalism, in the quantitative portion of their study, DeMitchell and Cobb found that teachers responding to a five point Likert style question (1 strongly disagree to 5 strongly agree) agreed (M=3.77) that the contract protected their professional activities.[70]   However, the subsequent question, which asked whether the contract fosters quality teaching, had a mean of 2.72, showing that most disagreed with the prompt.[71]   Fifty-seven percent of the respondents strongly disagreed or disagreed with the statement: "The artistic/creative elements of teaching can be addressed in a contract" and only 27 percent agreed or strongly agreed with the statement.[72]

---

[67] Todd A. DeMitchell & Casey D. Cobb, *Teacher as Union Member and Teacher as Professional: The Voice of the Teacher,* 220 EDUC. LAW REP. 25, 31-4 (2007) (finding the following themes of support, protection, advocacy, support).

[68] *Id.* at 34-6 (finding the following themes of harm to the profession, blind protection, work of the union, divisiveness, and the union label.).

[69] *Id.* at 37.

[70] Todd A. DeMitchell & Casey D. Cobb, *Teachers: Their Union and Their Profession. A Tangled Relationship*, 212 EDUC. LAW REP. 1, 18 (2006).

[71] *Id.*

[72] *Id.* The mean for the question is 2.66. The lowest mean for the survey instrument is 2.45, mid-way between strongly disagree and disagree with "Quality teaching can be standardized into a contract." *Id.*

Menuey conducted a mixed methodology study of over 200 elementary school teachers in Virginia on their perceptions of incompetence and barriers to dismissal.[73] He found that the teachers in their study identified union protection, the expense of dismissal, and the time and difficulty of documenting the incompetence as barriers to principals dismissing incompetent teachers.[74] This generally mirrors the NCES data discussed in this research. However, this study also found that teachers perceived that the "lack of resolve or strength of character by principal" and "lack of skill by the principal to achieve dismissal" were also barriers but with a lower mean score than protection and documentation.[75] It should be noted that the NCES barrier question did not include an option that focused on the evaluation skills of the principal.

Teacher unions have often been characterized as, at a minimum, tolerating incompetent teachers, and possibly making their dismissal harder.[76] Part of the argument is that unions prolong the time necessary to remove an incompetent teacher from the front of the classroom. Consequently, there is a push for developing a more expedient dismissal process. Unions contend that they are protecting the due process rights of teachers who face employment sanctions such as dismissal. Scholarly research on this issue both casts light and raises questions. Bireda asserted: "Dismissal reform should not be focused on eliminating due process for teachers but rather on creating more efficient methods of identifying and terminating the employment of those teachers who no longer belong in the classroom."[77] Hess and West argued that the collective bargaining agreement, arguably the most important work of a union, is "restrictive in matters related to termination."[78] Paige, a professor and former school law attorney, responded to legislative enactments that make teacher evaluation a prohibited subject of bargaining by raising the issue of whether union involvement through collective bargaining "could undermine teacher evaluation reform."[79] DeSander's

---

[73] Brendan P. Menuey, *Teachers' Perceptions of Professional Incompetence and Barriers to the Dismissal Process,* 18 J. PERS. EVAL. EDUC. 309 (2005), *available at* http://link.springer.com/content/pdf/10.1007%2Fs11092-007-9026-7.pdf.

[74] *Id.* at 315.

[75] *Id.*

[76] Suzanne R. Painter, (2000). *Principals' Perceptions of Barriers to Teacher Dismissal,* 14 J. PERS. EVAL. EDUC. 253 (2000).

[77] SABA BIREDA, CTR. FOR AM. PROGRESS, DEVIL IN THE DETAILS: AN ANALYSIS OF STATE TEACHER DISMISSAL LAWS 2 (June 2010), *available at* http://www.americanprogress.org/issues/2010/06/pdf/sabateacherdismissal.pdf.

[78] Hess & West, *supra* note 64 at 27.

[79] Mark Paige, *Applying the "Paradox Theory": A Law and Policy Analysis of Collective*

found that in a 20 year study of dismissal cases for incompetence there was no significant difference between dismissal cases between union and non-union states.[80]

Data Analysis of the NCES Survey

Over 60 percent of the principals responding regarded unions and the length of time that it takes to dismiss a teacher as barriers. But are the two concerns related? Of the principals who perceived that unions were a barrier to dismissal, 73.1 percent also perceived that the length of time necessary for dismissal was also a barrier; whereas, 39.8 percent of the principals who marked that unions were not a barrier stated that the length of time was a barrier. A Spearman rank-correlation between the two variables shows a moderate correlation (r_s=.330) that is statistically significant (p<.001).[81] In other words, principals who believed that unions were a barrier to dismissing incompetent teachers were nearly twice as likely to consider length of time a barrier as well as compared to teachers who do not perceive unions to be a barrier. However, it must be remembered that this does not establish that unions cause the length of time necessary for dismissal; it only indicates a relationship between the two as perceived barriers to removing incompetent teachers.

Bridges found that the ability to properly, responsibly, and fairly document teaching behaviors is central to effective supervision.[82] Documentation was listed as the second most selected barrier (67%). Continuing the line of discussion of the impact of unions on the evaluation of teachers, a crosstab on unions and documentation shows that 78 percent of the principals who considered unions to be an obstacle to dismissal also selected documentation as a barrier, while 48.6 percent of those principals who stated that unions were not a barrier said that documentation was a barrier. A Spearman rank-order correlation between unions and documentation is moderate (r_s=.302) and statistically significant (p<.001).

Bargaining Rights and Teacher Evaluation Reform from Selected States, 2013 BYU EDUC. & L.J. 21, 42 (2013) ("As unions and their membership are excluded from bargaining teacher evaluations, unions will become more vigilant in protecting their employees when management mismanages the evaluation system"). *Id.* at 42-3.

[80] Marguerita Kalekas Desander, *Tenured Teacher Dismissal for Incompetence and the Law: A Study of State Legislation and Judicial Decisions,* 1983-2003 (2005) (Unpublished doctoral dissertation, College of William & Mary) (on file with Swem Library, College of William and Mary).

[81] *See* THOMAS URDAN, STATISTICS IN PLAIN ENGLISH (3d ed. 2010) (Correlations from 0 to .2 are weak, from .2 to .5 are moderate, and above .5 are strong)

[82] Bridges, *supra* note 34.

In other words, three-quarters of the principals who considered unions to be a barrier also believed that documentation is a barrier. Principals link unions and documentation.[83]

Documentation and the length of time required for dismissal are perceived barriers. Both have a moderate correlation to unions. Whereas the length of time that it takes to dismiss an incompetent teacher may largely be out of the control of a principal through external due process requirements, documentation is not. However, the length of time it takes to terminate an ineffective teacher probably has a relationship to the amount of time it takes to properly document the case for dismissal. Since the burden of proof in a dismissal proceeding of a tenured teacher is placed on the school district, the quality of the documentation is critical.[84] A crosstab on these two factors reveals that 79.4 percent of the principals who consider documentation to be a barrier to dismissal also found the length of time required to also be a barrier. A Spearman rank-order correlation between length of time for dismissal and documentation is strong (r_s=.548) and is statistically significant (p<.001). Principals believe that preparing the documentation necessary to support a dismissal and the length of time that it takes to dismiss have a strong positive relationship. For example, a middle school principal in Queens characterized the onerousness of paperwork and grievance hearings necessary in a teacher dismissal proceeding as "taking on another job."[85] The question of how principals are prepared and in-serviced to document teacher behavior is, therefore, a critical finding from these data.

The two potential barriers that received the lowest positive rating as a barrier were the stress or discomfort (14.6% answered yes) that accompanies confrontation. The lowest potential barrier is parents (4.7% answered yes). Why discomfort with dismissing an employee is not considered a barrier is suspect. Bridges noted that dismissing a teacher is

---

[83] An example of appropriate documentation in a school district with a union is found in Cohn v. Bd. of Educ., 960 N.Y.S.2d 362 (N.Y. App. Div. 2013) in which the principal and two assistant principals observed the teacher and provided detailed reports of the observations of his poor performance in classroom management, lesson planning, and engagement of students. The court also noted that a professional development plan was developed including professional support.

[84] This burden of proof is well-established. Newton Edwards, writing in 1932, stated: "A teacher cannot, however, be dismissed because of general dissatisfaction on the part of parents and pupils. Such evidence is not conclusive of incompetency. When a teacher is dismissed for incompetency, the burden of proof is upon the board of education." Newton Edwards, *Law Governing the Dismissal of Teachers. I*, 33 ELEMENTARY SCH. J. 255m 264-5 (1932).

[85] STEVEN BRILL, CLASS WARFARE 151 (ebook, NOOK) (2011).

"unpleasant."[86] Meuney writes, the "[d]ismissal of incompetent teachers is often described as one of the hardest and most frustrating processes a principal will go through during his or her term of leadership."[87] Similarly, Streshly, Gray, and Frase stated "(c)onfronting the failure of a teacher to perform adequately is uncomfortable."[88]

However, as stressful as it may be, "[t]he cost of keeping incompetent staff members in the classroom is staggering and multi-faceted."[89] Nolan and Hoover asserted that identifying and developing an approach to remediating deficiencies has a positive impact on the school as an organization and it sends two messages to teachers in the school: Poor teaching is not acceptable; and the administration will work with teachers to help them improve their performance.[90]

As noted above, parents were not generally perceived as a barrier to dismissal by the responding principals. They would intuitively be considered to be an ally of the principal in removing an incompetent teacher because teacher incompetence impacts their children. Additional research may be needed, however, to address the role of parents as facilitator or inhibitor of dismissal proceedings.

Conclusion

Because competent teachers are central to education, the importance of credentialing for entry into the profession[91] and retaining qualified teachers is an imperative for education. The secondary analysis above-- concerning the data on principal perceptions of the evaluation--is important to understanding how principals retain qualified teachers or dismiss them. The data reveal four major perceived barriers to dismissing incompetent teachers. In order of the highest percentage, the four variables were "tenure" (70.8%); "effort required for documentation" (67%); "teacher association or union" (62.7%); and "length of time required for termination process" (60.7%). Tenure was set aside as entangled with the other three variables and the statutory rights involved with defining tenure. It must be noted, however, that concerning these

---

[86] Bridges, *supra* note 34, at 56.

[87] Menuey, supra note 73, at 309.

[88] WILLIAM A. STRESHLY, ET AL., THE NEW MANAGEMENT BY WANDERING AROUND 250 (2012).

[89] Menuey, *supra* note 73, at 309.

[90] JAMES NOLAN, JR. & LINDA A. HOOVER, TEACHER SUPERVISION AND EVALUATION: THEORY INTO PRACTICE 108 (2011).

[91] Ralph D. Mawdsley, & P. Williams, *Teacher Assessment and Credentialing: The Role of the Federal Government in a State Function,* 262 EDUC. L. REP. 735 (2011).

statutory rights, tenure is not a lifetime guarantee of job security as is commonly held, and does not mean that an incompetent teacher cannot be dismissed. But sufficient administrative skill, will, and support are necessary in order for a principal to discharge an incompetent teacher effectively and efficiently.

The other three factors noted above are interrelated. Because state law and government regulations may structure the length of time for dismissal, the two remaining levers that are within the control of school administrators are documentation and union relations. Tenure provides a process for termination, albeit, a difficult one at times, but it is not a bar to termination. Documentation is a necessary skill that can be taught and must be learned by principals. With the use of proper of documentation practices, principals and supervisors "can increase morale and minimize future legal problems."[92] School districts that train, value, and hold principals accountable for effective and efficient documentation reduce the effect of the perceived documentation barrier.

The issue of length of time it takes to dismiss a teacher can be influenced by the school district's relationship with its union. School districts should seek to negotiate reasonable time limits into the collective bargaining agreement. Another approach is to build trust between the union and the school district; good faith should not just be reserved for the bargaining table but should pervade the relationship. As unions and school districts mutually strengthen and publically share their commitment to quality teaching, by achieving a balance between rights and responsibilities, a new dynamic of general ally and occasional adversary may be forged which allows unions to meet their legal obligation of protecting the interests of their membership while also serving the public good.[93] The union, with the help and support of school administrators, can persuade the majority of its members that concern for the public good does not mean giving up its traditional role of securing the bread-and-butter issues of bargaining and protecting their interests. To the contrary, a fair and rigorous system of supervision serves the interest of teachers generally, helping to assure that they work with competent colleagues who share their commitment to the profession and the education of students.

Teachers and principals play different but essential roles in the operation of schools. Price argues that "[w]hen principals establish trusting school spaces, serious school improvement and success can

---

[92] Jeffrey Horner, *Fifteen Tips for Better Documentation of Employee Performance,* 146 EDUC. L. REP. 613, 616 (2000).

[93] *See* Todd A. DeMitchell, *A Reinvented Union: A Concern for Teaching, Not Just Teachers*, 11 J. PERS. EVAL. EDUC. 255 (1998).

occur."[94]   An understanding of perceived barriers to dismissing incompetent teachers is important for school leaders and policy makers to understand.   That knowledge can inform practices and assist in policy adjustments that reduce the impact of these potential barriers.   High quality training in principal preparation programs, continual in-servicing in their school districts, and appropriate support from superintendents are imperative to give principals the tools and assistance that they need to carry out this essential function.

---

[94] Price, *supra* note 19, at 42.

Teacher Tenure: The Times, They Are a Changin'

Ann Elizabeth Blankenship, J.D., Ph. D.[*]

As dissatisfaction with the American public school system grows, so do efforts to change it. In efforts to repair what is perceived by some as a broken system, federal and state policy makers have attempted various legislative approaches to improve low student test scores and unsatisfactory student achievement. As a result, lawmakers have passed a flood of education related legislation in the areas of national standards, testing, school choice, teacher licensure, pay for performance, and teacher evaluations designed to increase student achievement. Acknowledging that teacher quality does positively impact student achievement, recent reform efforts specifically have focused on getting the right teachers in the classroom.[1] Some posit that part of getting the right teachers in the classroom is getting rid of the wrong ones, which has put teacher tenure under fire.

Since January 2009, teacher tenure legislation has come under particular scrutiny. While tenure for K-12 public school teachers has been challenged periodically in the past, recent events made it possible for the theoretical debate over tenure to turn into a large-scale reform movement. Between January 2009 and the end of June 2013, 28 states made substantive changes to their teacher tenure laws and an additional four states have proposed legislation pending.[2] This article examines the

---

[*] Ann Elizabeth Blankenship is an Assistant Professor in the College of Education & Psychology, Department of Educational Leadership and School Counseling, at the University of Southern Mississippi with experience in legal practice and expertise in personnel law.

[1] Ann L. Elrod, *Teacher Tenure Reform: Problem Definition in Policy Formation*, Paper presented at the 1994 ANNUAL MEETING OF THE AMERICAN EDUCATIONAL RESEARCH ASSOCIATION (1994, Apr. 4-8). *See also*, Linda Darling-Hammond, *Teacher Quality and Student Achievement: A Review of State Policy Evidence*, 8 EDUC. POL'Y ANALYSIS ARCHIVES 1, 1-44 (2000); Eric A. Hanushek, *The Trade-Off Between Child Quantity and Quality*, 100 J. OF POLITICAL ECON. 1, 84-117 (1992); Eric A. Hanushek and Steven G. Rivkin, *Teacher Quality*, *in* HANDBOOK OF THE ECONOMICS OF EDUCATION (Eric A. Hanushek and Finis Welch eds. 2006); Barbara Nye, Spyros Konstantopoulos, & Larry V. Hedges, *How Large Are Teacher Effects?*, 26 EDUC. EVALUATION & POL'Y ANALYSIS 3, 237-257 (2004).

[2] For the big picture view of this reform movement, each state will be counted only once, as a change state, a proposal state, or a no-change state. Florida, Indiana, Maryland,

evolution of teacher tenure legislation, particularly over the past four years. The first section of this article provides an overview of teacher tenure and the history of K-12 teacher tenure legislation. The second section of this article provides a review of the specific legislative changes that were passed and proposed between January 2009 and June 2013. The legislative changes are organized into categories based upon the nature of the change to allow a thorough understanding of the character of the particular changes and the popularity of each type of change. This article will conclude with a brief discussion of how these teacher tenure changes might impact teachers' employment rights and educational and legal practices.

Overview and History of K-12 Teacher Tenure

Tenure Defined

The concept of teacher tenure in the United States is complex and ever evolving. While the concept of tenure is most often associated with college and university faculty, similar employment protections are or have been available to elementary and secondary teachers in all 50 states and the District of Columbia.[3] Because tenure is a product of state law, it

---

Minnesota, Mississippi, and Washington have all both passed tenure reform and have proposed legislation pending. For purposes of this paper, these states will generally be counted as "change" states, rather than "proposal" states. Therefore, the four states counted as proposal states for this article are Alaska, Kentucky, North Carolina, and Oklahoma. As is discussed later in this paper, North Carolina passed relevant legislation after the conclusion of the data collection for this article. Therefore, for purposes of this discussion, it remains a proposal state. For a visual depiction of the change and proposals made, please see Figures 1 and 2. Furthermore, the time period selected for this article was dictated by the data. Change began to take shape in 2009, therefore, that is where this article begins. It also happens to mark the beginning of the Obama administration and the period in which the Race to the Top grant program went into effect. The impact of the aforementioned on the tenure reform movement is touched on later in this article and will be discussed in greater detail in future articles by this author.

[3] Scott Grubbs, *Quality of Graduate Experience in a Georgia Case Study: The Elimination of Teacher Tenure in Georgia as Viewed Through the Policy Formulation Process Model Environment*, 3 GEORGIA EDUCATIONAL RESEARCHER 1 at 1(2005). Note that Mississippi claims that it does not offer teacher tenure. According to general education provisions of Mississippi law, before being suspended or dismissed, all Mississippi teachers are entitled to a notification of the charges and a right to a public hearing on the charges. Miss. Code Ann. § 37-9-59 (West 2013). Mississippi also enacted the School Employment Procedures Law of 2001 which applies in situations in which a teacher's contract is not renewed. It requires that a teacher be provided with notice of the reasons for nonrenewal, an opportunity for the non-renewed teacher to

manifests itself differently in legislation depending upon the state. For example, while states generally require a probationary period of service before tenure protections take effect, probationary time periods range from one year (Hawaii[4]) to seven years (Ohio[5]).[6] However, the basic principles remain the same. Therefore, for the purposes of this article, tenure is defined as the "expectation and provision of job security through the guarantee of due process, generally following a probationary period."[7]

Teacher tenure rights are triggered when a teacher's employment status is negatively impacted. Each state lists the grounds upon which a teacher may be removed from his or her position (either by termination, demotion, or suspension). Some common grounds for negative employment action include: Incompetency/poor performance, insubordination, willful neglect of duties, reduction in force, and failure to maintain proper certification and/or licensure. For example, in Georgia, a teacher may be dismissed for the following: (1) Incompetency; (2) Insubordination; (3) Willful neglect of duties; (4) Immorality; (5) Inciting, encouraging, or counseling students

---

respond to the "charges", and a hearing. Miss. Code Ann. § 37-9-101. Sub-section 101 specifically states: "It is the intent of the Legislature not to establish a system of tenure." By applying the definitions set forth in sub-section 103 of the School Employment Procedures Law, teachers are only entitled to the aforementioned employment protections in cases of non-renewal if they have been employed by the local school district for a period of two (2) continuous years or two (2) years of employment in any Mississippi school district and one year of employment in the school district of current employment. Miss. Code Ann. § 37-9-103 (West 2013). Therefore, while Mississippi's intent is not to create tenure protections for its teachers, it has done so by default. All teachers are entitled to written notice and an opportunity to be heard before being suspended or dismissed. Furthermore, all teachers who have worked the number of years designated in sub-section 103 have the right to notice and a hearing in cases of non-renewal. Despite the difference in vocabulary, in application, Mississippi does offer its teachers all of the due process rights associated with teacher tenure.

[4] HAW. REV. STAT. § 302A-608 (2013) (read in conjunction with the 2008 Senate Bill No. 2449, which reduced the probationary period from four semesters to two semesters).

[5] OHIO REV. CODE ANN. § 3319.08 (West 2013). Teachers employed after January 1, 2011 are eligible for a "continuing contract" after working as a teacher for at least 7 years and some graduate education. It is important to note that the 7 year requirement is for licensure and is not a probationary period. Ohio also requires employment in a district for at least 3 years out of a five year period for receipt of tenure rights. This time period is more consistent with probationary periods in other states. OHIO REV. CODE ANN. § 3319.08 (D)(3) (West 2013). Teachers who were licensed to teach in Ohio prior to January 1, 2011 can earn a continuing contract with just graduate coursework. OHIO REV. CODE ANN. § 3319.08 (D)(2) (West 2013).

[6] Additionally, the vocabulary and definitions used in each state may vary but have similar operations.

[7] Holly Robinson, *Tenure: What are the Benefits for Children?*, GEORGIA PUBLIC POLICY FOUNDATION (Feb. 4, 2003).

to violate any valid state law, municipal ordinance, or policy or rule of the local board of education; (6) To reduce staff due to loss of students or cancellation of programs; (7) Failure to secure and maintain necessary educational training; or (8) Any other good and sufficient cause.[8]

Some grounds for dismissal are easier for supervisors to prove than others. Insubordination and failure to secure proper certification/licensure are relatively straightforward in terms of identification and documentation of violations. However, traditionally, teacher incompetency/poor performance has been poorly defined by both state legislation and case law, making it difficult for supervisors to identify and document it for employment actions. Likewise, reduction in force decisions have become more complicated of late. With smaller budgets and a strong focus on student test scores, the needs of the school and teacher performance increasingly are being considered in reduction in force decisions. Consequently, as is discussed in the second half of this article, those are areas in which many states chose to make legislative changes.

Procedural Due Process

As used today, tenure laws are designed to protect public school teachers from arbitrary dismissal without just cause and due process.[9] Teacher tenure is not intended to be a guarantee of lifetime employment. Rather, it is a procedural due process which guarantees that teachers receive notice of the grounds for termination and a hearing before he or she can be terminated.[10] Some jurisdictions also require that the teacher be provided names of witnesses, grant the power of subpoena to compel the production of supporting documents and witness testimony, allow the teacher to be represented by an attorney, and guarantee the right to appeal.[11]

In the 1972 U.S. Supreme Court case *Board of Regents of State College v. Roth,*[12] the Court stated that the requirements of procedural due process apply only when a teacher has been deprived of his or her interests encompassed by the Fourteenth Amendment's protection of liberty or property. A tenured teacher has a vested property interest in that

---

[8] Georgia Fair Dismissal Act of 1975, GA. CODE ANN. § 20-2-940 (West 2013).
[9] AM. FED'N OF TEACHERS, ASSURING TEACHER QUALITY: IT'S UNION WORK (1999); Sidney E. Brown, *Teacher Tenure*, 91(1) EDUCATION 12 (1978); Perry A. Zirkel, *Teacher Tenure Is Not the Real Problem*, 91(9) PHI DELTA KAPPAN 76 (2010).
[10] Zirkel, *supra* note 9; U.S. CONST. amend XIV, §1.
[11] Andy Nixon, Abbot Packard & Gus Douvanis, *Non-Renewal of Probationary Teachers: Negative Retention*, 131(1) EDUCATION 43 (2010).
[12] *Bd. of Regents of State Coll. v. Roth*, 408 U.S. 564, 569 (1972).

employment because he or she has a legal expectation of continued employment. Since the Fourteenth Amendment prohibits states from, "depriving any person of life, liberty, or property, without due process of law"[13] a tenured teacher is constitutionally entitled to due process before being terminated.[14]

Historical Context

Teacher tenure regulations have been a part of the American elementary and secondary education system for over 100 years.[15] At the turn of the 20th century, many teachers faced over-crowded classrooms, uncomfortable working conditions, and interference from demanding parents and administrators trying to dictate lesson plans and curriculum.[16] Teachers were not only poorly paid, often with no pension or benefits, but teaching jobs were often subject to the whim of politicians.[17] Furthermore, by the turn of the century, nearly 75% of all American K-12 teachers were women, but few were promoted to positions of authority.[18]

---

[13] U.S. CONST. amend XIV, §1.

[14] *Bd. of Regents*, 408 U.S. at 569. *See also* Nixon, Packard, & Douvanis, *supra* note 11. While some states require a record of satisfactory evaluations for teachers to be eligible for tenure, generally tenure is a right that has been automatically granted after the expiration of the probationary period. Emily Cohen & Kate Walsh, *Invisible Ink in Teacher Contracts*, 10 EDUCATION NEXT 18 (2010); EDUC. COMM'N OF THE STATES, TEACHER TENURE/CONTINUING CONTRACT LAWS: UPDATED FOR 2007 (2007), *available at* http://www.ecs.org/clearinghouse/75/64/7564.pdf. During the probationary period, teachers are considered "at-will" employees and a district may choose to terminate the employment relationship at the end of any contract year. Teachers are generally not entitled to due process during the probationary period. If a non-tenured teacher's employment is terminated mid-contract, he or she is entitled to due process of law. However, a teacher's right to his or her reputation has been recognized as a constitutionally protected liberty interest. Therefore, if grounds for termination of a non-tenured teacher are made public and can be construed as defamatory, it may entitle that teacher to the protections of procedural due process. *Bd. of Regents*, 408 U.S. at 569. *See also* Nixon, Packard, & Douvanis, *supra* note 11.

[15] Julianne Coleman, Stephen T. Schroth, Lisa Molinaro & Mark Green, *Tenure: An Important Due Process Right or a Hindrance to Change in the Schools?* 18(3) J. PERS. EVAL. EDUC. 219 (2005); Josh Marshall, *Look at the Map*, TPM (TALKING POINTS MEMO), Feb. 18, 2011.

[16] Coleman et al., *supra* note 15; M.J. Stephey, *A Brief History of Tenure*, TIME MAGAZINE, Nov. 17, 2008.

[17] Coleman et al., *supra* note 15; Thomas A. Kersten, *Teacher Tenure: Illinois School Board Presidents' Perspectives and Suggestions for Improvement*, 37 (3 & 4) PLANNING & CHANGING 234 (2006).

[18] Coleman et al., *supra* note 15.

By this time, working conditions for teachers deteriorated to the extent that reform was necessary in order to preserve the profession.

Championed by the National Education Association (NEA)[19] and inspired by federal legislation protecting the rights of United States civil service employees, teacher tenure laws began to take shape.[20] In 1909, New Jersey became the first state to grant teachers fair dismissal rights.[21] By 1950, 21 states adopted some form of teacher tenure regulation; 20 additional states had at least one school district that had tenure-like teacher contracts ranging from one to five years.[22] By the late 1960s, nearly all states offered some sort of employment protection to their teachers, either in the form of formal tenure laws or automatically renewing contract policies.[23]

Despite dramatic policy changes in other areas of education, teacher tenure legislation remained relatively stable for nearly 50 years, from the late 1960s to the late 2000s.[24] Tenure reform *has* been a topic of discussion on the political agenda for decades; but for the most part, discussion failed to inspire actual change. For example, in the 1970s, shortly after the enactment of the Elementary and Secondary Education Act of 1965,[25] many scholars considered the relationship between "accountability" in education and tenure.[26] In his paper presented at the

---

[19] The NEA is now the nation's largest teachers' union.

[20] Kersten, *supra* note 17.

[21] *Id.*

[22] Marshall, *supra* note 15. In 1950, only seven states had no state or district regulations providing continuing contracts and/or fair dismissal rights.

[23] *Id.*

[24] Periodically, isolated changes have been made to state teacher tenure legislation. *See, e.g.*, Elrod, *supra* note 1. For example, in the early 1990s, Colorado made significant revisions to its teacher tenure legislation. *Id.* In 1997, Oregon replaced its teacher tenure system with a "modified tenure" system in which teachers were offered two-year renewable contracts and provided with a rehabilitation program for teachers deemed ineffective. *See* Stephey, *supra* note 16. In 2000, under the direction of Governor Roy Barnes, Georgia repealed the Fair Dismissal Act of 1975 and its job protections for teachers as part of the Georgia's educational reform efforts. Barnes' victory in eliminating teacher tenure increased the resolve of Georgia teachers to run Barnes out of office. After winning the Georgia Governorship in 2003, Sonny Perdue became the first Republican Governor of Georgia since Reconstruction. With Purdue's support, job protections for teachers were restored in 2004. Grubbs, *supra* note 3, at 1. While Georgia teachers regained their tenure protections just four years later, Georgia's repeal of tenure is one of the more dramatic examples of isolated tenure legislation reform.

[25] 20 U.S.C. §70 (1965).

[26] The Elementary and Secondary Education Act of 1965 called for annual evaluations of the programs it was funding which increased the focus on accountability. Worth (1972) notes that "in an era of tax revolt, inflation, recession, and social unrest, when the goals

1974 convention of the American Association of School Administrators, Charles Blaschke noted that political and economic changes led to and/or required a change in educational management, the increased popularity of accountability, and an increase in administrative flexibility.[27]   He argued that tenure "is designed to protect teachers from being fired unless proven to be incompetent; yet, teachers don't have to demonstrate competencies to be given tenure."[28]   Blaschke also contended that tenure increasingly hampered the efficient allocation of school resources and that it was counterproductive as a tool for teacher motivation.[29]

Recent political, social, and economic events have made it possible for the theoretical debate over tenure to turn into actual legislative change.[30] The following section documents the remarkable nationwide movement to reform teacher tenure legislation that that took place between January 2009 and the end of June 2013.   During that time, 28 states made substantive changes to their teacher tenure laws and an additional four states had proposed legislation pending.[31]

---

of education and the means used to achieve them are very much in question, funding sources…are demanding to know what we teachers are trying to do and how successful we are at it." George W. Worth, *Evaluation and Tenure*, 5 THE BULLETIN OF THE MIDWEST MODERN LANGUAGE ASS'N 21 (1972); *See also*, Charles L. Blaschke, *Should Performance Contracts Replace Tenure?* Paper presented at the 1974 ANNUAL CONVENTION OF THE AMERICAN ASSOCIATION OF SCHOOL ADMINISTRATORS (1974, Feb 22-24). During this time period, the United States was going through a dramatic economic downturn and experiencing extreme political partisanship, not unlike today.

[27] Blaschke, *supra* note 26, at 1. Blaschke's piece was actually written in response to Kenneth Hansen & William J. Ellena, *Teacher Tenure "Ain't" the Problem*. Paper presented at the 1973 ANNUAL CONVENTION OF THE AMERICAN ASSOCIATION OF SCHOOL ADMINISTRATORS (1973).

[28] *Id.*

[29] *Id.*

[30] How and why this reform movement came to pass is a long and complicated discussion--one that cannot be appropriately addressed within the confines of this article. The author is currently drafting additional articles analyzing the social, political, and economic factors contributing to this reform movement.

[31] *See* note 2. In preparation for the drafting of this article, the author did a review of each state's teacher tenure laws, legislative history, news reports, and other relevant documents (reports, collective bargaining agreements, etc.). Once all of the laws were collected, substantive changes were noted and analyzed. During this process, common themes of legislative change emerged. Note that only substantive changes are discussed, meaning any change to due process and/or employment rights for teachers. Some states made changes to their tenure laws which are not included in this article because they were not "substantive" (they did not affect the operation of the law or teaches' employment rights). For example, changes correcting grammar used in a provision or renumbering a law (or subparts) to comply with a new numbering system are not included herein.

Legislative Changes to K-12 Teacher Tenure Laws (January 2009-June 2013)

Based upon a state-by-state review of changes made to teacher tenure legislation from January 2009 through June 2013, the following five types of legislative change were most common:

A. Change in length of the probationary period;

B. Teacher performance/evaluation considered in granting of tenure;

C. Poor performance added as a grounds for "just cause" dismissal;

D. Reduction in force decisions not based entirely on seniority; and

E. Loss of tenure protections after receipt of poor performance evaluations.

This section contains a discussion of each category of change. Figures 1 and 2 below and Appendices A and B provide visual overviews of the categorical changes.

In addition to these five categorical changes, a few states have experienced other legislative events that potentially impact teachers' tenure rights but that do not fall into one of the above mentioned categories. Many of these consisted of procedural legislative changes but they still warrant discussion. Therefore, some of these outlier changes will be addressed briefly at the conclusion of this section.

A. Change in Length of Probationary Period

Thirteen states made changes to the length of their probationary periods and three additional states have proposed legislation pending.[32] The majority of the states increased their probationary period from a set number of years to a greater set number of years. Maine,[33] Maryland,[34]

---

[32] Note that there does not seems to be a discernable logic behind the particular changes made to teacher probationary periods. There is no indication that states are using any sort of research or "best practices" to inform legislative action.

[33] ME. REV. STAT. ANN. tit. 20-A, § 13201 (2011). Maine increased its probationary period from 2 to 3 years. It will increase to 4 years for new teachers hired for the 2015-16 school year.

[34] MD. CODE ANN., Education § 6-202 (West 2010). Maryland increased its probationary period from two to three years.

and Nevada[35] all increased their probationary periods to three years. New Jersey[36] now has four year probationary period, while Michigan,[37] New Hampshire,[38] and Tennessee[39] have moved to five years. Alaska also has proposed to increase its probationary period from three to five years.

Illinois,[40] Kansas,[41] Oklahoma,[42] South Carolina,[43] and Virginia[44] increased the length of their probationary periods as well, but the increase is variable depending on teacher performance. For example, in Kansas a teacher must serve a probationary period of at least 3 years, but it may be extended to four or five years at the agreement of the teacher and the board of education based on the teacher's performance evaluations.[45] Similarly, in Virginia, the minimum probationary period is three years but may be extended for an additional two years.[46]

In 2009, Ohio added requirements to its teacher tenure law, increasing the time it takes new teachers to earn tenure to seven years.[47] In addition

---

[35] NEV. REV. STAT. ANN. § 391.311 (West 2011). Nevada increased its probationary period from two to three years.

[36] N.J. STAT. ANN. § 18A:28-5 (West 2012). New Jersey increased its probationary period from three to four years for teachers hired after the effective date of the legislative change.

[37] MICH. COMP. LAWS ANN. § 38.81 (West 2011). Michigan increased its probationary period from four to five years.

[38] N.H. REV. STAT. ANN. § 189:14-a (2011). New Hampshire increased its probationary period from three to five years.

[39] TENN. CODE ANN. §§ 49-5-503 (West 2011). Tennessee increased its probationary period from three to five years (during a seven year period).

[40] 105 ILL. COMP. STAT. 5/24-11 (West 2011). The probationary period for teachers hired on or after the PERA implementation date varies from two to four years based on the teachers' performance evaluations.

[41] KAN. STAT. ANN. § 72-5445 (West 2011). Each Kansas teacher is required to serve a probationary period of three years. If, at the end of that three years, the teacher has not made sufficient progress to warrant receipt of tenure, the teacher and the board of education may enter into an additional contract for a fourth year or a fourth and fifth year of probationary status. Such teachers are entitled to written plans of assistance from the district.

[42] OKLA. STAT. ANN. tit. 70, § 6-101.3 (West 2013). While this law did not become effective until July 1, 2013 (after the data collection cutoff date), it was passed in May 2013 so its inclusion is appropriate.

[43] S.C. CODE ANN. §59-26-40 (2012). South Carolina changed its one year induction period to a variable one to three year induction period, at the discretion of the school district.

[44] VA. CODE ANN. § 22.1-303 (West 2013). The probationary period in Virginia is a minimum of three years with an optional additional two years, at the discretion of the school district.

[45] KAN. STAT. ANN. § 72-5445 (West 2011).

[46] VA. CODE ANN. § 22.1-303 (West 2013).

[47] OHIO REV. CODE ANN. §§ 3319-08 to 3319-11 (West 2009).

to an actual probationary period of three years, Ohio teachers must hold an educators license for at least seven years to be eligible for tenure ("continuous contract").

Figure 1: Number of Legislative Changes from January 9009 through June 2013[48]

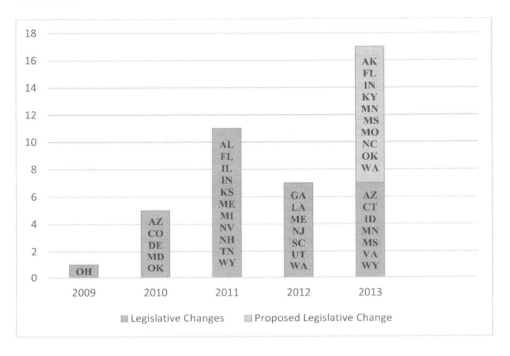

Perhaps most notable in this category are the states that are considering decreasing their probationary periods. While just last year, in April of 2012, the Missouri Senate was considering a bill to increase teacher probationary period from five to ten years,[49] they are now considering a bill to decrease the period from five to four years.[50] Equally interesting are the competing proposals in the Mississippi State Senate. In January

---

[48] For purposes of this chart, states may be listed more than once if they passed or proposed more than one law during the given time frame. Only those proposed changes that are still live and pending a final vote are listed on Figure 1.

[49] In April 2012, Missouri Senate Bill 806 proposed to increase the probationary period from 5 to 10 years. The bill failed when it was brought to a vote in the Missouri Senate. S. 806, 96th Gen. Assemb., Reg. Sess. (Mo. 2012).

[50] Missouri House Bill 631 proposes to decrease the probationary period from 5 to 4 years. However, it also adds the requirement that the teacher must receive an evaluation rating of effective or highly effective each of those years. H. 631, 97th Gen. Assemb., Reg. Sess. (Mo. 2013).

2013, two proposals were put forth in the Senate, one to increase the teacher probationary period from three to four years,[51] and one to decrease it from three years to one year.[52]   Both states appear to be facing an internal struggle over the direction of their tenure policies.[53]

Figure 2: Number of Legislative Changes and Proposals by Category

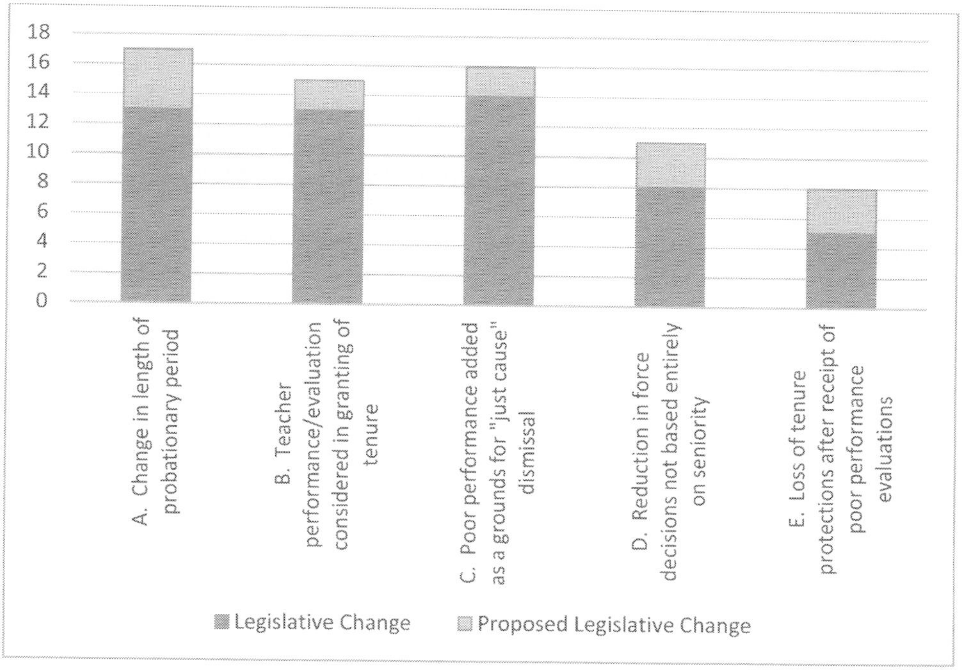

B. Teacher Performance/Evaluation Considered in Granting of Tenure

Of the changes that have been made to teacher tenure legislation in the last four years, linking the award of tenure or continuing contract status to performance evaluations is one of the most prevalent. Thirteen states have already made legislative changes that fall under this category and two additional states have proposed legislation pending. Within this category, there are several different varieties of change.

---

[51] S. 2351, 128th Leg. Sess., (Miss. 2013).
[52] S. 2120, 128th Leg. Sess., (Miss. 2013).
[53] Note that Hawaii in 2008, Hawaii decreased its probationary period to 1 year to bring the state legislation in line with the provisions of the collective bargaining agreement. *See* HAW. REV. STAT. §§ 302A-608 (West 2008). This change is not counted in this study because it occurred outside of the determined study period.

Many states now require a particular number of positive evaluations before a teacher is eligible for tenure status. Nine states (DE,[54] LA,[55] MI,[56] NV,[57] NJ,[58] OK,[59] TN,[60] WA,[61] and WY[62]) added a positive evaluation requirement to an existing probationary period.[63] For example, Delaware's probationary period is three years; additionally, a teacher must receive a rating of at least "satisfactory" on the "student improvement" component of the teacher appraisal for at least two of the three years of the probationary period.[64] Similarly, the new Michigan law increases the probationary period from four to five years and requires that a teacher be rated as "effective" or "highly effective" on at least three of the last five year-end performance evaluations. Tennessee is unique in that it considers teacher evaluations only in the last two years of its five year probationary period.[65]

Colorado,[66] Illinois,[67] and Indiana[68] now require a teacher to receive a certain number of positive evaluations in lieu of a set probationary period. For example, prior to May 2010, Colorado required a probationary period of three years of consecutive service in order to earn tenure. The new law requires a teacher to receive three years of positive evaluations ("demonstrated effectiveness") in order to receive tenure.[69]

Kansas[70] includes teacher evaluations in the award of tenure but does so at the discretion of local officials. A teacher in Kansas must complete a probationary period of at least three years. But that period may be

---

[54] DEL. CODE ANN. tit. 14, § 1403 (West 2010).

[55] LA. REV. STAT. ANN. § 17:442 (2012).

[56] MICH. COMP. LAWS ANN. § 38.83b (West 2011).

[57] NEV. REV. STAT. ANN. § 391.3197 (West 2011).

[58] N.J. STAT. ANN. § 18A:28-5 (West 2012).

[59] OKLA. STAT. ANN. tit. 70, § 6-101.3 (West 2013).

[60] TENN. CODE ANN. § 49-5-503 (West 2011).

[61] WASH. REV. CODE. ANN. § 28A-405.220 (West 2012).

[62] WYO. STAT. ANN. § 21-7-102 (West 2013). As it was originally passed, the Teacher Accountability Act of 2011 was initially supposed to go into place for the 2013-14 school year. However, in March 2013, it was amended to delay implementation until the 2016-17 school year.

[63] North Carolina is considering similar legislation. See H. 719, 2013 Gen. Assemb., Reg. Sess. (N.C. 2013).

[64] DEL. CODE ANN. tit. 14, § 1403 (Wet 2010). The "satisfactory" ratings do not have to be consecutive.

[65] TENN. CODE ANN. § 49-5-503 (West 2011).

[66] COLO. REV. STAT. ANN. § 22-63-103 and § 22-9-105.5 (West 2010).

[67] 105 ILL. COMP. STAT. 5/24-11 (West 2011).

[68] IND. CODE. ANN. §§ 20-28-6-7.5 (West 2011).

[69] COLO. REV. STAT. ANN. § 22-63-103(7) (West 2010).

[70] KAN. STAT. ANN. § 72-5445 (West 2011).

extended to four or five years upon agreement by the district's board of education and the teacher based on the teacher's performance.[71]

C. Poor Performance Added as a Grounds for "Just Cause" Dismissal

Poor performance has traditionally been included as a ground for dismissal of both probationary and tenured teacher. However, states often failed to specifically define poor performance either in the legislation or in case law, making use of the provision difficult and risky for principals attempting to terminate underperforming teachers. However, in recent years, a number of states refined their teacher dismissal laws, using unsatisfactory teacher evaluations as evidence of poor performance, and thus grounds for termination. Thirteen states[72] already made legislative changes addressing termination for receipt of unsatisfactory evaluations and an additional two states have proposed legislation pending.

Indiana[73] and Oklahoma[74] are using negative evaluations as grounds for non-renewal of its probationary teachers. While technically a state is not required to have "grounds" for dismissing a probationary teacher since they are at-will employees,[75] states are certainly permitted to give guidelines for when non-renewal is most appropriate. For example, Indiana law states that a probationary teacher may not be renewed if he or

---

[71] KAN. STAT. ANN. § 72-5445(c)(1) (West 2011). Missouri is also considering a proposal that would give the school principal and superintendent discretion over the length of a teacher's probationary period. S. 332, 197th Gen. Assemb. Reg. Sess. (Mo. 2013) states that in addition to receiving 4 consecutive effective or highly effective evaluation ratings, a teacher shall undergo a formal review and conferral process by the principal and superintendent before gaining permanent teacher status. In 2012, the Kentucky State Senate considered a similar proposal. Senate Bill 122 stated that teachers hired after July 1, 2012 who served 4 years of continuous active service could request that they be considered for continuing contract status. S. 122, 2012 Reg. Sess. (Ky. 2012). Continuing contracts would be awarded by a school based committee consisting of 4 faculty members with continuing contract status and the school principal. Teachers seeking continuing contract status will be judged on their effectiveness using evaluation data and a portfolio of other information. A teacher who is not awarded continuing contract status by the conclusion of his or her 6th year will not be offered a renewal contract for a seventh or subsequent year. Senate Bill 122 died in committee without a vote of the full state senate.

[72] Oklahoma is discussed twice in this section because its revised legislation falls into more than one category but is counted only once.

[73] IND. CODE. ANN. § 20-28-6-7.5(b)(2) (West 2011).

[74] OKLA. STAT. ANN. tit. 70, § 6-101.22(D)(1) (West 2013).

[75] A probationary teacher generally can be dismissed at the end of any contract period.

she receives one rating of "ineffective" or two ratings of "improvement necessary."[76]

Arizona,[77] Connecticut,[78] Louisiana,[79] Oklahoma,[80] Tennessee,[81] Utah,[82] Virginia,[83] and Wyoming[84] all added provisions stating generally that poor performance in the classroom constitutes grounds for dismissal.[85] For example, Arizona added "inadequacy of classroom performance" as grounds for dismissal.[86] Also, Tennessee expanded its definition of "inefficiency" as a grounds for termination to include receipt of an evaluation of "below expectation" or "significantly below expectation."[87]

Four states (FL,[88] ME,[89] MI,[90] and WA[91]) specified the particular number of unsatisfactory or negative evaluations which constitute grounds for dismissal.[92]   For example, under Florida law, a teacher may be terminated for receiving two consecutive annual performance ratings of "unsatisfactory" (either consecutively or two within a three year period), or three consecutive annual performance ratings of "needs improvement," or a combination of "needs improvement" and "unsatisfactory."[93]   In Maine, two consecutive unsatisfactory evaluations constitute grounds for dismissal.[94]

---

[76] IND. CODE. ANN. § 20-28-6-7.5(b)(2) (West 2011). Additionally, North Carolina House Bill 719 proposes that teachers who receive a rating of "in need of improvement" by the end of his or her 4th year teaching should not be renewed for a 5th year (effectively terminating employment). H. 719, 2013 Gen. Assemb., Reg. Sess. (N.C. 2013).

[77] ARIZ. REV. STAT. ANN. §§ 15-538.01 through 15-548 (2010).

[78] CONN. GEN. STAT. ANN. §10-151(d) (West 2013) (effective July 1, 2014).

[79] LA. REV. STAT. ANN. § 17:443(B) (2012).

[80] OKLA. STAT. ANN. tit. 70, § 6-101.22 (West 2010).

[81] TENN. CODE ANN. §§ 49-5-501 and 49-5-511(a)(2) (West 2011).

[82] UTAH CODE ANN. § 53A-8-503 (Wet 2012).

[83] VA. CODE ANN. § 22.1-307 (West 2013).

[84] WYO. STAT. ANN. § 21-7-110(a)(vii) (West 2011). However, note that this provision does not go into effect until the 2016-17 school year.

[85] A similar provision was proposed in New Mexico but it died in committee. See H. 251, 50th Leg. Sess., 2d Sess. (N.M. 2012).

[86] ARIZ. REV. STAT. ANN. §§ 15-538.01 through 15-548 (2010).

[87] TENN. CODE ANN. §§ 49-5-501 and 49-5-511(a)(2) (West 2011).

[88] FLA STAT. ANN. § 1012.33(1)(a) (West 2011).

[89] ME. REV. STAT. ANN. tit. 20-A, § 13703 (2012).

[90] MICH. COMP. LAWS ANN. § 380.1249(h) (West 2011).

[91] WASH. REV. CODE. ANN. § 28A.405.100(4)(c) (West 2012).

[92] Additionally, Missouri Senate Bill 332 proposes to change the definition of incompetency (as a grounds for dismissal) as two consecutive evaluation ratings of ineffective. S. 332, 197th Gen. Assemb. Reg. Sess. (Mo. 2013).

[93] FLA STAT. ANN. § 1012.33(1)(a) (West 2011).

[94] ME. REV. STAT. ANN. tit. 20-A, § 13703 (2012).

D. *Reduction in Force Decisions Not Based Entirely on Seniority*

As of the end of June 2013, 8 states passed legislation addressing the use of teacher tenure status and/or seniority in making reduction in force decisions; an additional three states proposed similar legislation. Six states (GA,[95] IN,[96] ME,[97] MI,[98] NV,[99] and VA[100]) made legislative changes that prohibited tenure status and/or seniority from being the *sole* factor considered in making reduction in force decisions. Minnesota,[101] Missouri,[102] and Washington[103] have similar proposed legislation awaiting a vote. Georgia's new law (as of May 2012) states that teacher seniority (including tenure status) is no longer the primary or sole factor used when implementing a reduction in force.[104] Similarly, Nevada law now states that reduction in force decisions cannot be made based solely on teacher seniority.[105]

Arizona[106] and Utah[107] passed laws that prohibit any use of tenure status and/or seniority as a factor in making reduction in force decisions. Instead, reduction in force decisions are made based exclusively on teacher effectiveness.

E. *Loss of Tenure Protections after Receipt of Poor Performance Evaluation*

In five states, a teacher may lose tenure status if he or she receives unsatisfactory evaluations. An additional three states have proposed

---

[95] GA. CODE ANN. § 20-2-948 (West 2012).

[96] IND. CODE. ANN. § 20-28-7.5-1(d) (West 2011).

[97] ME. REV. STAT. ANN. tit. 20-A, § 13703 (2011).

[98] MICH. COMP. LAWS ANN. §§ 38.82(a) and 380.1248 (West 2011).

[99] NEV. REV. STAT. ANN. § 288.151 (West 2011).

[100] VA. CODE ANN. § 22.1-304 (West 2013).

[101] *See* H.F. 980, 88th Leg. Sess., 1st Reg. Sess. (Minn. 2013), proposing that teachers be placed on unrequested leave (reduction in force) based on their subject matter licensure and most recent evaluation outcomes.

[102] *See* S. 408, 97th Gen. Assemb., 1st Reg. Sess. (Mo. 2013), proposing that the primary basis for placing teachers on leave (reduction in force) be teacher evaluation results.

[103] *See* S. 5246, 63d Leg., Reg. Sess. (Wash. 2013) (proposing that seniority must not be weighed as more than 10% after other factors are considered in making all human resource and personnel decisions).

[104] GA. CODE ANN. § 20-2-948 (West 2012).

[105] NEV. REV. STAT. ANN. § 288.151 (West 2011).

[106] ARIZ. REV. STAT. ANN. § 15-502(H) (2010).

[107] UTAH CODE ANN. § 53A-8a-505 (West 2012).

similar legislation.   In Colorado,[108] Louisiana,[109] and Nevada,[110] if a teacher receives a particular number of negative and/or unsatisfactory annual evaluations, he or she may lose tenure status and be required to serve an additional full probationary period. For example, in Louisiana, if a teacher receives a performance rating of "ineffective," he or she shall lose tenure status.[111] In order to re-earn tenure status, a Louisiana teacher must again be rated "highly effective" for five years within a six year period. Under Colorado and Nevada law, a teacher will lose tenure status after receiving two consecutive poor evaluations.[112]

In Arizona[113] and Tennessee,[114] a teacher who receives two consecutive evaluation ratings of "below expectations" or "significantly below expectations" loses tenure status.[115] In order to re-earn tenure status, the teacher does not have to serve a second full probationary period, but re-earns tenure by receiving a certain number of positive evaluations (fewer than the initial probationary period). For example, in Tennessee, a teacher who loses tenure status must receive two consecutive evaluation ratings of "above expectations" or "significantly above expectations" to have tenure protections reinstated.[116]

Alaska's proposed legislation focuses more on keeping tenure status rather than losing it.[117] It proposes to review a teacher's tenure every five years of continuous employment. After such a review, the district may terminate the teacher's tenure rights if it finds one of the following: the teacher did not meet its goals for student achievement for two or more of the five years; the teacher's performance did not improve as required under a plan of improvement; or, the teacher did not adequately assist the school district with the implementation of change to the instructional model.[118]

---

[108] COLO. REV. STAT. ANN. §22-63-103(7) (West 2010).

[109] LA. REV. STAT. ANN. § 17:442(C)(1) (2012).

[110] NEV. REV. STAT. ANN. § 391.3129 (West 2011).

[111] LA. REV. STAT. ANN. § 17:442(C)(1) (2012) (This rule was first implemented during the 2013-2014 school year).

[112] COLO. REV. STAT. ANN. §22-63-103(7) (West 2010); NEV. REV. STAT. ANN. § 391.3129 (West 2011).

[113] ARIZ. REV. STAT. ANN. § 15-538.01(C) (2013).

[114] TENN. CODE ANN. § 49-5-504(e) (West 2011).

[115] For similar proposed legislation, see H.R. 631, 97th Gen. Assemb., Reg. Sess. (Mo. 2013); H.R. 719, 2013 Gen. Assemb., Reg. Sess. (N.C. 2013).

[116] Id.

[117] See H.R. 162, 28th Leg., 1st Sess. (Alaska. 2013).

[118] Id. (A similar idea was put forth by the Governor of Connecticut in early 2012. He proposed that teachers be required to prove continued effectiveness in order to retain tenure rights. However, this idea was never realized in legislation.)

Other Notable Legislative Events

In addition to the aforementioned categories of legislative change, other less widespread but interesting legislative events took place that deserve mention. First is the attempt of several states to eliminate entirely automatically renewing contracts. In 2011, Florida passed legislation eliminating automatically renewing contracts for all teachers hired on or after July 1, 2011. Non-tenured teachers now are renewed on an annual basis based on performance evaluations (using an evaluation system also introduced in 2011). While this annual renewal system persists in Florida, the constitutionality of the evaluation system on which it is built has been challenged in federal court.[119] Four additional states attempted to pass similar legislation with less success. The state legislatures in both Idaho and South Dakota passed legislation replacing automatically renewing

---

[119] On April 16, 2013, 7 Florida teachers and 3 local unions (Alachua County Education Association, Hernando Classroom Teachers Association, and Escambia Education Association) filed suit against the Florida Commissioner of Education, the Florida State Board of Education, and the 3 relevant county school boards. In their complaint, Plaintiffs claim that Florida Senate Bill 736, codified throughout Chapter 1012, Florida Statutes (passed on March 24, 2011) ("the Act") is arbitrary, irrational, and unfair as it applies to classroom teachers that do not teach classes tested by the state standardized tests. Specifically, Plaintiffs note that the Act requires that classroom instructors be evaluated annually using a value added formula. The Act requires the use of state approved assessments to measure student growth. Currently, only statewide assessments for reading and math for students in grades 4-10 ("FCATs") are available for calculating student growth. School districts are permitted to develop and implement assessments for subjects and grade levels not covered by the FCATs; however, as a result of limited time and resources, none of the named counties have developed such assessments. Consequently, all teachers, regardless of subject and/or grade level are evaluated in part using each school district's FCAT scores. For example, an elementary school art teacher can be evaluated using the FCAT reading scores for all of the elementary schools in the district. In other words, the teacher may be evaluated based on test scores of students and a subject he or she does not teach. The Act requires that the evaluation results be used to determine teacher contract renewal, raises, promotions, and placement. Furthermore, the Act requires school districts to notify parents annually of students assigned to a classroom teacher with negative performance ratings, potentially harming a teacher's professional reputation. Plaintiffs claim that the evaluation system created under the Act is a violation of both the Due Process Clause and the Equal Protection Clause of the 14th Amendment to the U.S. Constitution. Complaint for Declaratory and Injunctive Relief, Cook v. Bennett, No. 1:13-cv-00072-MW-GRJ (N.D. Fla. Apr. 16, 2013). The Florida legislature is considering several amendments to remedy the particular issues addressed in the lawsuit. See S. 822, 115th Reg. Sess. (Fla. 2013); S. 980, 115th Reg. Sess. (Fla. 2013); S. 1336, 115th Reg. Sess. (Fla. 2013); S. 147, 115th Reg. Sess. (Fla. 2013); H.R. 197, 115th Reg. Sess. (Fla. 2013); H.R. 907, 115th Reg. Sess. (Fla. 2013).

contracts with renewable annual or multi-year employment contracts for teachers. However, in both states the legislation was challenged, put to a popular vote, and failed.[120] Likewise, similar proposals have been made and failed in the North Carolina[121] and Virginia[122] state legislatures. While it appears that there is interest in moving away from automatically renewing contracts, some states are having difficulties passing and/or implementing such laws.

Two states made changes to the procedural operation of their teacher tenure system, making the teacher termination process easier, faster, or both. Alabama's Students First Act of 2011 streamlines its teacher dismissal procedure, terminates salary and benefits for dismissed teachers (during the appeals process), and eliminates appellate rights for teachers who are laid off or transferred as a result of reductions in force.[123] Similarly, under revised Idaho tenure laws, teachers terminated for reasons

---

[120] The Idaho legislature attempted to eliminate automatically renewing contracts, moving instead to a system of 1-2 year contracts. *See* S.L. ch. 96, § 4 (Idaho. 2011); S.L. ch. 295, § 2 (Idaho. 2011). The legislation was challenged and the changes were put to a popular vote by referendum, known as the Idaho Teachers' Collective Bargaining Veto Referendums (Propositions 1-3). It appeared on the November 6, 2012 ballot and the Idaho constituency voted to repeal the new law at a rate of 58% to 42%, thus reinstating tenure and returning issues like workload and class size to contract negotiations. S.L. ch 102, § 49 (S.D. 2012). which would have amended S.D. CODE ANN. §§13-43-6-6.6, proposed the following legislative changes: Teachers who had not earned tenure (continuing contract status) before July 1, 2016 would not acquire it; teaching contracts would be for 1 year (as opposed to 1-3 years); and, 2 consecutive evaluation ratings of unsatisfactory would constitute grounds for termination of a tenured or non-tenured teacher. The amendment was referred to the voters by referendum petition and was rejected on November 6, 2012 by a vote of 114,590 for and 235, 064 against.
[121] H.R. 950, 2011 Gen. Assemb., 2011 Reg. Sess. (N.C. 2011), proposed to replace continuously renewing contracts for teachers with 1-4 year contracts. This provision of the bill was eliminated before ratification. However, Senate Bill 402, passed on July 26, 2013, eliminates career status for teachers who did not receive it before the 2013-14 school year. Teachers without career status are to be offered 1 or 4 year contracts. The 4 year contracts will go to the top performing 25% of teachers, as identified by superintendents. Remaining teachers will receive 1 or 2 year contracts. While this is a significant legislative change, it passed after the conclusion of data collection for this particular paper so is not considered in study results. S. 402, 2013 Gen. Assemb., 2013 Reg. Sess. (N.C. 2013).
[122] House Bill 576 proposed to immediately increase the probationary period for untenured teachers from three to five years. It also proposed to eliminate the option of tenure or "continuing contract status" for teachers that had not earned it before the 2013-14 school year. Instead, it proposed offering teachers renewable three years contracts. H.R. 576, 2012 Gen. Assemb., 2012 Reg. Sess. (Va. 2012). The bill died in committee and the Virginia legislature instead passed a variable year increase to the probationary period.
[123] ALA. CODE §§ 16-24C-1-14 (2011) (see in particular sections 4 and 6).

other than unsatisfactory service are no longer entitled to individual due process proceedings.[124] Instead, there is a single, informal review hearing for all employees impacted by a termination event, such as a lay-off.[125]

Finally of interest are the states that have not made legislative changes to their tenure policies but have made some effort to change how they implement their current policies. While the District of Columbia made no changes to its legislation,[126] in 2010 it entered into a revised collective bargaining agreement with the Washington Teachers' Union that provided a new bonus structure in exchange for weakened teacher seniority protections.[127] In particular, the agreement gave principals the power to use performance rather than seniority as the primary determinant in making layoff decisions and more control over which teachers would be hired at new schools.[128] Districts in New York and Texas changed the application of their existing tenure laws to reduce the number of teachers awarded tenure status. For example, in 2005, nearly 99% of New York City teachers received tenure, whereas in 2011, approximately 58% of teachers eligible for tenure received it.[129] By using stricter evaluation guidelines, New York deferred granting tenure to 39% of eligible teachers

---

[124] IDAHO CODE ANN. §§ 33-514 and 33-515 (West 2013).

[125] These due process rules apply only until July 1, 2014.

[126] The District of Columbia has a one year probationary period, during which time a "probationary employee" can be terminated without notice or evaluation. After completion of the probationary period, in order to terminate an employee, he or she must be provided with a 15-day separation notice and been evaluated at least once within six months preceding notice (at least 30 days prior to notice), unless he or she has committed a crime that impacts job duties (including all felonies). D.C. CODE §1-608.01a(b)(2)(C) (2012).

[127] Bill Turque, *D.C. Teachers' Union Ratifies Contract, Basing Pay on Results, Not Seniority*, WASHINGTON POST (June 3, 2010), *available at* http://www.washingtonpost.com/wp-dyn/content/article/2010/06/02/AR2010060202762.html; *Collective Bargaining Agreement between the Washington Teachers' Union (Local #6 of the American Federation of Teachers) and the District of Columbia Public Schools, 2007-2012,* WASHINGTON POST (March 19, 2010), *available at* http://media.washingtonpost.com/wp-srv/metro/documents/teachercontract060210.pdf?sid=ST2010060202812

[128] *Id.*

[129] Adam Lisberg & Meredith Kolodner, *Mayor Bloomberg Vows to Tenure Only Good Teachers and Boot Bad Ones*, NY DAILY NEWS (Sept. 27, 2010), *available at* http://articles.nydailynews.com/2010-09-27/local/27076511_1_tenure-city-teachers-united-federation; Sharon Otterman, *Once Nearly 100%, Teacher Tenure Rate Drops to 58% as Rules Tighten*, NY TIMES (July 27, 2011), *available at* http://www.nytimes.com/2011/07/28/nyregion/tenure-granted-to-58-of-eligible-teachers-in-city.html?_r=1.

without making any changes to tenure legislation.[130] In the same vain, in response to budgetary challenges, Texas school districts dramatically decreased the number of continuing contracts awarded or ceased offering them at all.[131] Houston Independent School District, Texas' largest school district, stopped offering continuing contracts in the late 1990s and a number of other districts joined suit in 2011.[132] While these states did not make formal legislative changes and are thus outside of the scope of this study, their changes in implementation of existing laws certainly impact the tenure rights of teachers in those states and should be noted.

Discussion

Race to the Top

In furtherance of President Obama's focus on economic growth and education, he signed into law the American Recovery and Reinvestment Act (ARRA) in 2009.[133] The ARRA provided $4.35 billion for the Race to the Top Fund (RTTT), a competitive grant program designed to encourage education innovation and reform, improvement in student achievement, and college and career readiness.[134] Out of its four core education reform areas, the third relates directly to teacher tenure; its focus being "recruiting, developing, rewarding, and retaining effective teachers and principals, especially where they are needed most."[135] Based on the RTTT application scoring rubric, using performance evaluations to inform key personnel decisions (such as tenure) was worth just over five percent of the total points available.[136] Of the 46 states (and the District of Columbia) that applied for a RTTT grant, the great majority of grant

---

[130] Otterman, *supra* note 129.

[131] Morgan Smith, *Budget Crisis May Cause Teachers to Lose Jobs, but Some Are Safe with Tenure*, THE TEXAS TRIBUNE (January 17, 2011), *available at* http://www.texastribune.org/texas-education/public-education/budget-crisis-may-cause-teachers-lose-jobs-some-ar/

[132] *Id. See e.g.*, North East Independent School District (San Antonio), Arlington Independent School District, and Fort Bend Independent School District.

[133] American Recovery and Reinvestment Act of 2009, Pub. L. No. 111-5, 123 Stat. 115 (2009). *See also*, U.S. Dept. of Educ., *Race to the Top Program: Executive Summary* (Nov. 2009*), available at* http://www2.ed.gov/programs/racetothetop/executive-summary.pdf.

[134] U.S. Dept. of Educ., *Executive Summary*, *supra* note 133.

[135] *Id.*

[136] U.S. Dept. of Educ., *Appendix B. Scoring Rubric* (2010), *available at* http://www2.ed.gov/programs/racetothetop/scoringrubric.pdf.

awardees made changes to their tenure laws despite the low number of points available.[137]

Given the apparent influence of the RTTT grant program on the tenure reform movement, it is not surprising that legislative changes focusing on the use of teacher performance indicators (particularly evaluations) in making personnel decisions, such as granting tenure and dismissal, were widespread. While such changes were not actually worth a great many points on the scoring rubric, it was a concrete way to demonstrate commitment to reform.

Waning Reform?

While the number of proposed changes seems to be holding strong, it appears that the general enthusiasm for gutting teacher tenure rights is beginning to wane. Several small yet significant events (or non-events) suggest that perhaps this reform movement is losing steam:

- Both Missouri and Mississippi have proposed legislation on the table that would actually reduce the length of the teacher probationary period.
- To date, lawsuits have been filed in at least Florida and California challenging some aspect of the states' teacher tenure system.
- The legislatures in Idaho and South Dakota passed laws making it more difficult (or impossible) for teachers to earn tenure. Both laws were rejected by the public when brought to a vote by referendum.
- Iowa, Massachusetts, New Mexico, Rhode Island, and South Dakota have all considered legislative changes to their teacher tenure provisions. For one reason or another, changes have failed in each of these states. Additionally, Nebraska has not made any changes to its tenure system, despite recommendations made in a report by the Platte Institute for Economic Research.[138] The report called for a teacher selection and evaluation process similar to the one currently used in Florida, tying teacher pay and tenure status to student achievement. For purposes of this study, they are all listed

---

[137] The influence of the Race to the Top grant program warrants extensive investigation and is more thoroughly explored in an upcoming article by this author.

[138] VICKI E. ALGER, TEACHER SELECTION AND EVALUATION IN NEBRASKA (Platte Institute for Economic Research, 2012), *available at* http://www.platteinstitute.org/docLib/20120109_Teacher_Selection_and_Evaluation_in_Nebraska.pdf

as having made no legislative change and having no pending proposals.

The next 12 to 24 months should reveal if this reform movement has, in fact, come to an end.

Implications for Practice

The teacher tenure reform movement could have lasting effects for both education in general and education policy specifically, even after this period of reform ends. In the education arena, teacher tenure may be over as we know it. Consequently, the role it plays in recruiting and retaining teachers may change. Additionally, the teacher tenure reform movement has been widely publicized. It may have a lasting impact on how the public perceives teachers and teacher tenure. Similarly, widespread legislative changes will effect teachers' employment rights and the practice of law with regards to personnel issues. Finally, the reform movement may also impact education policy. The growing influence of the executive branch may impact state and local control over public schools. However it manifests itself in the future, the teacher tenure reform movement is certainly going to have lasting effects on education.

Impact on Education

Teacher tenure, as it was known in 2008, may be over. Over half of the states have already passed some variety of teacher tenure reform, and more are considering changes. Instead of using tenure as a general employment protection, many states now are using it as a reward for certain levels of teacher performance. This begs the question, how will changes in teacher tenure impact teacher recruitment and retention? The job security that tenure offers is a benefit that should not be discounted. Little research has been conducted on the impact of teacher tenure on recruitment and retention;[139] however, Brunner and Imazeki attempt to address this issue by "using cross-state variation in tenure policies to identify the effects, if any, of the length of the probationary period on entry-level teacher salaries."[140] The authors investigate whether states off-

---

[139] Susanna Loeb & Jeannie Myung, *Economic Approaches to Teacher Recruitment and Retention, in* INTERNATIONAL ENCYCLOPEDIA OF EDUCATION 473, 478 (Penelope Peterson, Eva Baker, & Barry McGaw eds., 3rd ed., 2010).

[140] Eric J. Brunner & Jennifer Imazeki, *Probation Length and Teacher Salaries: Does Waiting Pay Off?*, 64 INDUSTRIAL & LABOR RELATIONS REV. 164, 164 (2010).

set longer probationary periods with higher wages.[141] The results indicate that states do offer higher wages for teachers that must undergo longer probationary periods, demonstrating that tenure has value as an employment benefit.[142] If teacher tenure becomes more difficult to earn and less frequently awarded, presumably, its value as an employment benefit also will decrease. In order to keep up with teacher recruitment, schools will have to create new benefits or increase existing benefits (such as wages) to make up for the diminished value of teacher tenure.

In addition to teacher recruitment and retention, the teacher tenure reform movement may also have a negative effect on the public perception of teachers and schools. Currently the general public has a fairly positive view of teachers and schools, particularly those in their own community.[143] However, their opinion of teachers' unions, collective bargaining, and teacher tenure is not as positive.[144] With an inundation of negative media coverage of teacher tenure and related issues, public sentiment regarding not only tenure, but the teaching profession in general, may suffer. Negative perceptions of teachers and schools could have the potential to impact education funding, strengthen the school choice movement, increase private school enrollment, and negatively impact teacher recruitment.

Impact on Employment Rights and Legal Practice

Changes to teacher tenure laws across the county will certainly affect teachers' employment rights and the practice of personnel law in education. Teachers' employment rights will change most dramatically in the states that eliminate automatically renewing contracts (currently only Florida). At the conclusion of each contract cycle, before contract

---

[141] *Id.* The thought is that higher wages is a way to compensate for the extended evaluative period.

[142] *Id.* at 178-179.

[143] William J. Bushaw & Shane J. Lopez, *Betting on Teachers: The 43rd Annual Phi Delta/Gallup Poll of the Public's Attitudes Toward the Public Schools*, 93 KAPPAN MAGAZINE 11, 18 (Sept. 2011); William G. Howell, Martin R. West, & Paul E. Peterson, *The Public Weighs In on Public School Reform*, EDUCATION NEXT, 12-13 (Fall 2011), *available at* http://educationnext.org/files/ednext_20114_feature_peterson_howell.pdf. Surveyors interviewed a nationally representative sample of 2,600 American citizens during April and May 2011.

[144] *Id.* Note that the push to change teacher tenure laws was closely linked to efforts to change legislation concerning teacher and/or administrator evaluation systems, teacher salary issues, and teacher collective bargaining rights. Therefore, in some cases, efforts made to change legislation in one are, or perceptions thereof, had an impact on legislation in the other areas during the same time period.

renewal, teachers will be treated as at-will employees. Unless otherwise prescribed by state law, teachers may be non-renewed at the discretion of the school district for any reason. Grounds for termination, such as incompetency and insubordination, do not apply to non-renewal decisions. This in and of itself is a dramatic change in employment protections for teachers. It also opens the door to increased litigation for alleged constitutional violations. Without access to the hearing and appeals process set up for tenured teachers (as a result of their due process rights), non-renewed teachers who feel that they have been wronged will be forced to go straight to the state court system in order to be heard. Additionally, since their legal options for challenging a non-renewal are more limited, they are likely to rely more heavily on constitutional (both state and federal) protections, particularly with regards to issues concerning academic freedom and discrimination of protected classes (age, race, gender, etc.).[145] However, it is important to note that teachers who are terminated, laid off, or non-renewed through no fault of their own may be eligible to collect unemployment benefits.[146] If an employer challenges the award of unemployment benefits on the grounds of employee misconduct, the employee will then be entitled to an administrative hearing.

In addition to tying acquisition and retention of tenure rights to teacher evaluations, many states have overhauled their teacher evaluation systems. A popular new trend in teacher evaluation is using students' standardized test scores as some percentage (up to 60%) of a teacher's evaluation.[147] The result is that teacher tenure is directly tied to students' standardized test scores. For a number of reasons, using student test scores to make such high-stakes decisions will likely lead to an increase in legal challenges.[148] Some object to the standardized tests themselves, claiming

---

[145] See Neal H. Hutchens, *Using a Legal Lens to Better Understand and Frame Issues Shaping the Employment Environment of Non-Tenure Track Faculty Members*, 55(11) AMER. BEHAVIORAL SCIENTIST 1443, 1453-1454 (2011).

[146] Generally, unemployment benefits are not paid to teachers and other education workers for school breaks (including summer) if they will be employed in any capacity the following school year, even if it is in a reduced capacity. Also note that resigning from a position generally disqualifies a teacher from later collecting unemployment benefits.

[147] These kinds of teacher evaluations are not just used tenure decisions. They are also used for calculating teacher salaries and/or bonuses in pay-for-performance and value-added systems.

[148] Mark Paige, *Using VAM in High-Stakes Employment Decisions*, 94(3) KAPPAN MAGAZINE 29, 30 (2012). *See also*, Xiaoxia A. Newton, Linda Darling-Hammond, Edward Haertel, & Ewart Thomas, *Value-Added Modeling of Teacher Effectiveness: An Exploration of Stability Across Models and Contexts*, 18(23) EDUC. POL'Y ANALYSIS

that they are biased and fail to accurately capture student achievement over time, instead focusing only on how the student performs on one particular test on one particular day. As such, such examinations would be an invalid basis for making employment decisions. Additionally, it may be argued that student test scores are an inaccurate measure of a teacher's instructional skill because there are so many other factors that may impact the student's score that are not within the teacher's control, from the student's socio-economic status and parental support to whether the student had breakfast the morning of the test. Therefore, using student standardized test scores to make high-stakes employment decisions, including decisions concerning teacher tenure, will certainly result in increased legal challenges.[149]

Impact on Education Policy

While the U.S. Constitution makes no provision for education, the federal government increasing has played a role in the creation and implementation of K-12 education policy.[150] From the time public schools began operating in the mid-nineteenth century, education has been the responsibility of the state and local governments.[151] However, the federal government, particularly the legislative branch, was pushed into the public education ring with the Supreme Court's decision in *Brown v. Board of Education*.[152] Since the Court's 1954 decision, the federal government's power over public schools has expanded, usurping state and local control.[153]

With RTTT, the executive branch exerted its own influence over education policy, separate from that of Congress. RTTT enabled President Obama to bring state policy in line with his own policy agenda. It was

---

ARCHIVES 1 (2010); Report, Econ. Policy Inst., Problems with the Use of Student Test Scores to Evaluate Teachers (Aug. 27, 2010), *available at* http://www.epi.org/publication/bp278/.

[149] *Id.* Florida is an excellent example of this. Complaint for Declaratory and Injunctive Relief, *Cook v. Bennett*, No. 1:13-cv-00072-MW-GRJ (N.D. Fla. Apr. 16, 2013).

[150] *See, San Antonio v. Rodriguez*, 411 U.S. 1 (1973). Under the Tenth Amendment of the U.S. Constitution, the power to control education is reserved for the states.

[151] Charles Barone & Elizabeth DeBray, *Education Policy in Congress: Perspectives from Inside and Out*, *in* CARROTS, STICKS, AND THE BULLY PULPIT: LESSONS FROM A HALF CENTURY OF FEDERAL EFFORTS TO IMPROVE AMERICA'S SCHOOLS, eds. Frederick M. Hess & Andrew P. Kelly (2012) at 61-82.

[152] 347 U.S. 483 (1954).

[153] Sarah G. Boyce, *The Obsolescence of San Antonio v. Rodriguez in the Wake of the Federal Government's Quest to Leave No Child Behind*, 61 DUKE L. J. 1025, 1037 (2012); Barone & DeBray, *supra* note, at 151.

particularly effective because it used high-dollar incentive grants during a time of economic crisis and it encouraged legislative change in targeted areas.

Based on the success of RTTT, the President already expressed interest in pursuing additional high-dollar incentive programs, such as RESPECT.[154] With schools still facing budget shortfalls, opportunities for additional funding remain attractive, regardless of the policy cost. Therefore, in addition to the influence that Congress already wields over states,[155] the executive branch's increased leverage may serve to further diminish state and local control over public schools.[156]

Conclusion

After decades of relatively little change, teacher tenure legislation currently is the focus of widespread reform efforts. As of the end of June 2013, 28 states passed legislation affecting teacher tenure rights, and an additional four states are considering proposed legislation. In fact, some of the states that have passed legislative amendments are currently considering additional proposals. A review of these legislative changes reveals that the most popular changes include: an increase (or decrease) in the length of probationary periods; consideration of teacher performance/evaluation in the grant of tenure; the use of poor performance (based on performance evaluations) as a grounds for "just cause" dismissal; reduction in force decisions not based entirely on seniority; and the loss of tenure protections after receipt of poor performance evaluations. Certain events over the last year suggest that this reform movement may be coming to a close. While this is left to be seen, this tenure reform movement is certain to have long-term effects on education and education policy.

---

[154] U.S. Dept. of Educ., *Obama Administration Seeks to Elevate Teaching Profession, Duncan to Launch RESPECT Project: Teacher-Led National Conversation* (Feb. 15, 2012), available at http://www.ed.gov/news/press-releases/obama-administration-seeks-elevate-teaching-profession-duncan-launch-respect-pro.

[155] Particularly as a result of the Elementary and Secondary Education Act of 1965, 20 U.S.C. §70 (1965), as drafted and as amended by reauthorization.

[156] The executive branch's influence would not necessarily be limited to education policy; the use of incentive grants could increase the President's influence over state and/or local policy in any area.

Appendix A

Categories of Legislative Change

A. Change in length of the probationary period	B. Teacher performance/evaluation considered in granting of tenure	C. Poor performance added as a grounds for "just cause" dismissal	D. Reduction in force decisions not based entirely on seniority	E. Loss of tenure protections after receipt of poor performance evaluations
Increase in probationary period (set): ME, MD, MI, NJ, NV, NH, OH, TN; AK & MS (proposed)	Positive evaluations + years of consecutive service: DE, LA MI, NV, NJ, OK, TN, WA, WY; NC (proposed)	Probationary teachers recieving bad evaluations not renewed: IN & OK; NC (proposed)	Reduction in force decisions not based solely on tenure status/seniority: GA, IN, ME, MI, NV, VA; MN, MO, WA (proposed)	Re-earn tenure by serving additional probationary period: CO, LA, NV
Increase in probationary period (variable): IL, KS, OK, SC, VA	Positive evaluations required in lieu of years of consective service: CO, IL, IN	Negative evaluation(s) grounds for termination (generally): AZ, CT, LA, OK, TN, UT, VA, WY	Reduction in force decisions cannot be made based on tenure status/seniority: AZ & UT	Re-earn tenure by receiving stated number of positive evaluation (varies from original probationary period): AZ & TN; MO & NC (proposed)
Probationary period decreased: MS & MO (proposed)	Tenure based on evaluations generally (discretionary): KS; MO (proposed)	Certain # of consecutive negative evals = grounds for dismissal: FL, ME, MI, WA; MO (proposed)		Periodic review of tenure status: AK (proposed)

Appendix B
Legislative Changes by State
(From January 2009 through June 2013)[1]

State	Tenure Law	Date of Legislative Change or Proposal	Nature of Legislative Change(s)
Alabama	ALA. CODE §§ 16-24C-1 through 16-24C-14	July 2011	F. Other[2]
Alaska	ALASKA STAT. ANN. §§ 14.20.150 through 14.20.215	Proposed March 2013 (HB 162)	A. Change in length of probationary period; E. Loss of tenure for poor performance; F. Other
Arizona	ARIZ. REV. STAT. ANN. §§ 15-538.01 through 15-548, and 15-502(H)	July 2010	C. Poor performance grounds for dismissal; D. RIF[3] decisions not based entirely on seniority
		June 2013	E. Loss of tenure for poor performance; F. Other
Arkansas	ARK. CODE ANN. §§ 6-17-1501 through 6-17-1510	None	None
California	CAL. EDUC. CODE § 44929.21	None	None

---

[1] Only legislative changes made between January 2009 and June 2013 and proposals pending on June 30, 2013 are included in this chart. Many legislative changes were proposed between 2009 and 2013 that failed for one reason or another. Those proposals are not included on this chart.

[2] "Other" refers to legislative changes that impact teacher tenure rights in some way but that do not fall into the categories of change identified as most popular in this study. These changes range from procedural changes to changes in the date of implementation.

[3] Reduction in force (RIF).

Colorado	COLO. REV. STAT. ANN. §22-63-103 and §22-9-105.5	May 2010	B. Teacher performance considered in grant of tenure; E. Loss of tenure for poor performance
Connecticut	CONN. GEN. STAT. ANN. §10-151	January 2013	C. Poor performance grounds for dismissal F. Other
Delaware	DEL. CODE ANN. tit. 14, §§ 1403, 1411-1414	July 2010	B. Teacher performance considered in grant of tenure
District of Columbia	D.C. CODE §1-608.01a	None	None
Florida	FLA STAT. ANN. §§ 1012.33, 1012.335, and 1012.22	July 2011	C. Poor performance grounds for dismissal F. Other
		Proposed January-March 2013 (SB 1336, SB 980, SB 1474, SB 822, HB 197, HB 907)	F. Other
Georgia	GA. CODE ANN. §§ 20-2-940, 20-2-942, and 20-2-948	May 2012	D. RIF decisions not based entirely on seniority
Hawaii	HAW. REV. STAT. § 302A-608	None	None
Idaho	IDAHO CODE ANN.	April 2013	F. Other

	§§33-514 and 33-515		
Illinois	105 ILL. COMP. STAT. 5/24-11	July 2011	B. Teacher performance considered in grant of tenure
Indiana	IND. CODE. ANN. §§ 20-28-6-2 through 20-28-6-8 and 20-28-7.5-1(d)	June 2011	B. Teacher performance considered in grant of tenure; C. Poor performance grounds for dismissal; D. RIF decisions not based entirely on seniority;
		Proposed May 2013 (HB 1339)	F. Other
Iowa	IOWA CODE ANN. §§ 279-13 and 279-19	None	None
Kansas	KAN. STAT. ANN. § 72-5445	July 2011	A. Change in length of probationary period; B. Teacher performance considered in grant of tenure
Kentucky	KY. REV. STAT. ANN. §§ 161.720 through 161.841	Proposed January 2013	F. Other
Louisiana	LA. REV. STAT. ANN. §§ 17:441 through 17:446	April 2012	B. Teacher performance considered in grant of tenure; C. Poor performance grounds for dismissal; E. Loss of tenure for poor performance; F. Other
Maine	ME. REV. STAT. ANN. tit. 20-A, §§ 13201 and 13701	September 2011	A. Change in length of probationary period
		April 2012	C. Poor performance grounds for dismissal

	through 13706		D. RIF decisions not based solely on seniority F. Other
Maryland	MD. CODE ANN., Education, § 6-202	May 2010	A. Change in length of probationary period F. Other
		Proposed February 2013	F. Other
Massachusetts	MASS. GEN. LAWS ANN. ch. 71, §§ 41 and 42	None	None
Michigan	MICH. COMP. LAWS ANN. §§ 38.71, 38.81 through 38.93 and 380.1249(h)	July 2011	A. Change in length of probationary period; B. Teacher performance considered in grant of tenure; C. Poor performance grounds for dismissal D. RIF decisions not based entirely on seniority
Minnesota	MINN. STAT. ANN. §122A.40-41	May 2013	F. Other
		Proposed February 2013 (HF 980)	D. RIF decisions not based entirely on seniority
		Proposed March 2013 (SF 1282)	F. Other
Mississippi	MISS. CODE ANN. §§ 37-9-103 through 37-9-113	April 2013	F. Other
		Proposed January 2013 (SB 2352 and SB 2120)	A. Change in length of probationary period

Missouri	MO. ANN. STAT. §§ 168.102 through 168.130	Proposed February 2013 (SB 408 and SB 332)	C. Poor performance grounds for dismissal; D. RIF decisions not based entirely on seniority; F. Other
		Proposed March 2013 (HB 631)	A. Change in length of probationary period; B. Teacher performance considered in grant of tenure; E. Loss of tenure for poor performance
Montana	MONT. CODE ANN. § 20-4-203	None	None
Nebraska	NEB. REV. STAT. ANN. §§ 79-824 through 79-842	None	None
Nevada	NEV. REV. STAT. ANN. §§ 391.311 through 391.3197, 288.151	July 2011	A. Change in length of probationary period; B. Teacher performance considered in grant of tenure; D. RIF decisions not based entirely on seniority E. Loss of tenure for poor performance
New Hampshire	N.H. REV. STAT. ANN. § 189:14-a	July 2011	A. Change in length of probationary period
New Jersey	N.J. STAT. ANN. §§ 18A:28-5 through 18A:28-10	August 2012	A. Change in length of probationary period B. Teacher performance considered in grant of tenure
New Mexico	N.M. STAT. ANN. §§ 22-10A-21 through 22-10A-24	None	None

New York	N.Y. EDUCATION LAW § 3012	None	None
North Carolina	N.C. GEN. STAT. ANN. §§ 115C-304 and 115C-325	Proposed April 2013 (HB 719)	B. Teacher performance considered in grant of tenure; C. Poor performance grounds for dismissal E. Loss of tenure for poor performance
North Dakota	N.D. CENT. CODE ANN. §§15.1-15-02 and 15.1-15-05	None	None
Ohio	OHIO REV. CODE ANN. §§ 3319-08 to 3319-11	October 2009	F. Other
Oklahoma	OKLA. STAT. ANN. tit. 70, §§ 6-101.3 and 6-101.22	May 2010	B. Teacher performance considered in grant of tenure; C. Poor performance grounds for dismissal
		May 2013	B. Teacher performance considered in grant of tenure
Oregon	OR. REV. STAT. ANN. §§ 342.815 through 342.895	None	None
Pennsylvania	24 PA. CONS. STAT. ANN. §11-1121	None	None
Rhode Island	R.I. GEN. LAWS ANN. § 16-13-3	None	None
South Carolina	S.C. CODE ANN. §59-	June 2012	A. Change in length of probationary period

South Dakota	26-40 S.D. CODIFIED LAWS §§13-43-6 through 13-43-6.6	None	None
Tennessee	TENN. CODE ANN. §§ 49-5-501 through 49-5-511	July 2011	A. Change in length of probationary period; B. Teacher performance considered in grant of tenure; C. Poor performance grounds for dismissal; E. Loss of tenure for poor performance
Texas	TEX. EDUC. CODE ANN. §§ 21.002 through 21.207	None	None
Utah	UTAH CODE ANN. §§ 53A-8-402 through 53A-8a-505	May 2012	C. Poor performance grounds for dismissal; D. RIF decisions not based entirely on seniority
Vermont	VT. STAT. ANN. tit. 16, § 1752	None	None
Virginia	VA. CODE ANN. §§ 22.1-303 through 22.1-307	March 2013	A. Change in length of probationary period; C. Poor performance grounds for dismissal; D. RIF decisions not based entirely on seniority
Washington	WASH. REV. CODE. ANN. §§ 28A-405.100 through 28A-	March 2012	B. Teacher performance considered in grant of tenure; C. Poor performance grounds for dismissal; F. Other

	405.220		
West Virginia	W.Va. Code Ann. §§ 18A-2-2 and 18A-2-6	None	None
Wisconsin	Wis. Stat. Ann. §§ 118.23 and 119.42	None	None
Wyoming	Wyo. Stat. Ann. §§ 21-7-102 and 21-7-110	February 2011	B. Teacher performance considered in grant of tenure; C. Poor performance grounds for dismissal F. Other
		March 2013	

Forthcoming Issues of the *Education Law & Policy Review*

Special Issue of the ELPR on Free Speech

Education, free speech, civility, and civic courage are the necessary foundations of liberty and democracy. If students do not learn to effectively exercise free speech in defense of fundamental human rights, justice, liberty, and democracy will soon fade from the common government and culture. In recognition of the essential role of free speech in education and the protection and promotion of liberty and democracy, the *Education Law & Policy Review* has a *Special Issue on Free Speech* in progress, with a forward by Mary Beth Tinker, famed plaintiff in *Tinker v. Des Moines*, 393 U.S. 503 (1969). This special issue features invited commentary from the nation's leading First Amendment scholars. We anticipate a landmark issue of the ELPR addressing this landmark case and its continuing influence on education, democracy, and our common government and culture. Commentaries will review legal developments since *Tinker*, and the current status of free speech law and policy in schools, universities, and the broader emerging global culture.

We could not be more pleased to have Mary Beth Tinker on board for this special issue of the ELPR along with many of the nation's leading free speech scholars. The *Tinker* decision is commonly cited in free speech cases, read by every U.S. law student, and it is included in nearly every American Civics education book and curriculum. But the battle for freedom is never over, and Mary Beth continues this essential work. The ELPR is a proud supporter of Mary Beth and the *Tinker Tour*. Last fall Mary Beth and First Amendment attorney Mike Hiestand traveled over 16,000 miles and spoke to over 20,000 students and teachers on the *Tinker Tour* promoting freedom of speech and press. The *Tinker Tour* included an evening at the U.S. Supreme Court at a special event hosted by Justice Samuel Alito, and the initial tour ended in Des Moines, Iowa, at the school where Mary Beth and her brother John were suspended nearly a half-century ago. Mary Beth stated: "I made a difference with just an armband. Can you imagine what a 13 year-old today can do with all of the extraordinary speech tools available?" Mary Beth changed our world for the better, and she is continuing this essential work of defending and promoting the First Amendment. Help Mary Beth continue this work by visiting: http://startsomegood.com/tinkertourwest

Call for Papers for the Next Regular Issue of the ELPR

The ELPR is issuing a call for papers for the next regular issue of the ELPR. As the only peer-reviewed open access education law and policy journal, the ELPR is an ideal forum for broadly disseminating your scholarly work and maximizing readers and the resulting impact on scholarship and practice. Please see the *Call for Papers and Instructions for Authors* on the following page.

Call for Papers and Instructions for Authors

Submission Dates: December 1, 2014 thru January 15, 2015

The Editors for the *Education Law & Policy Review* (ELPR) will be accepting papers for consideration for publication in the next regular issue of the ELPR between the dates of December 1, 2014 and January 15, 2015. Please plan on having your article ready for submission and consideration for publication in the ELPR by these dates. The ELPR does not accept unsolicited manuscripts on a rolling basis. To assure full consideration for publication in the ELPR, please submit publication ready manuscripts between the designated dates.

The ELPR is an academically rigorous peer-reviewed law and policy journal providing scholarly reviews and commentary on national and international issues in education law and policy in K-12 and Higher Education. Preference for publication will be given to articles that address current and significant issues in education law and policy, and that help support positive changes in educational institutions through law and policy improvements.

Articles accepted for review by the ELPR Editors are submitted to a rigorous peer-review process by law and policy scholars on the ELPR Faculty Editorial Board. Articles accepted for publication are thoroughly reviewed and cite checked by the ELPR Student Editorial Board, and finally edited and approved by ELPR Editors prior to publication.

To maximize its impact, scholarship must be published in a timely manner. It is the policy of the ELPR to move from article submission to publication without undue delay. Articles that do not initially meet ELPR standards of academic rigor or that are not otherwise appropriate for the ELPR will not be accepted for review. Reviewed and accepted articles will be edited and published without delay in order to transmit the most current law and policy scholarship to scholars, policymakers, judges, lawyers, educators, and all ELPR readers.

Authors are invited to submit publication ready manuscripts for consideration for publication and scholarly peer-review. Articles should address current issues in education law and policy of national or international significance. Manuscripts should conform to the style and academic rigor of articles published in other scholarly law journals. Citations should be formatted as footnotes and follow THE BLUEBOOK: A UNIFORM SYSTEM OF CITATION (19TH ED.). See the current issue of the ELPR for style and formatting examples for all manuscript submissions. Send publication ready manuscripts and inquiries to the ELPR Editors at jdayton@uga.edu.

Invitation to Join the *Education Law Association*

The *Education Law Association*, established in 1954, is a national, nonprofit association offering unbiased information about current legal issues affecting education, and the rights of those involved in education, in public and private K-12 schools, universities, and colleges. Together, our professional community--including attorneys, administrators, and professors--anticipates trends in education law and supports scholarly research through high-value print and electronic publications, conferences, seminars, and forums, including a partnership with the *Education Law & Policy Review*. Member benefits include:

PUBLICATIONS

Monthly Issues of the School Law Reporter: Citations and summaries for current reported education law decisions; an online database with analyses of selected cases prepared by recognized authorities in education law
Quarterly Issues of the ELA Notes: Commentaries on significant legal developments; case notes on important education law decisions; information on ELA activities; new publications; and education law events
Publication Discounts: 35% discount on ELA's high-quality books and monographs (print and electronic publications)

SEMINARS, CONFERENCES, WEBINARS, AND PODCASTS

Discounts on ELA Conferences and Seminars: CLE and CEU credits available
Free Webinars for Members: Non-members pay a fee
Two Free Samples from the ELA K-12 Legal Issues Podcast Catalog: Series of audio files providing easy-to-understand overviews of current issues in education law, prepared by well-known experts in the field

RESOURCES AND NETWORKING

Access to the SLR Express: A searchable online case database; now offering access to feature articles
Connection with other ELA members via Listserv: Featuring the popular *School Law Blog*, written by Mark Walsh
Free access to a Teaching School Law Folder for Sharing Materials: E-mail ela@educationlaw.org for access
Partnerships with NASPA and the *Education Law Consortium*: ELA members have limited access to our partners' newsletters and journals
Networking, Presenting and Publishing Opportunities

For more information and to join ELA, go to: www.educationlaw.org

Invitation to Support the *Pro Bono* Work of the *Education Law Consortium*

Education will always remain the key to the American Dream of social and economic progress. For over two centuries enlightened Americans have understood that quality education is essential to the Nation's freedom, security, prosperity, and quality of life. Further, they have recognized that it is the central duty of each generation to provide an education for succeeding generations that will prepare them for the challenges of life, self-governance in a free and just democracy, and protecting and advancing the American Dream for all persons.

The *Education Law Consortium* (ELC) is a non-profit, non-partisan, university-based group of leading scholars, policy analysts, and practitioners, dedicated to the advancement of education, and the promotion of the common good, through law and policy improvement. The ELC seeks to play a vital role in promoting education law and policy improvement thru non-partisan research and model policy development, and the free dissemination of information to all persons, including thru the *Education Law & Policy Review* (ELPR), which is provided free by the ELC and its partners to all readers.

We hope that you will consider supporting future educational improvement by supporting the *pro bono* work of the ELC. Helping support the work of the ELC is fast and easy thru the University of Georgia's *Georgia Education Law Consortium Fund* account. Contributions in any amount are most welcomed. Just cut and paste or copy the link below into your Internet browser:

https://gail.uga.edu/give?id=fc97320f-deb9-432b-82b4-d4935069dc31

Everyone working with the ELC and the ELPR thanks you for your support. We look forward to continuing our work in promoting education law and policy improvement through non-partisan research and model policy development, and the free dissemination of information to all persons including free access to the *Education Law & Policy Review*.